Study Guide and Workbook to Accompany

THE ECONOMICS OF MONEY, BANKING AND FINANCIAL MARKETS

Study Guide and Workbook to Accompany

THE ECONOMICS OF MONEY, BANKING AND FINANCIAL MARKETS

Third Edition

Frederic S. Mishkin

Prepared by

JOHN McARTHUR
Wofford College

FREDERIC S. MISHKIN
Columbia University

HarperCollins*Publishers*

Study Guide and Workbook to accompany, THE ECONOMICS OF MONEY, BANKING AND FINANCIAL MARKETS. By John McArthur and Frederic S. Mishkin.

ISBN: 0-673-52176-1
92 93 94 95 96 9 8 7 6 5 4 3

Contents

How to Use this
Study Guide and Workbook

The only way to effectively learn the economics of money, banking, and financial markets is by continual, and active, application of the basic concepts in this field. To assists in this endeavor, we have written this Study Guide and Workbook as a tool to help you learn the material contained in The Economics of Money, Banking, and Financial Markets. This Study Guide and Workbook has one chapter for every chapter in the textbook, and it contains the following learning tools.

Chapter Synopsis/Completions. Rather than just providing you with a conventional chapter synopsis that briefly covers all the material in a textbook chapter, the chapter synopsis here requires you to fill in blanks with key words and phrases. This will make your review of a chapter a more active enterprise, one that presents you with a challenge.

Exercises. Following the chapter synopsis are a series of exercises that give you hands-on practice with the basic concepts taught in this course. The exercises are intended to provide you with a healthy workout. By pushing your way through them, you are strengthening your ability to make use of the concepts that are essential to learning the material in the textbook. The exercises vary in their approach in order to keep you interested (and awake!); some ask you to do calculations; others, to connect items in different columns; some to fill in key words; and others, to draw graphs. Each exercise comes with a heading that tells you what material is covered so that you can pick exercises on topics where you need the most work.

Self-Test. Each chapter ends with a self-test that allows you to gauge how well you are mastering the material. Typically, the self-test includes 15 true-false questions, which function as a warmup, and then 10 multiple-choice questions. If your performance on the self-test is strong, then you should have no problem with the exam in the course.

Answers. The answers to the chapter synopsis/completions, exercises, and self-test are all provided in the back of the book so that you can readily check your progress. The answers to the exercises are sufficiently detailed so that even when you have trouble with an exercise, the answer should help you to learn the necessary concepts.

STRATEGIES FOR STUDYING WITH THE STUDY GUIDE
AND WORKBOOK

There are many possible strategies to improve your course performance with the Study Guide and Workbook. One is to first loosen up by filling in the blanks of the chapter synopsis and then to look up the answers. If you feel comfortable with the material, then you might want to go directly to the self-test. If your self-test performance is good, then you can rest easy and proceed to the next chapter. On the other hand, if you find that you are weak in some areas, then you can do those exercises which cover the topics you are having trouble with.

Alternatively, you might not feel very comfortable with the material after working your way through the chapter synopsis/completions. In this case, you might be better off to go right to the exercises and work your way through all of them. Then, when you think you are in better control of the material, you can take the self-test and evaluate your performance.

Some students may even find that taking the self-test alone is enough practice for them. Feel free to experiment with the Study Guide and Workbook. It is a flexible tool that should help you learn the material without too much strain and pain.

Acknowledgements

Special thanks are extended to Professor Dawn M. Saunders who provided us with a list of corrections that have been incorporated into this addition. Thanks also to Professors Terry Ferguson and David Whisnant of Wofford College for helpful advice concerning the computer hardware and software used in the production of this book. Without their help this book might still be in production. Professor King Banaian of St. Cloud State University offered a number of useful suggestions for which we are grateful. Finally, we thank Bruce Kaplan, Katherine Lee, and Arlene Bessenoff of HarperCollins for their patience during the production of this edition.

John McArthur
Frederic S. Mishkin

Study Guide and Workbook to Accompany

THE ECONOMICS OF MONEY, BANKING AND FINANCIAL MARKETS

Chapter 1

Why Study Money, Banking, and Financial Markets?

CHAPTER SYNOPSIS/COMPLETIONS

The study of money is an extremely important part of both economics and finance. Research has found money to play an important role in the determination of aggregate output, the aggregate price level, the rate of inflation, and the level of interest rates.

(1)_____, the condition of a continually rising price level, has exhibited a close relation to the money supply over so many countries and so many time periods that Nobel Laureate Milton Friedman has stated that "Inflation is always and everywhere a monetary phenomenon." Evidence indicates that those countries with the highest rates of inflation are also the ones with the (2)_____ money growth rates.

The upward and downward movements in economic activity, commonly referred to as (3)_____ _____, also have exhibited a close relationship to money growth. Indeed, every recession in the United States in the twentieth century has been preceded by a (4)_____ in the rate of money growth.

In addition, economic theory suggests, and historical evidence indicates, that money has an important influence on the level of interest rates. Since interest rates play such an important role in people's (5)_____ and (6)_____ decisions, it should not be surprising that this has been one of the more intensively studied relationships in economics. For example, (7)_____ interest rates are typically blamed for the depressed conditions experienced by the housing industry from time to time. Thus while high interest rates may cause people to put off buying a house, it may encourage them to save in hopes of buying one in the future.

Also of concern to economists has been the recent volatility of (8)_____ _____. In the 15-year period 1970 to 1985, interest rates became much more volatile than they had in the previous 15 years. Concern that these substantial fluctuations might reduce investment has led to additional research of this relationship. A related area concerns the interconnection between (9)_____ growth, interest rates, and budget deficits. Clearly, the study of money is diverse and intimately related to many important economic events.

The other major area of study in this course is the business of banking. Banks play an important role in determining the quantity of money in an economy. At one time, banks were unique among financial institutions in their roles as monetary policy players. Now a large number of (10)_____ _____ can have important effects on the nation's money supply. However, since the financial intermediary that people deal with most frequently is a commercial (11)_____, that will be the institution most discussed throughout the book.

Financial intermediaries are an important part of a modern industrial economy. They play an important role in transferring funds from those who wish to (12)_____ to those who wish to (13)_____, thereby ensuring that resources are put to more productive uses. This process of channeling funds by way of an intermediary or middleman is known as (14)_____ _____. Without the services provided by financial intermediaries, Americans could not enjoy the present high standard of living to which they have become accustomed. (15)_____ markets such as the bond market, the stock market, and foreign exchange market have become increasingly important areas of study. Small movements in bond and stock prices can have significant effects, and changes in (16)_____ _____ --the price of one country's currency in terms of another's-- not only affect those individuals involved in international trade, but all consumers and producers.

The bond market is important since (17)_____ rates are determined in this market, while the (18)_____ _____ is the most widely followed financial market in the United States.

Exchange rates are determined in foreign currency markets and have important effects on international trade. For example, a (19)_____ dollar means that the value of the dollar rises relative to foreign currencies and foreign goods become less expensive to Americans--good news for consumers. Unfortunately, a stronger dollar means that goods produced in the United States become more (20)_____ to foreign purchasers, who are now likely to purchase fewer American goods--bad news for producers. Thus we see that a stronger dollar is really a double-edged sword.

EXERCISES

Exercise 1: Definitions and Terminology

Match the following terms in the column on the right with the definition or description in the column on the left. Place the letter of the term in the blank provided next to the appropriate definition. Terms may be used once, more than once, or not at all.

_____ 1. Fluctuations in aggregate output.

a. Money

_____ 2. Anything generally accepted in payment for goods and services.

b. Aggregate price level

_____ 3. Periods of declining aggregate output.

c. Inflation rate

_____ 4. The average price of goods and services in the economy.

d. Aggregate output

_____ 5. Price paid for the rental of borrowed funds.

e. Business cycles

_____ 6. The rate of change in the aggregate price level.

f. Recessions

_____ 7. Excess of government expenditures over tax revenues.

g. Interest rate

_____ 8. The total production of goods and services in the economy.

h. Budget deficit

_____ 9. The management of money and interest rates.

i. Exchange rate

_____ 10. Price of one county's currency in terms of another's.

j. Monetary policy

4

Exercise 2: Money and Inflation

Money growth and inflation rates are reported for a number of selected countries in the table below. Graph the money growth-inflation coordinate for each country, creating a scatter diagram in Figure 1A. Sketch a single line to illustrate the general relationship between money growth and inflation depicted in the scatter diagram. Does the line slope upward to the right?

Country	Average Annual Rate of Money Growth (1975-1984)	Average Annual Rate of Inflation (1975-1984)
Chile	59.4	54.4
Ecuador	24.5	19.0
France	11.9	10.5
Germany	6.3	4.2
Italy	17.3	16.1
Mexico	39.2	40.1
Portugal	15.3	22.8
Turkey	39.5	45.3
United Kingdom	13.0	11.4
United States	7.5	7.6

Source: *International Financial Statistics*

FIGURE 1A

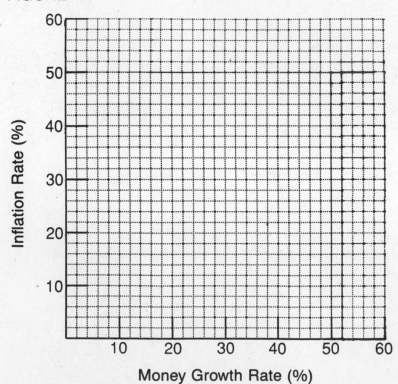

Exercise 3: Money and Business Cycles

A. At the time the Second Bank of the United States closed its doors in 1836, the money supply in the United States was approximately $280 million. By 1843, the money supply had fallen by more than $100 million. Predict what happened to the price level and economic activity during the period 1836 to 1843.

_____

_____

B. Referring to the effects of an expansion in the quantity of currency in 1723, the governor of colonial Pennsylvania said, "It is inconceivable to think what a prodigious good Effect immediately ensued on all the Affairs of the Province." What do you suppose he means by "all the Affairs of the Province"?

_____

_____

Exercise 4: Bond, Stock, and Foreign Exchange Markets

Some of the most important financial markets are discussed briefly in Chapter 1. The statements below refer to three of these markets in the United States: the bond market, the stock market, and the foreign exchange market. Indicate to which of the three markets the statement refers. Let B = bond market, S = stock market, and F = foreign exchange market.

_____1. The market where interest rates are determined.

_____2. The market where claims on the earnings of corporations are traded.

_____3. The market that made major news when the Dow-Jones industrial average fell 508 points on October 19, 1987.

_____4. Individuals trying to decide whether to vacation in California or France might be influenced by the outcomes in this market.

_____5. The most widely followed financial market in America.

_____6. The prices of Japanese video cassette recorders sold in the United States is affected by trading in this market.

SELF-TEST

Part A: True-False Questions

Circle whether the following statements are true (T) or false (F).

T F 1. Empirical evidence suggests that the price level and the money supply move closely together over long periods of time.

T F 2. Money is defined as anything that is generally accepted in payment for goods or services or in the repayment of debts.

T F 3. The condition of a continually rising price level is known as a recession.

T F 4. There is a strong negative association between inflation and the growth rate of money.

T F 5. Economists frequently talk about "the interest rate" because most interest rates move up and down together.

T F 6. The budget deficit is the excess of government tax revenues over government expenditures.

T F 7. Monetary policy is defined as the management of money and interest rates.

T F 8. Some economists express concern that huge government budget deficits cause the money supply to grow more rapidly, causing inflation.

T F 9. Financial intermediaries are essentially unproductive middlemen.

T F 10. Financial intermediation is an important activity because it allows funds to be channeled to those who can put them to productive use.

T F 11. One can reasonably assume that financial intermediaries would not exist unless they provided services that people valued.

T F 12. The foreign exchange market is likely to be of interest to those corporations that do a lot of overseas business.

T F 13. Economists tend to disregard events in the stock market since stock prices tend to be extremely stable and are therefore of little interest.

T F 14. The price of one country's currency in terms of another's is called the concentration ratio.

T F 15. A stronger dollar means that American goods become more expensive in foreign countries and so foreigners will buy fewer of them.

Part B: Multiple-Choice Questions

Circle the appropriate answer.

1. Money appears to have a major influence on

   a. inflation.
   b. the business cycle.
   c. interest rates.
   d. each of the above.
   e. only (a) and (c) of the above.

2. Budget deficits are important to study in a money and banking class because

   a. budget deficits cause banks to fail.
   b. without budget deficits banks would not exist.
   c. budget deficits may influence the conduct of monetary policy.
   d. of each of the above.
   e. of none of the above.

3. An increase in the growth rate of the money supply is most likely to be followed by

   a. a recession.
   b. a decline in economic activity.
   c. inflation.
   d. none of the above.
   e. all of the above.

4. A sharp decrease in the growth rate of the money supply is most likely to be followed by

   a. a decline in economic activity.
   b. an upswing in the business cycle.
   c. inflation.
   d. all of the above.

5. The process of channeling funds from individuals with surplus funds to those desiring additional funds in which the security issued by the borrower is not purchased by the saver is known as

    a. theft.
    b. redistribution.
    c. barter.
    d. financial intermediation.

6. Banks are an important part of the study of how money affects the economy, since

    a. banks play a critical role in the creation of money.
    b. banks have been important in the rapid pace of financial innovation.
    c. both (a) and (b) are correct.
    d. neither (a) nor (b) are correct.

7. Suppose that due to a fear that the United States is about to enter a long period of stagnant growth, stock prices fall by 50% on average. Predict what would happen to spending by consumers.

    a. Spending would probably increase.
    b. Spending would probably fall.
    c. Spending would probably be unaffected.
    d. The change in spending would be ambiguous.

8. An increase in interest rates is likely to cause spending on houses to
    a. fall.
    b. rise.
    c. rise in the short run if interest rates are expected to fall in the future.
    d. remain unchanged.

9. Assume that large budget deficits have significant impacts on the level of interest rates. In which market will budget deficits have their biggest impact directly?

    a. The stock market
    b. The bond market
    c. The wheat market
    d. The gold market

10. An increase in the value of the dollar relative to all foreign currencies means that the price of foreign goods purchased by Americans

    a. increases.
    b. falls.
    c. remains unchanged.
    d. There is not enough information to answer.

Chapter 2

What is Money?

CHAPTER SYNOPSIS/COMPLETIONS

Chapter 2 deals with a problem that has received increased attention among economists since the mid-1970s: just what is money or the money supply? This topic is given expanded treatment in a later chapter, but raising the issue here allows us to consider the importance of money, discovering why it evolves in all but the most primitive societies.

Economists define (1)_____ as anything that is generally accepted in payment for goods and services or in the repayment of debts. This usually means (2)_____ to most people, but to economists this definition is far too narrow. Economists include checking account deposits and travelers checks with currency to come up with a narrow definition of the (3)_____ _____ referred to as M1.

Before discussing the significance of money, it is important that one distinguish money from income. Money is a (4)_____; that is, it represents a measure at a point in time. For example the money stock, M1, was $766.9 billion on March 21, 1988. Income is a (5)_____ of earnings per unit of time.

Money serves a purpose, or in economists' jargon, it is productive. If money was not productive, we would abandon its use. Money's productivity results largely from its ability to reduce (6)_____ costs and encourage (7)_____.

Money has three primary functions: It is a (8)_____ _____ _____, a (9)_____ _____ _____, and a (10)_____ _____ _____, which all act to reduce transaction costs and encourage specialization. Generally regarded as its most important function, money's ability to serve as a medium of exchange is what distinguished it from other assets, both financial and physical. Without money, exchanges would be strictly (11)_____ transactions. And while barter can be an efficient system for small groups of people, transaction costs rise significantly as the population grows because people find it increasingly difficult to satisfy a double coincidence of wants. Money reduces the high search costs that are characteristic of barter exchange.

Money also lowers information and exchange costs by serving as a unit of account. Comparison shopping is extremely time-consuming and costly when goods are not priced in a common unit, whether the units be dollars, cigarettes, or beaver pelts.

Finally, money serves as a store of value. This function of money facilitates the exchange of goods over (12)_____. Although money is not unique as a store of value, it is the most (13)_____ of all assets, and thus it tends to be the preferred store of value for most people most of the time. To illustrate just how strong this tendency is, consider that people did not completely abandon the use of German currency even during the hyperinflationary 1920s, though barter did become much more prevalent.

Money's evolution over time has been driven by efforts designed to reduce transaction costs further. The introduction and subsequent acceptance of (14)_____ _____ and (15)_____ greatly reduced transportation costs and the loss from theft, respectively. More recently, there has been progression toward a checkless society. Although concerns about fraud have slowed development of an (16)_____ _____ _____ _____ (EFTS), one continues to observe movements in this direction.

Unfortunately, it is much easier to identify the virtues of money than it is to identify which assets actually function as money. In general, economists take two approaches to obtain a precise definition of money: the (17)_____ approach and the (18)_____ approach.

The theoretical approach suggests that assets that act as a (19)_____ _____ should be summed to calculate the money supply. The theoretical definition, however, is inherently ambiguous since many assets have moneylike qualities. For example, in a discussion among Federal Reserve Board members several years ago, someone commented that money market mutual funds should not be included within the narrow money definition because most funds required a $500 minimum on all their checks. Chairman Volker's response was to the effect that the minimum requirement had not often prevented his wife from spending from their account. Volcker's comment, though lighthearted, illustrates one problem of the theoretical approach to measuring money.

The empirical approach suggests using that measure which does the best job of predicting the (20)_____ _____ and inflation. To date, the results of this approach have proved mixed, with measures providing little consistency from one time period to the next.

Because of such confusion, the Fed monitors closely the movements of several (21)_____ _____. Most important are the two narrowest definitions, M1 and M2. If both measures moved together and exhibited a high degree of correlation with economic activity, the Fed's job would be much easier. Such is not the case, however, and there seems little optimism among economists that a solution will be found soon to the measurement problem.

Further complicating matters is the unreliability of (22)_____ money statistics. Given all these problems, it is no wonder that some commentators refer to monetary policymaking as an art rather than a science. At the same time, it is this kind of controversy and uncertainty that makes the study of money and banking so interesting.

EXERCISES

Exercise 1: The Functions of Money

List the three primary functions of money.

1. _____

2. _____

3. _____

Exercise 2: The Functions of Money

Money has three primary functions: It is a medium of exchange, a store of value, and a unit of account. The statements below provide examples of these three functions. Indicate which of the three primary functions of money is illustrated by each statement. Let M = medium of exchange, S = store of value, and U = unit of account.

_____1. Erin purchases tickets to the Guns and Roses concert by writing a check.

_____2. Christopher drops the change from his pocket into the wine bottle bank on his study desk.

_____3. So that they might avoid calculating relative prices of goods in terms of all other goods, the traders at the trading post agreed to value their wares in terms of beaver pelts.

_____4. Everyone understood, including nonsmokers, that the prices of commodities traded in the prisoner-of-war camp were to be stated in terms of cigarettes.

_____5. Although he loved to smoke, Andrew saved his cigarettes for he knew that he would be able to purchase chocolate bars on more favorable terms as the supply of cigarettes dwindled in the POW camp.

_____6. Anthony calculated that the opportunity cost of his time was $10.00 per hour.

_____7. Meghan purchases for $29.95 the videotape she plans to give to her parents for Christmas.

_____8. This function of money is important if people are to specialize at what they do best.

_____9. Function of money that reduces transaction costs in an economy by reducing the number of prices that need to be considered.

_____10. The role of money that would not be provided if bananas were to serve as money.

Exercise 3: Medium of Exchange

Assume that there are three students on campus named Allen (A), Barbi (B), and Clyde (C). They live in the same dorm and know each other well. Allen owns a CD by the rap group Run DMC (R), Barbi owns a Bruce Springsteen (S) CD, and Clyde has a CD by Randy Travis (T). Furthur assume that Allen prefers the Bruce Springsteen CD to the one by Run DMC and that he prefers the Run DMC CD to the one by Randy Travis. Barbi prefers the Randy Travis CD to her Bruce Springsteen CD, but likes Run DMC the least. Clyde prefers the Run DMC CD to his Randy Travis CD, liking the Bruce Springsteen CD the least. If we rank each student's preferences for the CDs, representing preference with the " > " symbol, we get the following table:

Individual	Preferences	Initial CD
A	S > R > T	R
B	T > S > R	S
C	R > T > S	T

Now assume an economy with no money, so that all trades are barter transactions. Note that when Allen (because he likes Bruce Springsteen better than Run DMC) approaches Barbi about trading CDs, Barbi will be unwilling to trade since she will be worse off (she prefers Bruce Springsteen to Run DMC). The same happens when any two individuals try to trade directly. Allen will be unwilling to give Run DMC for Randy Travis in a trade with Clyde, and Clyde will be unwilling to trade away Randy Travis in an exchange with Barbi.

Thus we see from in this example that barter between any two individuals-- because there is not a double coincidence of wants--prevents the three individuals from getting their most preferred musical artist.

However, if we assume that Barbi is aware of Clyde's willingness to trade his Randy Travis for the Run DMC CD, then Barbi will be willing to accept the Run DMC CD in exchange for her Bruce Springsteen since she knows that she will be able to exchange with

Clyde at a later date.

Finish filling in the table below showing the movement of the CDs among Allen, Barbi, and Clyde.

Individual	Initial CD	Intermediate CD	Final CD
A	R	____	____
B	S	____	____
C	T	____	____

What has the Run DMC CD functioned as? _____

_____.

Exercise 4: Functions of Money--Unit of Account

The price of one good in terms of another is referred to as the barter price or exchange rate. The benefits of using money are best appreciated by thinking of a barter economy. Between any two goods there is one barter price or exchange rate. But as the number of goods increases, the number of barter prices or exchange rates grows more rapidly. Complete the following table which dramatically illustrates the virtues of a unit of account.

Number of Prices in a Barter Versus a Money Economy

Number of Goods	Number of Prices in a Barter Economy	Number of Prices in a Money Economy
5	_____	5
25	_____	25
50	_____	_____
500	124,750	_____
5000	_____	_____

Exercise 5: Measuring Money--The Federal Reserve's Monetary Aggregates

After each asset, indicate in the space provided which monetary aggregate--M1, M2, M3, or L--includes the asset. As an aid, the first one has already been completed.

1. Currency   <u>M1, M2, M3, L</u>

2. Savings bonds _____

3. Overnight repurchase agreements _____

4. Checkable deposits _____

5. Short-term Treasury securities _____

6. Small-denomination time deposits _____

7. Money market deposit accounts _____

8. Money market mutual fund balances (institutional) _____

9. Savings deposits _____

SELF-TEST

Part A: True-False Questions

Circle whether the following statements are true (T) or false (F).

T F 1. Since checks are accepted as payment for purchases of goods and services, economists consider checking account deposits as money.

T F 2. Of its three functions, it is as a unit of account that distinguishes money from other assets.

T F 3. Money is productive because it promotes economic efficiency by lowering transactions costs and thereby encouraging specialization.

T F 4. Money is a unique store of value, since physical goods depreciate over time.

T F 5. Money can be traded for other goods quickly and easily compared to all other assets. Thus money is said to be liquid.

T F 6. Money proves to be a good store of value during inflationary episodes, since the value of money is positively related to the price level.

T F 7. Hyperinflation refers to very high rates of inflation.

T F 8. Paper currency evolved because it is less costly to transport than is commodity money.

T F 9. Inflation may reduce economic efficiency if it induces people to resort to barter.

T F 10. The major impetus behind the move to expand the EFTS is the relatively high cost of transporting and processing checks.

T F 11. In times past when only currency functioned as money, defining money would have been conceptually much easier.

T F 12. The empirical approach to defining money is the one economists most generally use, since repeated studies indicate that empirical definitions predict economic activity better than do theoretical definitions over long periods of time.

T F 13. The problem of defining money has become less troublesome than in the past due to financial innovation.

T F 14. The past behavior of M1 and M2 indicates that using only one monetary aggregate to guide policy is sufficient, since they move together very closely.

T F 15. The initial data on the monetary aggregates reported by the Fed is a reliable guide to the short-run behavior of the money supply.

Part B: Multiple-Choice Questions

Circle the appropriate answer.

1. When an economist talks about the impossibility of barter, he or she really is not saying that barter is impossible. Rather, he or she means to imply that

   a. barter transactions are relatively costly.
   b. barter has no useful place in today's world.
   c. it is impossible for barter transactions to leave the parties to an exchange better off.
   d. each of the above is true.
   e. none of the above is true.

2. The resources expended trying to find potential buyers or sellers and negotiating over price and terms are called

   a. barter costs.
   b. transaction costs.
   c. information costs.
   d. enforcement costs.

3. If cigarettes serve as a medium of exchange, a unit of account, and a store of wealth, cigarettes are said to function as

   a. bank deposits.
   b. reserves.
   c. money.
   d. loanable funds.

4. Because money reduces both the time it takes to make exchanges and the necessity of a double coincidence of wants, people will find that they can more easily pursue their individual comparative advantages. Thus money

   a. encourages nonproductive pursuits.
   b. encourages specialization.
   c. forces people to become too specialized.
   d. causes a waste of resources due to the duplication of many activities.

5. The narrowest definition of money consists of

   a. currency.
   b. currency, checking account deposits, and money market mutual funds.
   c. currency, checking account deposits, and money market deposit account funds.
   d. currency, checking account deposits, and traveler's checks.

6. As the transaction costs of selling an asset rise, the asset is said to become

   a. more valuable.
   b. more liquid.
   c. less liquid.
   d. more moneylike.

7. Which of the following are problems with a payments system based largely on checks?

   a. Checks are costly to process.
   b. Checks are costly to transport.
   c. Checks take time to move through the check-clearing system.

d. All of the above.

e. Only (a) and (b) of the above.

8. Which of the following approaches to money definitions have economist considered?

a. The theoretical approach
b. The empirical approach
c. Weighted average approach
d. All of the above
e. Only (a) and (b) of the above

9. Which of the following is not included in the money aggregate M2?

a. Currency
b. Money market deposit accounts
c. Overnight repurchase agreements
d. Savings bonds

10. Which of the following best describes the behavior of the money aggregates M1 and M2?

a. While both M1 and M2 tend to rise and fall together, they often grow at very different rates.
b. M1 tends to grow at a much faster rate than M2.
c. While both M1 and M2 tend to move closely together over periods as short as a year, in the long run they tend to move in opposite directions.
d. While both M1 and M2 tend to move closely together over periods as short as a year, in the long run their growth rates are vastly different.

Chapter 3

An Overview of the Financial System

CHAPTER SYNOPSIS/COMPLETIONS

The financial system is a critical element in a well-functioning economy. Chapter 3 examines the general structure and operation of financial markets and institutions.

Financial markets perform the essential function of channeling funds from savers who have excess funds to (1)_____ who have insufficient funds. In (2)_____ finance, borrowers obtain funds directly from lenders in financial markets through the sale of securities. In (3)_____ finance, funds move from lenders to borrowers with the help of middlemen called (4)_____ _____. Financial markets improve the economic welfare of the society because they move funds from those without productive investment opportunities to those with such opportunities. They also directly improve the well-being of (5)_____ by allowing them to make their purchases when they desire them most.

Financial markets can be classified as debt or (6)_____ markets, primary or (7)_____ markets, organized exchanges or (8)_____-_____-_____ markets, and money and (9)_____ markets. A debt instrument is a contractual agreement by the borrower to pay the holder of the instrument fixed dollar amounts at regular intervals. A debt instrument is (10)_____-term if its maturity is a year or less, is intermediate-term if its maturity is from one to 10 years, and is long-term if its maturity exceeds 10 years. An (11)_____ is a claim to share in the net income and the assets of a business firm. A (12)_____ market is a financial market in which new issues of a security are sold to initial buyers by the corporation or government agency borrowing the funds. A secondary market is a financial market in which the securities that have been previously issued can be resold. Secondary markets can be organized in two ways. One is to organize (13)_____ , where buyers and sellers of securities meet in one central location to conduct trades. The other is to have an over-the-counter market, in which dealers at different locations buy and sell securities. The (14)_____ _____ is a financial market in which only short-term debt instruments are traded, while the capital market is the market in which longer-term debt and equity instruments are traded.

Financial intermediaries are financial institutions that acquire funds from lenders-savers by issuing (15)_____ and then, in turn, use the funds to make loans to borrowers-spenders. Financial intermediaries allow small savers and borrowers to benefit from the existence of financial markets, thus extending the benefits of these markets to nearly everyone in the economy.

The principal financial intermediaries fall into three categories: depository institutions (banks), contractual savings institutions, and a miscellaneous category. (16)_____ _____ are financial intermediaries that accept deposits from individuals and institutions and use the acquired funds to make loans. They include commercial banks, savings and loan associations, mutual savings banks, and credit unions. (17)_____ _____ institutions --life insurance companies, fire and casualty insurance companies, and pension funds-- are financial intermediaries that acquire funds at periodic intervals on a contractual basis. The miscellaneous category includes finance companies, mutual funds, and money market mutual funds.

The principal money market instruments (debt instruments with maturities of less than (18)_____ _____) are commercial paper, bankers' acceptances, repurchase agreements, federal funds, and Eurodollars. The principal (19)_____ market instruments (instruments with maturities greater than one year) are U.S. government securities, mortgages, corporate bonds, U.S. government agency securities, state and local government bonds, and consumer and bank commercial loans.

The financial system is among the most heavily regulated sectors of the American economy. A combination of economic and political forces have shaped past and current government regulatory policy, explaining governments' active role in: (a) providing (20)_____ to investors, (b) ensuring the (21)_____ of the financial system, (c) improving control of (22)_____ policy, and (d) encouraging (23)_____ ownership. Regulations include: requiring disclosure of information to the public, restrictions on who can set up a financial intermediary, restrictions on what assets financial intermediaries can hold, the provision of deposit insurance, the requirement that depository institutions maintain minimum levels of capital, and the requirement that depository institutions keep a certain fraction of their deposits in accounts at the Federal Reserve (called (24)_____).

In the 1960s, 1970s and early 1980s, volatile interest rates made for dynamic financial markets as new types of financial instruments emerged in response to investor demands. Change in the financial markets since the early 1980s has come primarily from a different source: the internationalization of financial markets. Nothing illustrates this trend more than the growth in Eurobonds and Euroequities. (25)_____ are bonds denominated in a currency other than that of the country in which it is sold. Growth in Eurobonds has been so substantial that the Eurobond market has now passed the U.S. corporate bond market as a source of new funds.

(26)_____ are new stock issues that are sold primarily to institutional traders abroad. Trading volume in Euroequities has risen at a time when interest in foreign stocks also has increased greatly, as evidenced by the growth in trading activity on various foreign stock exchanges. For instance, until quite recently, the stock market in the United States was by far the largest in the world. Beginning in the mid-1980s, however, the value of stocks traded in Japan has at times exceeded the value of stocks traded in the United States. Importantly, the internationalization of financial markets has facilitated the financing of domestic corporate and government debt; without these funds, the United States economy would be far less healthy.

EXERCISES

Exercise 1: Direct versus Indirect Finance

For each of the following financial transactions indicate whether it involves direct finance or indirect finance by writing in the space provided a D for direct finance and an I for indirect finance.

_____ 1. You take out a car loan from a finance company.

_____ 2. You buy a U.S. savings bond.

_____ 3. You buy a share of GM stock.

_____ 4. You buy a share of a mutual fund.

_____ 5. You borrow $1000 from your father.

_____ 6. You obtain a $50,000 mortgage from your local S&L.

_____ 7. You buy a life insurance policy.

_____ 8. GM sells a share of its stock to IBM.

_____ 9. Chase Manhattan Bank issues commercial paper to AT&T.

_____ 10. AT&T issues commercial paper to Mobil Oil Corp.

Exercise 2: Structure of Financial Markets

Put the following instruments in the appropriate box or boxes below:

U.S. Treasury bills   Federal funds
U.S. Treasury bonds   Common stocks
Corporate bonds   Commercial paper
Negotiable CDs

	Money Market Instrument	Capital Market Instrument
Traded in an Organized Exchange		
Traded in an Over-The-Counter Market		

Exercise 3: Financial Intermediaries

A. Next to each of the following financial intermediaries, write the letter corresponding to its primary assets.

Intermediary	Primary Assets
_____ 1. Commercial banks	a. mortgages
_____ 2. Savings and loans	
	b. consumer loans
_____ 3. Mutual savings banks	
_____ 4. Credit unions	c. money market instruments
_____ 5. Life insurance companies	
	d. business loans
_____ 6. Pension funds	
_____ 7. Fire and casualty insurance companies	e. corporate bonds
	f. U.S. government securities
_____ 8. Mutual funds	
_____ 9. Money market mutual funds	g. corporate stock
_____ 10. Finance companies	h. municipal bonds

B. Next to each of the following financial intermediaries, write the letter corresponding to its primary liabilities.

Intermediary	Primary Liabilities
_____ 1. Commercial banks	a. checkable deposits
_____ 2. Savings and loans	b. premiums from policies
_____ 3. Mutual savings banks	
_____ 4. Credit unions	c. savings deposits
_____ 5. Life insurance companies	
_____ 6. Pension funds	d. employer and employee contributions
_____ 7. Fire and casualty insurance companies	e. corporate bonds
_____ 8. Mutual funds	f. shares
_____ 9. Money market mutual funds	g. corporate stock
_____ 10. Finance companies	h. commercial paper

Exercise 4: Financial Instruments

A. List the nine principal capital market instruments in order from those with the smallest amount outstanding to those with the largest outstanding for the year 1980.

1. _____

2. _____

3. _____

4. _____

5. _____

6. _____

7. _____

8. _____

9. _____

B. List the seven principal money market instruments in order from those with the smallest amount outstanding to those with the largest outstanding for the year 1980.

1. _____

2. _____

3. _____

4. _____

5. _____

6. _____

7. _____

C. Is the order of capital and money market instruments any different in 1990 than in 1980?

Exercise 5: Financial Regulation

Match the regulatory agency to whom it regulates. Remember that some financial institutions are regulated by more than one agency.

	Regulatory Agency	Who it Regulates

_____1. Office of the Comptroller of the Currency

a. Savings and loans

_____2. National Credit Union Association

b. Commercial banks

_____3. State Banking and Insurance Commissions

c. Organized exchanges

_____4. Federal Reserve System

_____5. Federal Deposit Insurance Corporation (FDIC)

d. Mutual savings banks

_____6. Office of Thrift Supervision

e. Credit unions

_____7. Securities and Exchange Commission

f. Insurance companies

_____8. Commodities Futures Trading Commission (CFTC)

g. Futures market traders

SELF-TEST

Part A: True-False Questions

Circle whether the following statements are true (T) or false (F).

T F 1. The primary function of financial markets is to channel funds from those who have saved surplus funds, because they spend less than their income, to those who have a shortage of funds, because they wish to spend more than their income.

T F 2. When financial markets enable a consumer to buy a refrigerator before she has saved up enough funds to buy it, they are helping to increase economic welfare.

T F 3. Direct finance does not involve the activities of financial intermediaries.

T F 4. The difference between a primary market and a secondary market is that in a primary market new issues of a security are sold, while in a secondary market previously issued securities are sold.

T F 5. An over-the-counter market has the characteristic that dealers in securities conduct their trades in one central location.

T F 6. Capital markets involve trading in short-term securities.

T F 7. Financial intermediaries are involved in the process of direct finance.

T F 8. Financial intermediaries only exist because there are substantial information and transactions costs in the economy.

T F 9. Liquidity of assets is as important a consideration for contractual savings institutions as it is for depository institutions.

T F 10. Money market mutual funds to some extent function as depository institutions.

T F 11. Federal funds are loans made by the Federal Reserve System to commercial banks.

T F 12. Eurodollars are U.S. dollars deposited in banks outside of the United States that are frequently borrowed by American banks.

T F 13. The volume of new corporate bonds issued in the United States is substantially greater than the volume of new stock issues.

T F 14. The Office of the Comptroller of the Currency is the chartering agency for all commercial banks.

T F 15. The primary role of the Securities and Exchange Commission is to make sure that adequate and accurate information can be obtained by investors.

Part B: Multiple-Choice Questions

Circle the appropriate answer.

1. Which of the following cannot be described as indirect finance?

   a. You take out a mortgage from your local bank.
   b. An insurance company lends money to General Motors Corporation.
   c. You borrow $1000 from your best friend.
   d. You buy shares in a mutual fund.
   e. None of the above.

2. Which of the following is a short-term financial instrument?

   a. U.S. Treasury bill
   b. Share of IBM stock
   c. New York City bond with a maturity of 2 years
   d. Residential mortgage

3. Which of the following statements about the characteristics of debt and equity is true?

   a. They can both be short-term financial instruments.
   b. Bond holders are a residual claimant.
   c. The income from bonds is typically more variable than that from equities.
   d. Bonds pay dividends.
   e. None of the above.

4. Which of the following markets in the United States is never set up as an organized exchange?

   a. Stock market
   b. Corporate bond market
   c. U.S. government bond market
   d. Futures market

5. Which of the following is traded in a money market?

   a. U.S. Treasury bonds
   b. Mortgages
   c. Common stocks
   d. Federal funds
   e. None of the above

6. Which of the following is a depository institution?

    a. Life insurance company
    b. Credit union
    c. Pension fund
    d. Finance company

7. The primary assets of a mutual savings bank are

    a. money market instruments.
    b. corporate bonds and stock.
    c. consumer and business loans.
    d. mortgages.

8. The primary liabilities of a savings and loan are

    a. bonds.
    b. mortgages.
    c. deposits.
    d. commercial paper.

9. Savings and loan associations are regulated by the

    a. Office of the Comptroller of the Currency.
    b. Federal Home Loan Bank System and FSLIC.
    c. Securities and Exchange Commission (SEC).
    d. The Office of Thrift Supervision.

10. A bond denominated in a currency other than that of the country in which it is sold is called a(n)

    a. foreign bond.
    b. Eurobond.
    c. equity bond.
    d. currency bond.

Chapter 4

Understanding Interest Rates

CHAPTER SYNOPSIS/COMPLETIONS

Interest rates are among the most important variables in the economy. This chapter explains how interest rates are measured and shows that the interest rate on a bond is not always an accurate measure of how good an investment it will be.

Credit market instruments generally fall into four types: a simple loan, a fixed-payment loan, a coupon bond, and a discount bond. A simple loan provides the borrower with an amount of funds that must be repaid at the (1)_____ _____ along with an interest payment. A (2)_____-_____ loan requires the borrower to make the same payment every period until the maturity date. A coupon bond pays the owner a fixed coupon payment every year until the maturity date, when the (3)_____ value is repaid. Its (4)_____ _____ equals the coupon payment expressed as a percentage of the face value of the bond. A (5)_____ bond is bought at a price below its face value, but the face value is repaid at the maturity date.

The concept of (6)_____ _____ tells us that a dollar in the future is not as valuable as a dollar today; that is, a dollar received n years from now is worth $\$1/(1 + i)^n$ today. The (7)_____ _____ _____, the economists' preferred measure of the interest rate, is the interest rate that equates the present value of future payments of a debt instrument with its (8)_____ today. Applications of this principle reveal that bond prices and interest rates are (9)_____ related; when the interest rate rises, the price of the bond falls, and vice versa.

There are two less accurate measures of interest rates that are commonly used to quote interest rates. The current yield, which equals the (10)_____ payment divided by the price of the coupon bond, is a better measure of the interest rate the (11)_____ the bond's price is to the bond's par value and the (12)_____ is the maturity of the bond. The yield on a discount basis (also called a discount yield) (13)_____ the yield to maturity; and the longer the maturity of the discount bond, the greater this understatement becomes. Even when either of these measures is a misleading guide to the level of the interest rate, a rise in either of these rates signals a (14)_____ in the yield to maturity, and a fall signals a fall in the yield to maturity.

How well you have done by holding a security over a period of time is measured by the security's (15)_____--the payments to the owner plus the change in its value, expressed as a percentage of the purchase price. The return is equal to the yield to maturity in only one special case: when the holding period is equal to the (16)_____ of the bond. For bonds with maturities greater than the holding period, capital gains and losses can be substantial when (17)_____ _____ change. Returns can therefore differ greatly from the yield to maturity. This is why long-term bonds are not considered to be safe assets with a (18)_____ return over short holding periods. The real interest rate is defined as the nominal interest rate minus the (19)_____ _____ _____ _____. It is a better measure of the incentives to borrow and lend than is the nominal interest rate and is therefore a better indicator of the tightness of (20)_____ _____ conditions than is the nominal interest rate.

EXERCISES

Exercise 1: Present Discounted Value

Calculate the present discounted value for the following payments:

1. $500 two years from now when the interest rate is 5%.   _____

2. $500 two years from now when the interest rate is 10%.   _____

3. $500 four years from now when the interest rate is 10%.   _____

4. What do the preceding calculations indicate about the present value of a payment as the interest rate rises?

   _____

5. What do the preceding calculations indicate about the present value of a payment as it is paid further in the future?

   _____

Exercise 2: Yield to Maturity

A. Suppose you are offered a $1000 fixed-payment car loan that requires you to make payments of $600 a year for the next two years.

1. Write down the equation that can be solved for the yield to maturity on this loan: that is, the equation that equates the present value of the payments on the loan to the amount of the loan.

   _____

2. Calculate the present value of the loan payments when the interest rate is 10%.

   _____

3. Must the yield to maturity be above or below 10%? _____

4. Calculate the present value of the loan payments when the interest rate is 15%.

   _____

5. Must the yield to maturity be above or below 15%? _____

   Verify that the present value of the loan payments is approximately $1000 when the interest rate is 13%, indicating that this is the yield to maturity.

B. Suppose you are thinking of buying a $1000 face-value coupon bond with a coupon rate of 10%, a maturity of 3 years, and a price of $1079.

1. Is the yield to maturity going to be above or below 10%? _____ Why?

   _____

2. Write down the equation that can be solved for the yield to maturity of this bond: that is, the equation that equates the present value of the bond payments to the price of the bond.

   _____

3. Calculate the present value of the bond when the interest rate is 8%.

_____

4. Must the yield to maturity be above or below 8%? _____

5. Calculate the present value of the bond when the interest rate is 5%.

_____

6. Must the yield to maturity be above of below 5%? _____

Verify that the present value of the loan payments is approximately $1079 when the interest rate is 7%, indicating that this is the yield to maturity.

Exercise 3: Yield to Maturity and Yield on a Discount Basis

For discount bonds with a face value of $1000, fill in the yield to maturity (annual rate) and the yield on a discount basis in the following table.

Price of the Discount Bond	Maturity	Yield on a Discount Basis	Yield to Maturity
$900	1 year (365 days)		
$950	6 months (182 days)		
$975	3 months (91 days)		

Note: For bonds with a maturity of 6 months, the yield to maturity at an annual rate equals $(1 + i_{six})^2$, where i_{six} is the return over 6 months; for bonds with a maturity of 3 months, the yield to maturity at an annual rate equals $(1 + i_{three})^4$, where i_{three} is the return over 3 months.

What does the preceding table indicate about the degree of understatement of the yield to maturity by the yield on a discount basis as the maturity of a discount bond shortens?

_____

_____

Exercise 4: Current Yield

For the five U.S. Treasury bonds on 9 March 1988, fill in the value of the current yield in the following table:

Coupon Rate	Maturity Date	Price	Yield to Maturity	Current Yield
7 3/8s	Jan 1990	100 11/32	7.17%	
10 1/2s	Jan 1990	105 22/32	7.15%	
10 1/2s	Nov 1992	110 14/32	7.79%	
9 3/8s	Feb 2006	107 5/32	8.58%	
10 3/8s	Nov 2007-2012	115 3/8	8.72%	

For which of these bonds is the current yield a good measure of the interest rate? Why?

_____

_____

Exercise 5: The Rate of Return

1. For a consol with a yearly payment of $100, calculate the return for the year if its yield to maturity at the beginning of the year is 10% and at the end of the year is 5%. (Hint: Calculate the initial price and end-of-year price first; then calculate the return.)

_____

2. For a 10% coupon bond selling at par with 2 years to maturity, calculate the return for the year if its yield to maturity at the beginning of the year is 10% and at the end of the year is 5%. (Hint: Calculate the initial price and end-of-year price first; then calculate the return.)

_____

Which of the bonds is a better investment? _____

Why do you think that this has happened? _____

_____

Exercise 6: Real Interest Rates

Calculate the real interest rate in the following situations:

1. The interest rate is 3% and the expected inflation rate is -3%   _____

2. The interest rate is 10% and the expected inflation rate is 20%.   _____

3. The interest rate is 6% and the expected inflation rate is 3%.   _____

4. The interest rate is 15% and the expected inflation rate is 15%.   _____

In which of these situations would you (everything else equal) be a lender?

_____ A borrower? _____

SELF-TEST

Part A: True-False Questions

Circle whether the following statements are true (T) or false (F).

T   F   1.   A bond that pays the bondholder the face value at the maturity date and makes no interest payments is called a discount bond.

T F 2. The yield to maturity of a coupon bond that is selling for less than its face value is less than the coupon rate.

T F 3. A dollar tomorrow is worth more to you today if the interest rate is 10 percent than if it is 5 percent.

T F 4. The present value of a security that pays you $55 next year and $133 three years from now is $150 if the interest rate is 10%.

T F 5. You would prefer to own a security that pays you $1000 at the end of 10 years than a security that pays you $100 every year for 10 years.

T F 6. The yield to maturity on a $20,000 face value discount bond that matures in one year's time and currently sells for $15,000 is 33 1/3 percent.

T F 7. The yield to maturity on a coupon bond can always be calculated as long as the coupon rate and the price of the bond are known.

T F 8. The current yield is the most accurate measure of interest rates, and it is what economists mean when they use the term interest rates.

T F 9. The yield on a discount basis understates the yield to maturity, and the longer the maturity of the discount bond the greater is the understatement.

T F 10. The current yield is a more accurate approximation of the yield to maturity, the nearer the bond's price is to the par value and the shorter the maturity of the bond.

T F 11. You would prefer to hold a 1-year Treasury bond with a yield on a discount basis of 10% to a 1-year Treasury bond with a yield to maturity of 9.9%.

T F 12. A 5-year $1000 coupon bond selling for $1008 with a 9% current yield has a higher yield to maturity than a 1-year discount bond with a yield on a discount basis of 8.9%.

T F 13. When interest rates rise from 4 to 5%, bondholders are made better off.

T F 14. If interest rates on all bonds fall from 8 to 6% over the course of the year, you would rather have been holding a long-term bond than a short-term bond.

T F 15. Business firms are more likely to borrow when the interest rate is 2% and the price level is stable than when the interest rate is 15% and the expected inflation rate is 14%.

Part B: Multiple-Choice Questions

Circle the appropriate answer.

1. A discount bond

   a. pays the bondholder the same amount every period until the maturity date.
   b. at the maturity date pays the bondholder the face value of the bond plus an interest payment.
   c. pays the bondholder a fixed interest payment every period and repays the face value at the maturity date.
   d. pays the bondholder the face value at the maturity date.

2. A $5000 coupon bond with a coupon rate of 5% has a coupon payment every year of

   a. $50.
   b. $500.
   c. $250.
   d. $100.
   e. none of the above.

3. With an interest rate of 5%, the present value of a security that pays $52.50 next year and $110.25 two years from now is

   a. $162.50.
   b. $50.
   c. $100.
   d. $150.

4. If a security pays you $105 next year and $110.25 the year after that, what is its yield to maturity if it sells for $200?

   a. 4%
   b. 5%
   c. 6%
   d. 7%

5. Which of the following $1000 face value securities has the lowest yield to maturity?

   a. 5% coupon bond selling for $1000
   b. 5% coupon bond selling for $1200
   c. 5% coupon bond selling for $900
   d. 10% coupon bond selling for $1000
   e. 10% coupon bond selling for $900

6. If a $5000 face value discount bond maturing in 1 year is selling for $4000, then its yield to maturity is

   a. 5%.
   b. 10%.
   c. 25%.
   d. 50%.
   e. none of the above.

7. The current yield on a $5000 10% coupon bond selling for $4000 is

   a. 5%.
   b. 10%.
   c. 12.5%.
   d. 15%.

8. The yield on a discount basis of a 180-day $1000 Treasury bill selling for $975 is

   a. 5%.
   b. 10%.
   c. 20%.
   d. 50%.
   e. none of the above.

9. What is the return on a 15% coupon bond that initially sells for $1000 and sells for $700 next year?

   a. 15%
   b. 10%
   c. -5%
   d. -15%
   e. none of the above

10. In which of the following situations would you rather be borrowing?

   a. the interest rate is 20% and expected inflation rate is 15%
   b. the interest rate is 4% and expected inflation rate is 1%
   c. the interest rate is 13% and expected inflation rate is 15%
   d. the interest rate is 10% and expected inflation rate is 15%

Chapter 5

A Simple Approach to Portfolio Choice: The Theory of Asset Demand

CHAPTER SYNOPSIS/COMPLETIONS

What criteria should an investor use in deciding which assets he should hold? This chapter answers the question by developing the theory of asset demand--one of the basic analytical tools for the study of money, banking, and financial markets. This theory outlines criteria that are important when deciding which assets are worth purchasing. In addition, the theory of asset demand explains why it is sensible to diversify and not put all your eggs in one basket.

An (1)_____ is a piece of property that is a store of value. Faced with the decision of whether to buy one asset or another, an investor must consider the following four factors: (2)_____ (3)_____ _____ (4)_____ and (5)_____.

The theory of asset demand consists of the following four propositions:

1. The quantity demanded of an asset is usually (6)_____ related to wealth, with the response being greater if the asset is a (7)_____ rather than a necessity.

2. The quantity demanded of an asset is (8)_____ related to its expected return (relative to alternative assets). Thus an increase in an asset's (9)_____ _____ relative to alternative assets increases the quantity demanded of the asset.

3. The quantity demanded of an asset is (10)_____ related to the risk of its return relative to alternative assets. Hence, if an asset's risk rises relative to that of alternative assets, the quantity demanded of the riskier asset will fall.

4. The quantity demanded of an asset is (11)_____ related to its liquidity relative to alternative assets. The more liquid an asset relative to alternative assets, the greater will be the quantity demanded.

(12)_____, the holding of more than one asset, is almost always beneficial to the risk-averse investor because it reduces risk as long as returns on securities do not move (13)_____ together (an extremely rare occurrence). The more the returns on two securities diverge, the (14)_____ the benefit (risk reduction) there is from diversification.

EXERCISES

Exercise 1: Wealth Elasticity--Necessities and Luxuries

Indicate which the following assets are necessities and which are luxuries by writing in the space provided an N if it is a necessity and L if it is a luxury.

1. An asset with a wealth elasticity of 3.5. _____

2. An asset whose quantity demanded increases
    by 90% when wealth doubles. _____

3. An asset whose quantity demanded does not
    rise proportionally with wealth. _____

4. An asset whose quantity demanded rises over
    time at a rate faster than wealth is growing. _____

5. An asset with a wealth elasticity of 0.4. _____

Exercise 2: Expected Returns

1. If an ACME Corporation bond has a return of 15% one-third of the time, 10% one-third of the time, and 5% the other third of the time, then its expected return is _____%.

2. If an XYZ Corporation bond has an 18% return 25% of the time, a 16% return 50% of the time, and a 6% return the other 25% of the time, then its expected return is _____%.

3. If the ABC Corporation stock has a 12% return half the time and a 10% return the other half of the time, then its expected return is _____%.

4. If the McHoops Corporation stock has a 12% return 75% of the time and a 4% return the remainder of the time, then its expected return is _____%.

5. If the Teddy Bear Corporation stock has an 8% return 50% of the time and a 6% return 50% of the time, then its expected return is _____%.

Exercise 3: Theory of Asset Demand

In the second column of the following table indicate with an arrow whether the quantity demanded of the asset will increase (+) or decrease (-):

Variable	Change in Variable	Change in Asset Demand
Wealth	-	
Liquidity of asset	-	
Riskiness of asset	-	
Expected return of asset	-	
Riskiness of other assets	-	
Liquidity of other assets	-	
Expected return of other assets	-	

Exercise 4: Risk Reduction and Diversification

Suppose that you own common stock in Solar Energy, Ltd., which has a return of -10% when energy prices are low and +20% when energy prices are high. If you buy an equal amount of the following securities, write down your total expected return in the two states of the world: low energy prices and high energy prices.

	Low Energy Prices	High Energy Prices
1. Stock in Mobil Oil Co. which has return of -10% when energy prices are low and of +20% when energy prices are high.	_____	_____
2. Treasury bonds which are just as likely to have a return of 10% or 20% when energy prices are high or low.	_____	_____
3. Stock in Energy Intensive Products, Inc., which has a return of +20% when energy prices are low and -10% when energy prices are high.	_____	_____

4. Which of these securities would you rather buy? Why? _____

_____

5. What general principle does this example illustrate? _____

_____

SELF-TEST

Part A: True-False Questions

Circle whether the following statements are true (T) or false (F).

T   F   1. An increase in wealth raises the quantity demanded of an asset, and the increase in the quantity demanded is greater if the asset is a luxury rather than a necessity.

T   F   2. An asset with a wealth elasticity of 2.5 is called a necessity.

T   F   3. The quantity demanded of an asset is positively related to its expected return relative to alternative assets.

T   F   4. Everything else equal, when the expected return on an asset falls, the quantity demanded rises.

T   F   5. Holding everything else constant, when the liquidity of an asset falls, the quantity demanded falls.

T   F   6. Holding everything else constant, when an asset becomes riskier, the quantity demanded rises.

T   F   7. Holding many risky assets exposes the investor to more risk.

T   F   8. Diversification is always beneficial if people are risk-averse.

T   F   9. If a person is a risk-lover, then he or she will probable not diversify.

T   F   10. The less returns on two securities move together (everything else equal), the more likely it is that investors will want to hold both.

Part: B: Multiple-Choice Questions

Circle the appropriate answer.

1. If the quantity demanded of savings bonds increases by 75% when wealth in the economy doubles, then for savings bonds the wealth elasticity of demand is_____ and the savings bonds are a _____.

   a. 0.75; luxury
   b. 0.75; necessity
   c. 2; luxury
   d. 2; necessity

2. If certificates of deposit are a luxury, then the wealth elasticity is _____ than one and the quantity demanded grows at a _____ rate than wealth grows.

   a. greater; faster
   b. greater; slower
   c. less; slower
   d. less; faster

3. If the expected return on AMF stock falls from 13 to 10% and the expected return on IBM stock remains unchanged, then the expected return from holding IBM stock _____ relative to AMF stock and the quantity demanded of IBM stock _____.

   a. rises; rises
   b. falls; rises
   c. rises; falls
   d. falls; falls

4. If the expected return on ITT stock falls from 10 to 8% and the expected return on AT&T bonds falls from 16 to 12%, then the expected return from holding AT&T bonds _____ relative to AMF stock and the quantity of AT&T bonds _____.

   a. rises; rises
   b. falls; rises
   c. rises; falls
   d. falls; falls

5. If interest rates begin to fluctuate more wildly, then, other things equal, the quantity demanded of stocks _____ and that of long-term bonds _____.

   a. increases; decreases
   b. increases; increases

    c. decreases; decreases

    d. decreases; increases

6. The quantity demanded of rare coins falls when (holding everything else constant)

    a. bonds are suddenly expected to fall in value.

    b. wealth rises.

    c. antiques are suddenly expected to appreciate in value.

    d. the volatility of stock prices declines.

    e. none of the above is true.

7. You would be more willing to buy gold (holding everything else constant) if

    a. the price of gold becomes more volatile.

    b. you realize that your house is worth more than you thought.

    c. bonds become easier to sell.

    d. all of the above occur.

    e. both (a) and (c) of the above occur.

8. For a person holding one security, diversifying by buying another security provides no benefits if

    a. the person is risk-averse.

    b. the returns on the two securities do not move together at all.

    c. the returns on the two securities tend to move in opposite directions.

    d. the returns on the two securities move perfectly together.

9. If I own shares of stock in Gulf Oil Company, then which of the following investments provides me with the least amount of risk reduction?

    a. stock in a T.V. network

    b. stock in General Electric Company

    c. stock in Mobil Oil Company

    d. U.S. Treasury bills

10. If Irving the Investor already owns stock in American Airlines Corp., then (everything else equal) he will be less likely to buy

    a. stock in Walt Disney Corp.

    b. stock in Delta Airlines Corp.

    c. stock in Greyhound Bus Company.

    d. stock in Anaconda Copper Corp.

Chapter 6

The Behavior of Interest Rates

CHAPTER SYNOPSIS/COMPLETIONS

Chapter 6 examines how interest rates are determined and the factors that influence their behavior. The supply and demand analysis developed here explains why interest rates have had such substantial fluctuations in recent years.

The supply and demand analysis for bonds, known as the (1)_____ _____ framework, provides one theory of how interest rates are determined. The (2)_____ for bonds is the relationship between the quantity demanded and the bond price (which is (3)_____ related to the interest rate) when all other economic variables are held constant.

With the interest rate plotted on the vertical axis, the demand curve has an upward slope because a higher interest rate, and hence a higher (4)_____ _____, results in a greater quantity demanded. The (5)_____ _____ for bonds, the relationship between the quantity supplied and the interest rate, is downward-sloping when the interest rate is plotted on the vertical axis: A lower interest rate is associated with a (6)_____ cost of borrowing and a greater quantity supplied. The market interest rate is the (7)_____ _____, which occurs when the quantity of bonds demanded equals the quantity supplied; that is, at the intersection of the supply and the demand curves.

The theory of asset demand developed in Chapter 5 indicates that there are four factors that cause the demand curve for bonds to shift. Specifically, the demand curve shifts to the right when wealth (8)_____, when the expected returns on bonds relative to alternative assets (9)_____, when the riskiness of bonds relative to alternative assets (10)_____ or when the liquidity of bonds relative to alternative assets (11)_____.

There are three factors that cause the supply curve for bonds to shift. Specifically, the supply curve shifts to the right when businesses have a (12)_____ amount of attractive investment opportunities as in a business cycle boom, when expected inflation (13)_____, or when the government increases the supply of debt by running high budget deficits. Changes in any of these factors cause interest rates to change. This supply and demand analysis indicates, for example, that a rise in expected inflation leads to a

rise in interest rates, a phenomenon known as the (14)_____
_____.

An alternative theory of how interest rates are determined is provided by the
(15)_____ _____ framework, which analyzes the supply
and demand for money. The demand curve for money slopes downward because, with a
lower interest rate, the expected return on bonds falls relative to the expected return on
money. According to the theory of asset demand, this causes the quantity of money
demanded to (16)_____. The demand curve for money shifts to the right
when income (17)_____, when the price level (18)_____,
or when inflation is expected to increase.

The central bank is assumed to control the quantity of money supplied at a fixed amount,
meaning that the supply curve for money is a vertical line. The equilibrium interest rate
occurs at the intersection of the supply and demand curves for money. The supply and
demand analysis of the money market indicates that the interest rate
(19)_____ when income or the price level rises, or when the money supply
(20)_____.

The liquidity preference and loanable funds frameworks indicate that there are four
possible effects of an increase in the rate of money supply growth on interest rates: (a) the
liquidity effect, (b) the income effect, (c) the price- level effect, and (d) the expected
inflation effect. The liquidity effect indicates that higher money supply growth leads to a
(21)_____ in interest rates; the other effects work in the
(22)_____ direction. The evidence seems to indicate that the income,
price-level, and expected inflation effects dominate the liquidity effect, implying that an
increase in money supply growth leads to permanently (23)_____ interest
rates. Whether interest rates initially fall rather than rise when money growth is increased
depends critically on how fast people's expectations about inflation adjust.

EXERCISES

Exercise 1: Supply and Demand Analysis of the Bond Market

The quantity of bonds demanded and supplied at different interest rates is listed in the
following table.

Point	Interest Rate	Quantity Demanded	Point	Interest Rate	Quantity Supplied
A	20%	40	E	20%	0
B	15%	30	F	15%	10
C	10%	20	G	10%	20
D	5%	10	H	5%	30

1. Draw the demand and supply curves for bonds in Figure 6A.

FIGURE 6A

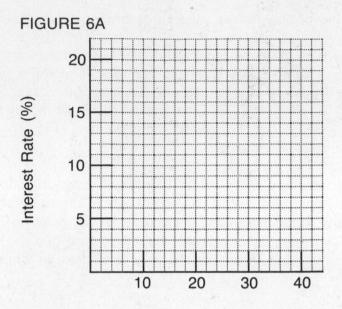

2. What is the equilibrium interest rate? _____

3. When the interest rate is 20%, then there is a condition of excess _____ in the bond market, the price of bonds will _____, and the interest rate will _____.

Exercise 2: Factors that Shift Supply and Demand Curves for Bonds

For each of the following situations (holding everything else constant), indicate in the space provided how the supply and demand curves for bonds shift: D --> for demand curve to the right, <-- D for demand curve to the left, S --> for supply curve to the right, and <-- S for supply curve to the left.

_____ 1. A decline in brokerage commission on bonds.

_____ 2. Expected inflation rises.

_____ 3. There is a new tax on purchases and sales of gold.

_____ 4. There is a large federal budget deficit.

_____ 5. Businessmen become more optimistic about the success of their investments in new plant and equipment.

_____ 6. Bond prices become more volatile.

_____ 7. The economy booms and wealth rises.

_____ 8. Stock prices become more volatile.

_____ 9. People suddenly expect a bear market (a decline in prices) for stocks.

_____10. People suddenly expect interest rates to rise.

Exercise 3: Analyzing a Change in the Equilibrium Interest Rate

Suppose the supply and the demand for long-term bonds are as marked in Figure 6B and market equilibrium is at point 1. Suppose that, as occurred in the early 1980s, the federal government begins to run a large budget deficit and at the same time the volatility of interest rates increases. Draw in the new supply and demand curves in Figure 6B.

FIGURE 6B

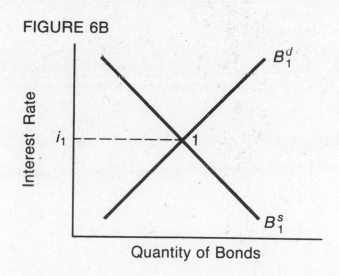

What happens to the interest rate? _____

_____

48

Exercise 4: Supply and Demand Analysis of the Money Market

Suppose the supply and the demand for money are as drawn in Figure 6C. Now the Federal Reserve decreases the money supply and as a result income falls. Draw the new supply and demand curves in Figure 6C.

FIGURE 6C

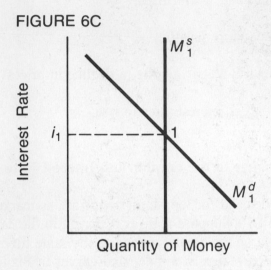

What happens to the interest rate? _____

Exercise 5: Money Growth and Interest Rates

Plot in Figure 6D the path of the interest rate, if at time T the rate of money growth is slowed from 10 to 7% and the liquidity effect is greater than the income, price-level, and expected inflation effects.

FIGURE 6D

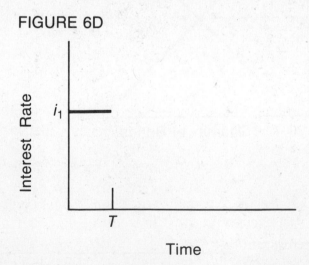

Plot in Figure 6E the path of the interest rate, if at time T the rate of money growth is slowed from 10 to 7%, while the liquidity effect is smaller than the income, price-level, and expected inflation effects, and there is slow adjustment of inflation expectations.

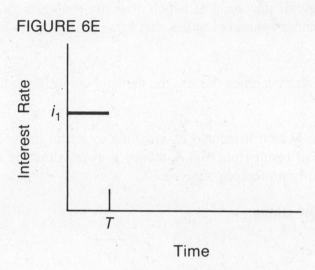

FIGURE 6E

SELF-TEST

Part A: True-False Questions

Circle whether the following statements are true (T) or false (F).

T F 1. The demand curve for bonds slopes downward because at a lower bond price, the expected return on the bonds is higher and the quantity demanded is higher.

T F 2. The loanable funds terminology relabels the demand curve for bonds as one for loanable funds and the supply curve for bonds as the one for loanable funds.

T F 3. A rise in the price of a bond shifts the demand curve for bonds to the left.

T F 4. When businessmen become optimistic about the future health of the economy, the supply curve for bonds shifts to the left.

T F 5. A rise in the expected future price of long-term bonds shifts the demand curve for long-term bonds to the right.

T F 6. A federal budget surplus will shift the supply curve for bonds to the right.

T F 7. The Fisher effect suggest that periods of high interest rates will also tend to be periods of high inflation.

T F 8. In Keynes's view of the world in which there are only two assets, an excess demand in the money market implies that there is an excess demand in the bond market.

T F 9. If the stock market becomes riskier, the demand curve for money shifts to the right.

T F 10. The reason that Milton Friedman is unwilling to accept the view that lower interest rates will result from higher money growth is that he disagrees with Keynes's liquidity preference analysis.

Part B: Multiple-Choice Questions

Circle the appropriate answer.

1. When the interest rate is below the equilibrium interest rate, there is an excess _____ for (of) bonds and the interest rate will _____.

    a. supply; fall
    b. supply; rise
    c. demand; rise
    d. demand; fall

2. When brokerage commissions in the housing market are raised from 6 to 7% of the sales price, the _____ curve for bonds shifts to the _____.

    a. demand; right
    b. demand; left
    c. supply; left
    d. supply; right

3. When rare coin prices become less volatile, the _____ curve for bonds shifts to the _____.

    a. demand; right
    b. demand; left
    c. supply; left
    d. supply; right

4. When the expected inflation rate decreases, the demand for bonds shifts to the _____, the supply of bonds shifts to the _____, and the interest rate _____.

   a. right; right; rises
   b. right; left; falls
   c. left; left; falls
   d. left; right; rises

5. When people revise downward their expectations of next year's short-term interest rate, the demand for long-term bonds shifts to the _____ and their interest rates _____.

   a. right; rises
   b. right; falls
   c. left; falls
   d. left; rises

6. In a recession, normally, the demand for bonds shifts to the _____, the supply of bonds shifts to the _____ and the interest rate _____.

   a. right; right; rises
   b. right; left; falls
   c. left; left; falls
   d. left; right; rises

7. In the money market, when the interest rate is below the equilibrium interest rate, there is an excess _____ for (of) money, people will try to sell bonds, and the interest rate will _____.

   a. demand; rise
   b. demand; fall
   c. supply; fall
   d. supply; rise

8. If the price level falls, the demand curve for money will shift to the _____ and the interest rate will _____.

   a. right; rise
   b. right; fall
   c. left; rise
   d. left; fall

9. If the Fed wants to permanently lower interest rates, then it should raise the rate of money growth if

    a. there is a fast adjustment of expected inflation.
    b. there is slow adjustment of expected inflation.
    c. the liquidity effect is smaller than the expected inflation effect.
    d. the liquidity effect is larger than the other effects.

10. When the growth rate of the money supply is increased, interest rates will rise immediately if the liquidity effect is _____ than the other money supply effects and there is _____ adjustment of expected inflation.

    a. larger; fast
    b. larger; slow
    c. smaller; slow
    d. smaller; fast

Chapter 7

The Risk and Term Structure of Interest Rates

CHAPTER SYNOPSIS/COMPLETIONS

The supply and demand analysis of interest rate behavior in Chapter 6, examined the determination of just one interest rate, even though there are many different interest rates in the economy. This chapter completes the interest rate picture by examining the relationship among interest rates on securities that differ in their riskiness, income tax treatment, and term to maturity.

The relationship among interest rates on different securities with the same term to maturity is called the (1)_____ _____ of interest rates. One attribute of a bond that influences its interest rate is its (2)_____ _____, the chance that the issuer of the bond will default, that is, be unable to make interest payments or pay off the face value when the bond matures. When default risk on a bond increases, the demand curve for this bond shifts to the (3)_____ and the demand curve for default-free bonds shifts to the (4)_____. The result is that as default risk increases, the (5)_____ _____ (the spread between this bond's interest rate and the interest rate on a default-free bond) (6)_____.

Another attribute of a bond that influences its interest rate is its (7)_____, that is, how quickly and cheaply it can be converted into cash if the need arises. Supply and demand analysis reveals that the less liquid a bond is, the (8)_____ its interest rate will be relative to more liquid securities. Therefore, the lower liquidity of corporate bonds relative to U.S. government bonds (9)_____ the spread between the interest rates on these two bonds and thus contributes to the size of the risk premium of corporate bonds.

Income tax rules also have an impact on the risk structure of interest rates. The tax exemption of municipal bonds (10)_____ their interest rate relative to Treasury securities. Similarly, the tax advantages of (11)_____ bonds, which can be cashed in at their par value to pay estate taxes, lowers their interest rates. The risk structure of interest rates is, therefore, explained by three factors: default risk, liquidity, and the (12)_____ _____ treatment of the bond.

54

The relationship among interest rates on bonds with different terms to maturity is called the (13)_____ _____ of interest rates. It is graphed as the (14)_____ _____, a plot of the yields on default-free government bonds with differing terms to maturity. Three theories have been proposed to explain the term structure of interest rates. The first theory, the expectations hypothesis, is derived using the assumption that bonds of different maturities are (15)_____ _____, implying that their expected returns must be equal. It indicates, therefore, that the interest rate on a long-term bond will equal an average of short-term interest rates that people expect to occur over the life of the long-term bond. Although the expectations hypothesis can explain the empirical fact that interest rates on bonds of different maturities tend to move together over time, it is unable to explain the fact that yield curves are usually (16)_____ sloping.

The (17)_____ _____ theory of the term structure sees markets as completely separated or segmented. It assumes that bonds of different maturities are not substitutes at all. Hence, the interest rate for each maturity bond is determined by the supply and demand for that maturity with no effects from (18)_____ _____ on bonds with either shorter or longer maturities. Although this theory can explain why yield curves usually slope upward, it cannot explain the empirical fact that interest rates on bonds of different maturities move together.

The preferred habitat theory of the term structure states the following: the interest rate on a long-term bond will equal an average of short-term interest rates expected to occur over the life of the long-term bond, plus a (19)_____ _____ that responds to supply and demand conditions for that bond. The theory takes the view that bonds of different maturities are (20)_____, so that the expected return on a bond of one maturity does influence the expected return of a bond with a different maturity, but it also allows investors to prefer one bond maturity over another.

The preferred habitat theory is able to explain the two empirical facts discussed above. It explains why interest rates on different maturity bonds move together over time. A rise in short-term interest rates indicates that short-term interest rates will, on average, be (21)_____ in the future and that long-term interest rates will rise along with them. Moreover, it explains why yield curves are usually upward-sloping, suggesting that the risk premium is (22)_____ because of people's preference for short-term bonds. Also, the theory explains a third empirical fact: when short- term interest rates are low, yield curves are more likely to have a steep (23)_____ slope; when short-term interest rates are high, yield curves are more likely to slope downward.

The preferred habitat theory has the additional attractive feature that it permits one to infer what the market is predicting for the movement of short- term interest rates in the future. A steep upward slope of the yield curve means that short-term rates are expected to

(24)_____; a mild upward slope means that short-term rates are expected to remain the same; a flat slope means that short-term rates are expected to (25)_____ moderately; and a downward slope means that short-term rates are expected to fall (26)_____.

EXERCISES

Exercise 1: Default Risk and Liquidity Effects on the Risk Structure

A. Figure 7A plots the supply and demand curves in the corporate bond market and the Treasury bond markets. If the health of the economy improves so that the probability of bankruptcy decreases, draw the new supply and demand curves in Figure 7A.

FIGURE 7A

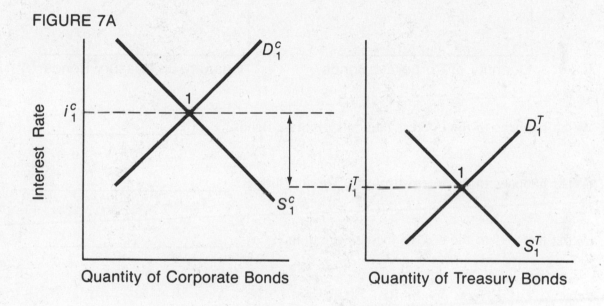

1. What happens to the interest rate on Corporate Bonds? _____

2. What happens to the interest rate on Treasury bonds? _____

3. What happens to the size of the risk premium? _____

B. Figure 7B is identical to Figure 7A. If new dealers enter the Treasury bond market and by so doing increase the liquidity of the Treasury bond market, draw the new supply and demand curves in Figure 7B.

FIGURE 7B

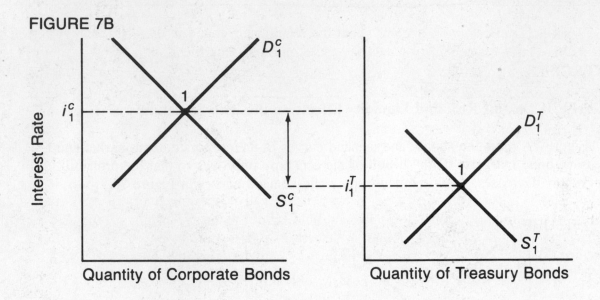

1. What happens to the interest rate on Corporate Bonds? _____

2. What happens to the interest rate on Treasury bonds? _____

3. What happens to the size of the risk premium? _____

Exercise 2: Tax Effects on the Risk Structure

Suppose your income tax bracket is 25%.

1. What is your after-tax return from holding a 1-year municipal bond with an 8% yield to maturity?

_____

2. What is your after-tax return from holding a 1-year corporate bond with a 10% yield to maturity?

_____

3. If both these securities have the same amount of risk and liquidity, then which one of them would you prefer to own?

_____

4. What does this example suggest about the relationship found in the bond market between interest rates on municipal bonds and those on other securities?

_____

Exercise 3: Expectations Hypothesis of the Term Structure

An investor is presented with the following two alternative investment strategies: Purchase a 3-year bond with an interest rate of 6% and hold it until maturity, or purchase a 1-year bond with an interest rate of 7%, and when it matures, purchase another 1-year bond with an expected interest rate of 6%, and when it matures, purchase another 1-year bond with an interest rate of 5%.

1. What is the expected return over the 3 years for the first strategy?

_____

2. What is the expected return over the 3 years for the second strategy?

_____

3. What is the relationship between the expected returns of the two strategies?

_____

4. Why does our analysis of the expectations hypothesis indicate that this is exactly what you should expect to find?

_____

58

Exercise 4: Deriving a Yield Curve

Given that the expectations hypothesis of the term structure is correct, plot in Figure 7C the yield curve when the expected path of 1-year interest rates over the next 10 years is the following: 1%, 2%, 3%, 4%, 5%, 5%, 4%, 3%, 2%, 1%.

FIGURE 7C

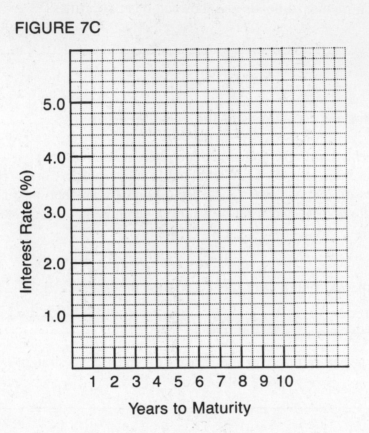

Years to Maturity

Exercise 5: Inferring Market Predictions of Future Interest Rates

A. What is the market predicting about the movement of future short-term interest rates (assuming there is a mild preference for shorter maturity bonds) if the yield curve looks like the one in Figure 7D?

_____

_____

_____

FIGURE 7D

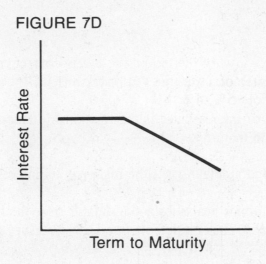

B. What is the market predicting about the movement of future short-term interest rates (assuming there is a mild preference for shorter maturity bonds) if the yield curve looks like the one in Figure 7E?

_____

_____

FIGURE 7E

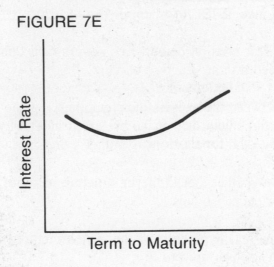

60

SELF-TEST

Part A: True-False Questions

Circle whether the following statements are true (T) or false (F).

T   F   1. The term structure of interest rates is the relationship among interest rates of bonds with the same maturity.

T   F   2. The greater is a bond's default risk, the higher is its interest rate.

T   F   3. Because municipal bonds bear substantial default risk, their interest rates tend to be higher than interest rates on default-free U.S. Treasury bonds.

T   F   4. Negotiable certificates of deposit tend to have lower interest rates than Treasury bills.

T   F   5. The risk premium on a bond only reflects the amount of risk this bond has relative to a default-free bond.

T   F   6. When income tax rates are lowered, the interest rates on Treasury bonds fall relative to the interest rate on state and local bonds.

T   F   7. An increase in estate tax rates would raise the interest rates on flower bonds.

T   F   8. The risk structure of interest rates is explained by three factors: default risk, liquidity, and the income tax treatment of the security.

T   F   9. A plot of the interest rates on default-free government bonds with different terms to maturity is called a term structure curve.

T   F   10. The difference between the expectations hypothesis of the term structure and the preferred habitat hypothesis is that the preferred habitat hypothesis allows for a risk premium while the expectations hypothesis does not.

T   F   11. The expectations hypothesis of the term structure assumes that bonds of different maturities are perfect substitutes.

T   F   12. The segmented markets hypothesis of the term structure is unable to explain why yield curves usually slope upward.

T   F   13. The preferred habitat hypothesis combines elements of both the segmented markets hypothesis and the expectations hypothesis.

T F 14. The preferred habitat hypothesis assumes that bonds of different maturities are not substitutes.

T F 15. The expectations hypothesis is unable to explain why interest rates on bonds of different maturities tend to move together over time.

Part B: Multiple-Choice Questions

Circle the appropriate answer.

1. Which of the following long-term bonds tend to have the highest interest rate?

   a. corporate Baa bonds
   b. U.S. Treasury bonds
   c. corporate Caa bonds
   d. municipal bonds

2. When the default risk on corporate bonds increases, other things equal, the demand curve for corporate bonds shifts to the _____ and the demand curve for Treasury bonds shifts to the _____.

   a. right; right
   b. right; left
   c. left; right
   d. left; left

3. When the corporate bond market becomes less liquid, other things equal, the demand curve for corporate bonds shifts to the _____ and the demand curve for Treasury bonds shifts to the _____.

   a. right; right
   b. right; left
   c. left; left
   d. left; right

4. The risk premium on corporate bonds falls when

   a. brokerage commissions fall in the corporate bond market.
   b. a flurry of major corporate bankruptcies occurs.
   c. the Treasury bond market becomes more liquid.
   d. both (b) and (c) of the above occur.

5. The interest rate on municipal bonds rises relative to the interest rate on corporate bonds when

   a. there is a major default in the municipal bond market.
   b. income tax rates are raised.
   c. Treasury securities become more widely traded.
   d. corporate bonds become riskier.

6. If all taxes were abolished,

   a. the interest rate on flower bonds would fall.
   b. the interest rate on municipal bonds would fall.
   c. the interest rate on municipal bonds would rise.
   d. the interest rate on flower bonds would rise.
   e. both (c) and (d) of the above would occur.

7. Which of the following theories of the term structure is able to explain the fact that when short-term interest rates are low, yield curves are more likely to slope upward:

   a. expectations hypothesis.
   b. segmented markets theory.
   c. preferred habitat theory.
   d. both (b) and (c) of the above.
   e. both (a) and (c) of the above.

8. If the expected path of 1-year interest rates over the next 3 years is 4, 1, and 1% then the expectations hypothesis predicts that today's interest rate on the 3-year bond is

   a. 1%.
   b. 2%.
   c. 3%.
   d. 4%.
   e. none of the above.

9. If the expected path of 1-year interest rates over the next 5 years is 2, 2, 4, 3, and 1%, the expectations hypothesis predicts that the bond with the highest interest rate today is the one with a maturity of

   a. 1 year.
   b. 2 years.
   c. 3 years.
   d. 4 years.
   e. 5 years.

10. If the yield curve slopes upward mildly for short maturities and then slopes sharply upward for longer maturities, the preferred habitat hypothesis (assuming a mild preference for short-term bonds) indicates that the market is predicting

    a. a rise in short-term interest rates in the near future and a decline further out in the future.

    b. constant short-term interest rates in the near future and a rise further out in the future.

    c. a decline in short-term interest rates in the near future and a rise further out in the future.

    d. a decline in short-term interest rates in the near future which levels off further out in the future.

Chapter 8

An Economic Analysis of Financial Structure

CHAPTER SYNOPSIS/COMPLETIONS

Lending is risky. Borrowers with ill intentions may choose to skip town and fail to leave a forwarding address, and even those with honest intentions may undertake actions that increase the probability that they will be unable to meet their payment obligations. Given these hazards, individuals may be understandably reluctant to lend. Although lending is risky for the lender, the channeling of funds from individuals with savings to others with productive investment opportunities is essential for economic growth. Channeling funds from savers to investors is beneficial for the economy and the parties to the exchange, but only if investors have incentives to honor their promises to invest the funds and to pay back the borrowed funds. The key to understanding the structure of financial markets is to ask how the observed financial arrangements (e.g., the dominance of (1)_____
_____ and complicated loan contracts) help to reduce the risk of loan defaults and the uncertainty of lending, thereby encouraging the financing of worthwhile business activities.

Although our financial system is complex in both structure and function, a few simple but powerful economic concepts provide the key insights necessary to understand its complexity. A careful examination of financial markets and institutions reveals that eight basic puzzles require explaining. Economic analysis of the eight puzzles indicates that our financial structure is best understood as a response to the problems of
(2)_____ _____ and (3)_____
_____.

The eight basic puzzles of financial markets in the United States include:

1. Stocks are not an important source of finance for American businesses. Since 1970, the stock market has accounted for only a very small fraction of the financing of American businesses. Moreover, since 1984, American corporations have repurchased such large numbers of shares that stock market financing has been (4)_____.

2. Issuing marketable securities is not the primary way businesses finance their operations. In the United States, (5)_____ are a far more important source of finance than are stocks, yet, combined, bonds and stocks supply less than (6)_____
_____ of the external funds corporations use to finance their activities.

64

3. Indirect finance, which involves the activities of (7)_____
_____, is many times more important than direct finance, in which businesses raise funds directly from lenders in financial markets. If direct finance is defined as the sale to households of marketable securities such as stocks and bonds, then direct finance accounts for less than five percent of the external financing of American business. Most securities are purchased by insurance companies, pension funds, and mutual funds.

4. Banks are the most important source of (8)_____ funds to finance businesses. Indeed, bank loans provide twenty-five times more financing of corporate activities than does the stock market.

5. The financial system is among the most heavily regulated sectors of the economy.

6. Only large, well-established corporations have access to securities markets to finance their activities.

7. (9)_____ is a prevalent feature of debt contracts for both households and businesses.

8. Debt contracts are typically (10)_____ legal documents that place substantial restrictions on the behavior of the borrower.

Two factors help to explain the dominant role played by financial intermediaries in our financial structure: transactions costs and problems that arise from (11)_____ _____. Banks reduce transactions costs by bundling the funds they attract from small savers into loans large enough to finance business undertakings. The bargaining, contracting, and administractive costs--that is, transactions costs--decline as a percentage of the loan amount as the size of the loan increases. Therefore, the administration of loans is subject to economies of scale. Economies of scale in financial markets also helps to explain the popularity of both mutual funds and money market mutual funds. (12)_____ _____--in this instance, brokerage commissions--are significantly reduced while, simultaneously, diversification is increased, both to the benefit of individual savers.

Financial intermediaries further reduce transactions cost through their expertise acquired from continual participation in financial markets. These costs are spread over many loan contracts, significantly reducing per unit costs.

Because borrowers know better the potential returns and associated risks of their investment alternatives than do lenders, financial markets are characterized by asymmetries of information. This informational disadvantage can create problems both before and after the financial transaction is made. (13)_____ _____ is the problem created by asymmetric information before the transaction occurs; (14)_____ _____ is the problem created by asymmetric information

66

after the deal has been made.

Adverse selection in financial markets occurs when bad credit risks are the ones who most actively seek financing and are thus the ones most likely to be financed. Moral hazard in financial markets occurs when borrowers have incentives to engage in activities that are undesirable (i.e., immoral) from the lenders point of view.

Solutions to adverse selection include: the private production and sale of (15)_____ (e.g., bond rating services), government regulation to increase information in securities markets, financial intermediation, requirements that collateral be pledged in loan contracts, and requirements that borrowers have sufficient (16)_____ _____.

The concept of adverse selection explains the first seven of the eight puzzles about financial structure. The first four puzzles emphasize the importance of financial intermediaries. Financial intermediaries--because they have expertise in evaluating (17)_____ _____ --are better able to identify and screen potential bad risks. Moreover, since financial intermediaries such as banks hold mostly non-traded bank loans, they are better able to avoid the (18)_____-_____ problem that would otherwise reduce their incentives to produce information concerning a borrower's creditworthiness. Puzzle five, that financial markets are heavily regulated, is explained by the problem of asymmetric information. Puzzles six and seven can be understood as mechanisms by which lenders (1) screen on the basis of net worth, and (2) reduce their risk exposure by asking that collateral be pledged. Borrowers who are good risks will neither want to lose their collateral nor have their net worth diminished, thus these requirements discourage bad risks from asking for loans and thereby reduce the "lemons problem" in financial markets.

Moral hazard in (19)_____ contracts is known as the principal-agent problem because the manager (the agent) has less incentive to maximize profits than do the stockholders (the principals). Because principals have an incentive to free-ride on others' information gathering efforts, it is likely that too few resources will be devoted to monitoring the agent. Government regulations that force firms to adhere to standard accounting principles, venture capital firms, and debt contracts are financial market mechanisms that reduce principal-agent problems.

The prevalence of debt contracts, relative to equity contracts, does not, however, imply that the use of debt is the sole solution to moral hazard problems. High net worth can reduce moral hazard problems in debt contracts by making them (20)_____ _____. Lenders further reduce their risks by requiring that borrowers comply with a (sometimes lengthy) list of conditions called (21)_____ _____. Finally, because of free-rider problems, financial intermediaries have a comparative advantage in reducing or avoiding moral hazard problems.

Although means have been devised for reducing adverse selection and moral hazard problems, (22)_____ _____ remind us that financial markets are not immune to the disruptions caused by the failure of a major financial or non-financial firm (such as the Knickerbocker Trust Company in 1907 or the Bank of United States in 1930). Financial crises occur when rising adverse selection and moral hazard problems prevent financial markets from channeling funds to those with productive investment opportunities, hastening the decline in economic activity. There are five factors which lead to financial crises: (1) increases in interest rates, (2) stock market declines, (3) increases in uncertainty, (4) bank panics, and (5) unanticipated declines in the price level.

The important economic concepts of adverse selection and moral hazard help us to better understand the structure of our financial system. In the next five chapters, we find that these two important concepts contribute additional insights to workings in financial markets and the behavior of financial market participants.

EXERCISES

Exercise 1: Financial Structure Definitions and Terminology

Match the terms on the right with the definition or description on the left. Place the letter of the term in the blank provided next to the appropriate definition or description.

____ 1. Problem of too little information gathering and monitoring activity because the person undertaking the activity cannot prevent others from benefiting from the information and monitoring.

a. Adverse selection

____ 2. Another term for equity capital, the difference between a firm's assets and its liabilities.

b. Moral hazard

____ 3. Problem that results when the manager behaves contrary to the wishes of stockholders due to the separation of ownership and control.

c. Collateralized debt

____ 4. Term describing the solution that high net worth provides to the moral hazard problem debt in contracts by aligning

d. Restrictive covenants

68

the incentives of the borrower to that
of the lender.

e. Collateral

_____ 5. Major disruptions in financial markets
characterized by sharp declines in asset
prices and the failures of many financial
and nonfinancial firms.

f. Financial crises

_____ 6. Property that is pledged to the lender if a
borrower cannot make his or her debt payments.

g. Incentive compatible

_____ 7. Clauses in bond and loan contracts that
either proscribe certain activities that
borrowers may have incentive to undertake,
or requires certain activities that
borrowers may not have incentive to undertake.

h. Principal-agent problem

_____ 8. The predominant form of household debt
contract, accounting for about 85 percent
of household debt.

i. Net worth

_____ 9. The problem in which borrowers have
incentives to use funds obtained from
external sources to finance riskier projects
than originally envisioned by the lender.

j. Free-rider problem

_____ 10. The lemons problem.

Exercise 2: Adverse Selection and Moral Hazard

The eight basic puzzles of financial markets in the United States are listed below. For each
of the following puzzles, indicate whether the puzzle can be explained by adverse selection
(A), moral hazard (M), or both (B).

_____ 1. Stocks are not an important source of finance for American businesses.

_____ 2. Issuing marketable securities is not the primary way businesses finance their
operations.

_____ 3. Indirect finance, which involves the activities of financial intermediaries, is many
times more important than direct finance, in which businesses raise funds directly

from lenders in financial markets.

_____ 4. Banks are the most important source of external funds to finance businesses.

_____ 5. The financial system is among the most heavily regulated sectors of the economy.

_____ 6. Only large, well-established corporations have access to securities markets to finance their activities.

_____ 7. Collateral is a prevalent feature of debt contracts for both households and businesses.

_____ 8. Debt contracts are typically extremely complicated legal documents that place substantial restrictions on the behavior of the borrower.

Exercise 3: Financial Crises and Aggregate Economic Activity

A. List the five factors in the economic environment that can lead to a substantial worsening of adverse selection and moral hazard problems in financial market, eventually leading to a financial crises.

1. _____

2. _____

3. _____

4. _____

5. _____

B. Most financial crises in the United States have begun with the following four factors:

1. _____

70

2. _____

3. _____

4. _____

SELF-TEST

Part A: True-False Questions

Circle whether the following statements are true (T) or false (F).

T F 1. Stocks are the most important source of external finance for American businesses.

T F 2. In the United States, bonds are a more important source of external finance for business than are stocks.

T F 3. Most American households own financial market securities.

T F 4. Financial intermediaries benefit savers by reducing transactions costs.

T F 5. The "lemons problem" is a term used to describe moral hazard.

T F 6. The free-rider problem helps to explain why adverse selection cannot be eliminated solely by the private production and sale of information.

T F 7. Banks avoid the free-rider problem by primarily making private loans rather than purchasing securities that are traded in financial markets.

T F 8. Collateral, which is property promised to the lender if the borrower defaults, reduces the consequences of adverse selection because it reduces the lender's losses in the case of default.

T F 9. Firms with higher net worth are the ones most likely to default.

T F 10. Equity contracts are subject to a particular example of moral hazard called the principal-agent problem.

T F 11. Moral hazard helps to explain why firms find it easier to raise funds with equity rather than debt contracts.

T F 12. Venture capitalists, unlike banks, are able to reduce moral hazard problems by placing individuals on the the board of directors of the firm receiving the loan.

T F 13. One way of describing the solution that high net worth provides to the moral hazard problem is to say that it makes the debt contract incentive compatible.

T F 14. The requirement that the borrower keep her collateral in good condition, as one of the conditions to receiving a loan, is called a restrictive covenant.

T F 15. Debt-deflation occurs when the price level rises, reducing the value of business firms' net worth.

Part B: Multiple-Choice Questions

Circle the appropriate answer.

1. Since 1984, American corporations

   a. have been repurchasing such large numbers of shares that stock issues have been a negative source of corporate finance in recent years.
   b. have been taking advantage of an especially strong stock market to issue record numbers of new shares in recent years.
   c. have generally abandoned corporate bond and commercial paper markets to concentrate on new stock issues.
   d. have done both (a) and (c) of the above.
   e. have done both (b) and (c) of the above.

2. Which of the following statements concerning external sources of financing for nonfinancial businesses in the U.S. are true?

   a. Since 1984, American corporations in the aggregate have not issued shares to finance their activities.
   b. Issuing marketable securities is not the primary way businesses finance their operations.
   c. Direct finance is many times more important than indirect finance as a source of external funds.
   d. All of the above.
   e. Only (a) and (b) of the above.

3. Poor people have difficulty getting loans because

   a. they typically have little collateral.

   b. they are less likely to benefit from access to financial markets.

   c. of both (a) and (b) of the above.

   d. of neither (a) nor (b) of the above.

4. Financial intermediaries provide their customers with

   a. reduced transactions costs.

   b. increased diversification.

   c. reduced risk.

   d. all of the above.

   e. only (b) and (c) of the above.

5. Because of the adverse selection problem,

   a. lenders are reluctant to make loans that are not secured by collateral.

   b. lenders may choose to lend only to those who "do not need the money."

   c. lenders may refuse loans to individuals with high net worth.

   d. all of the above.

   e. only (a) and (b) of the above.

6. That most used cars are sold by intermediaries (i.e., used car dealers) provides evidence that these intermediaries

   a. help solve the adverse selection problem in this market.

   b. profit by becoming experts in determining whether an automobile is of good-quality or a lemon.

   c. are unable to prevent purchasers from free-riding off the information they provide.

   d. do all of the above.

   e. do only (a) and (b) of the above.

7. Mishkin's analysis of adverse selection indicates that financial intermediaries in general, and banks in particular because they hold a large fraction of non-traded loans,

   a. play a greater role in moving funds to corporations than do securities markets as a result of their ability to overcome the free-rider problem.

   b. provide better-known and larger corporations a higher percentage of their external funds than they do to newer and smaller corporations, which tend to rely on the new issues market for funds.

   c. both (a) and (b) of the above.

   d. neither (a) nor (b) of the above.

8. The principal-agent problem arises because

   a. principals find it difficult and costly to monitor agents' activities.

b. agents' incentives are not always compatible with those of the principals.
c. principals have incentives to free-ride off the monitoring expenditures of other principals.
d. of all of the above.
e. of only (a) and (b) of the above.

9. Equity contracts

a. are agreements by the borrowers to pay the lenders fixed dollar amounts at periodic intervals.
b. have the advantage over debt contracts of a lower cost of state verification.
c. are used much more frequently to raise capital than are debt contracts.
d. are none of the above.

10. Factors that lead to worsening conditions in financial markets include

a. declining interest rates.
b. declining stock prices.
c. unanticipated increases in the price level.
d. only (a) and (c) of the above.
e. only (b) and (c) of the above.

Chapter 9

The Banking Firm and Bank Management

CHAPTER SYNOPSIS/COMPLETIONS

Banks are the most important financial intermediaries in the United States. In this chapter we examine the basic principles of bank management in order to improve our understanding of how banks operate in our economy.

The bank balance sheet, which lists assets and liabilities, can be thought of as a list of the sources and uses of bank funds. It has the characteristic that total assets equal total liabilities plus bank (1)_____ _____. The bank's liabilities are its (2)_____ of funds, which include: checkable deposits, nontransactions deposits, borrowings, and bank equity capital. The bank's assets are its uses of funds, and include: reserves, cash items in process of collection, deposits at other banks, securities, loans, and other assets (mostly physical capital). (3)_____ are either bank deposits held at the Fed or currency that is physically held by banks (called (4)_____ _____). Reserves are held for two reasons. First, by law a certain fraction of deposits must be held as reserves, called (5)_____ _____. Additional reserves, called (6)_____ reserves, can be used by a bank to meet obligations to depositors. Banks also hold U.S. government securities, sometimes referred to as (7)_____ _____ because of their high liquidity.

The basic operation of a bank is to make profits by engaging in the process of asset (8)_____. Banks issue liabilities such as deposits and use the proceeds to buy income-earning assets such as loans. An important consideration for a bank engaged in this process is that when it receives additional deposits, it (9)_____ an equal amount of reserves, but when it loses deposits, it loses an equal amount of reserves.

Banks must ensure that they have enough ready cash to pay their depositors in the event of (10)_____ _____. To keep enough cash on hand, the bank must engage in (11)_____ management, the acquisition of sufficiently liquid assets to meet the obligations of the bank to depositors. Specifically, banks hold (12)_____ and secondary reserves to escape the costs of (a) calling in or selling loans, (b) selling less liquid securities, (c) borrowing from the Fed, and (d) borrowing from other banks or corporations. Excess reserves are (13)_____ against the cost of deposit outflows. The higher are the costs associated with deposit outflows, the

74

(14)_____ excess reserves banks will want to hold.

Banks manage their assets using the following four principles. First, they try to find borrowers who will pay high interest rates and are unlikely to (15)_____ on their loans. Second, banks try to purchase securities with (16)_____ expected returns and low risk. Third, banks attempt to minimize risk by (17)_____ their holdings of both loans and securities. Fourth, banks must manage the liquidity of their assets so they can satisfy reserve requirements without incurring huge costs. This means that banks will hold liquid assets--even if they earn a somewhat (18)_____ return than other assets.

Before the 1960s, liability management was a staid affair. For the most part, banks took their liabilities as (19)_____ and spent their time trying to achieve an optimal mix of assets. Starting in the 1960s, large banks in key financial centers began to explore ways in which liabilities on their balance sheets could provide them with reserves and liquidity. This led to an expansion of (20)_____ _____ markets, such as the federal funds market, and the development of new financial instruments such as (21)_____ _____ (introduced in 1961). Large banks no longer took their sources of funds (liabilities) as given; instead, they aggressively set target goals for (22)_____ growth, acquiring funds by issuing liabilities as they were needed.

With the increased volatility of interest rates in the early 1980s, banks have become more concerned about their exposure to (23)_____ - _____ _____ --the riskiness of earnings and returns that is associated with changes in interest rates. Interest rate fluctuations can significantly impact bank profits. For example, if a bank has (24)_____ rate-sensitive liabilities than assets, a rise in interest rates will reduce bank profits, while a decline in interest rates will raise bank profits.

Bank managers can measure the sensitivity of bank profits to changes in interest rates using two techniques. Under (25)_____ analysis, the difference of rate-sensitive assets and rate-sensitive liabilities (that is, the gap) is multiplied by the change in the interest rate to obtain the effect on bank profits. Alternatively, duration analysis is based on Macauly's concept of (26)_____ , which measures the average lifetime of a security's stream of payments. If the average duration of a bank's assets exceeds the average duration of its liabilities, then rising interest rates will reduce the bank's net worth.

Once a bank has calculated the sensitivity of its profits to fluctuations in interest rates, it can then consider alternative strategies for reducing its interest-rate risk. Although a bank can reduce interest-rate risk by altering its balance sheet, such a strategy may prove costly. In response to the desire of banks to reduce interest-rate risk, financial instruments have been developed which allow banks to manage this risk at a lower cost. Banks' attempts to manage interest-rate risk have led to trading in financial futures, options for debt instruments, and interest-rate swaps.

(27)_____-_____ swaps enable a financial institution that has more rate-sensitive assets than rate-sensitive liabitities to swap payment streams with a financial institution that has more rate- sensitive liabilities than rate-sensitive assets, thereby reducing interest-rate risk for both parties. Banks also can use the financial futures market and the options market for debt instruments to reduce interest-rate risk by hedging. The operation of these markets are discussed in greater detail in Chapter 13.

Another important banking development to emerge in recent years has been the growth in off-balance-sheet activities. (28)_____-_____-_____ activities consist of trading financial instruments and the generation of income from fees, both of which affect bank profits but are not visible on bank balance sheets. Although these activities can increase bank profitability, many believe that they expose banks to increased risk.

EXERCISES

Exercise 1: Definitions and Terminology

Match the terms on the right with the definition or description on the left. Place the letter of the term in the blank provided next to the appropriate definition.

_____ 1. A financial transaction in which two borrowers exchange interest rate payments on a particular amount of money for a specified length of time.

    a. Gap and duration analysis

_____ 2. The riskiness of earnings and returns that is associated with changes in interest rates.

    b. Bank liabilities

_____ 3. Methods employed to measure interest-rate risk.

    c. Nontransaction deposits

_____ 4. Trading financial instruments and the generation of fee income, for example.

    d. Interest rate risk

_____ 5. Commercial banks' sources of funds.

    e. Negotiable CDs

_____ 6. Commercial banks' uses of funds.

    f. Off-balance-sheet activities

_____ 7. The primary source of bank funds.

    g. Bank assets

_____ 8. A simplified balance sheet that lists the changes that occur in balance sheet items.

h. Liquidity management

_____ 9. The acquisition of sufficiently liquid assets to meet the obligations of the bank to depositors.

i. T-account

_____ 10. Financial instruments developed in 1961 that enabled money center banks to quickly acquire funds.

j. Interest rate swaps

Exercise 2: The Bank Balance Sheet

A. List the six major categories of assets in the balance sheet of commercial banks, from the least liquid to the most liquid.

1. _____

2. _____

3. _____

4. _____

5. _____

6. _____

B. List the four major categories of liabilities in the balance sheet of commercial banks, from the smallest as a percentage of total liabilities to the largest.

1. _____

2. _____

3. _____

4. _____

Exercise 3: T-Accounts, and Deposits and Withdrawals

A. Fill in the T-account of the First National Bank if Sheila Student deposits $2000 in cash into her checking account at this bank.

FIRST NATIONAL BANK

Assets	Liabilities

B. Fill in the T-accounts of the First National Bank and the Second National Bank when Sheila writes a $1000 check written on her account at the First National Bank to pay her tuition at State University, which in turn deposits the check in its accounts at the Second National Bank.

| First National Bank | | Second National Bank | |
Assets	Liabilities	Assets	Liabilities

C. What is the net effect of the transactions in A and B on the reserve position at the two banks?

Exercise 4: Bank Response to Deposit Outflows and Liquidity Management

Suppose that the First National Bank has the following balance-sheet position and that the required reserve ratio on deposits is 20%.

Assets		Liabilities	
Reserves	$25 million	Deposits	$100 million
Loans	$75 million	Bank capital	$10 million
Securities	$10 million		

A. If the bank suffers a deposit outflow of $6 million, what will its balance sheet now look like? Show this by filling in the amounts in the following balance sheet.

Assets		Liabilities	
Reserves		Deposits	
Loans		Bank capital	
Securities			

Must the bank make any adjustment in its balance sheet? _____

Why? _____

B. Suppose the bank now is hit by another $4 million deposit outflow. What will its balance-sheet position look like now? Show this by filling in the amounts in the following balance sheet.

Assets		Liabilities	
Reserves		Deposits	
Loans		Bank capital	
Securities			

Must the bank make any adjustment in its balance sheet? _____

Why? _____

C. If the bank satisfies its reserve requirements by selling off securities, how much will it have to sell?

_____

Why? _____

D. After selling off the securities to meet its reserve requirements, what will its balance sheet look like? Show this by filling in the amounts in the following balance sheet:

Assets	Liabilities
Reserves	Deposits
Loans	Bank capital
Securities	

E. If after selling off the securities the bank is now hit by another $10 million of withdrawals of deposits and it sells off all its securities to obtain reserves, what will its balance sheet look like? Again show this by filling in the amounts in the following balance sheet:

Assets	Liabilities
Reserves	Deposits
Loans	Bank capital
Securities	

If the bank is now unable to call in or sell any of its loans and no one is willing to lend funds to this bank, then what will happen to the bank and why?

_____

_____

Exercise 5: Asset Management

List the four main concerns of bank asset management.

1. _____

2. _____

3. _____

4. _____

Exercise 6: Liability Management

List three of the changes in the way banks operate as a result of the flexibility in liabilities management that occurred after 1960.

1. _____

2. _____

3. _____

Exercise 7: Gap Analysis

Suppose that the First State Bank has the following balance sheet:

Assets		Liabilities	
Variable-rate loans	$20 million	Variable-rate CDs	$30 million
Short-term securities	10 million	Money market deposit accounts	15 million
Reserves	10 million	Federal funds	5 million
Long-term loans	40 million	Checkable and savings deposits	30 million
Long-term securities	10 million	Long-term CDs	20 million

A. Calculate the gap by subtracting the amount of rate-sensitive liabilities from rate-sensitive assets.

Gap = _____.

B. If interest rates suddenly increase by two percentage points, will First State Bank's profits increase or decrease? _____.

C. By how much do profits change? _____.

D. If, instead, interest rates were to drop by three percentage points, what will be the change in First State's profits? _____.

82

SELF-TEST

Part A: True-False Questions

Circle whether the following statements are true (T) or false (F).

T F 1. A bank's assets are its sources of funds.

T F 2. Bank capital equals the total assets of the bank minus the total liabilities.

T F 3. Savings accounts are the most common type of nontransaction deposit.

T F 4. Bank capital is listed as a liability in the bank balance sheet.

T F 5. State and local government securities are also called secondary reserves.

T F 6. Checkable deposits are usually the lowest-cost source of bank funds.

T F 7. Checkable deposits are the primary source of bank funds.

T F 8. Interest paid on deposits makes up over half of total bank operating expenses.

T F 9. Banks are only able to borrow reserves from the Fed.

T F 10. Collectively, reserves, cash items in process of collection, and deposits at other banks, are referred to as cash items in a bank balance sheet.

T F 11. Loans provide banks with most of their revenue.

T F 12. A bank failure occurs whenever a bank is not allowed to borrow from the Fed.

T F 13. Asset management is primarily concerned with the acquisition of sufficiently liquid assets to meet the obligations of the bank to depositors.

T F 14. If a bank has more rate-sensitive assets than liabilities, a rise in interest rates will reduce bank profits.

T F 15. Interest-rate swaps allow financial institutions to swap payment streams, thereby reducing interest-rate risk for both parties.

Part B: Multiple-Choice Questions

Circle the appropriate answer.

1. Which of the following bank assets is the most liquid?

   a. Consumer loans
   b. State and local government securities
   c. Physical capital
   d. U.S. government securities

2. Reserves

   a. equal the deposits banks hold at the Fed.
   b. include bank holdings of U.S. government securities.
   c. can be divided up into required reserves plus excess reserves.
   d. equal both (a) and (c) of the above.

3. When a $1000 check written on the Chase Manhattan Bank is deposited in an account at the Bank of America, then

   a. the liabilities of Chase Manhattan Bank increase by $1000.
   b. the reserves of Chase Manhattan Bank increase by $1000.
   c. the liabilities of Bank of America fall by $1000.
   d. the reserves of Bank of America increase by $ 1000.

4. When you deposit a $100 check in your bank account at the First National Bank of Chicago and you withdraw $50 in cash, then

   a. the liabilities of First National Bank rise by $100.
   b. the reserves of First National Bank rise by $100.
   c. the assets of the First National Bank rise by $100.
   d. the liabilities of the First National Bank rise by $50.
   e. none of the above occurs.

5. If a bank has $1 million of deposits and a required reserve ratio of 5%, and it holds $100,000 in reserves, then it must rearrange its balance sheet if there is a deposit outflow of

   a. $51,000.
   b. $20,000.
   c. $30,000.
   d. $40,000.
   e. none of the above.

6. A bank will want to hold less excess reserves (everything else equal) when

   a. it expects to have deposit inflows in the near future.
   b. brokerage commissions on selling bonds rise.
   c. both (a) and (b) of the above occur.
   d. neither (a) nor (b) of the above occurs.

7. When a bank faces a reserve deficiency because of a deposit outflow, it will try to do which of the following first?

   a. Call in loans
   b. Borrow from the Fed
   c. Sell securities
   d. Borrow from other banks

8. A bank failure is more likely to occur when

   a. a bank holds more U.S. government securities.
   b. a bank suffers large deposit outflows.
   c. a bank holds more excess reserves.
   d. a bank has more bank capital.

9. When interest rates are expected to fall in the future, a banker is likely to

   a. make short-term rather than long-term loans.
   b. buy short-term rather than long-term bonds.
   c. buy long-term rather than short-term bonds.
   d. do both (a) and (b) of the above.

10. If Bruce the Bank Manager determines that his bank's gap is a positive $20 million, then a five percentage point increase in interest rates will cause bank profits to

    a. increase by $1 million.
    b. decrease by $1 million.
    c. increase by $10 million.
    d. decrease by $10 million.

Chapter 10

The Banking Industry

CHAPTER SYNOPSIS/COMPLETIONS

This chapter provides a brief overview of the development of the banking structure of the United States. In addition, it examines several issues that are currently being debated in public forums and promise to be of interest for at least the next several years as regulatory changes and innovations continue to transform the banking industry.

The U.S. banking industry is unique in the sense that a multiplicity of regulatory agencies with overlapping jurisdictions monitor the activities of the nation's banks. For example, the Federal Reserve regulates (1)_____ _____ _____ and state banks that are members of the Federal Reserve System; the Comptroller of the Currency regulates (2)_____ banks; and the FDIC and state banking authorities jointly supervise the 7000 (3)_____ banks that are not members of the Federal Reserve System. Additionally, state banking regulatory agencies have sole authority over those relatively few (less than 500) state banks without FDIC insurance.

The multilayered regulatory structure strikes many as an inefficient system with unnecessary duplication and leads them to wonder how such a system evolved. Ironically, today's (4)_____ banking system is the result of the federal government's attempt to eliminate state banks during the Civil War. The attempt failed because state-chartered banks were able to substitute checking account deposits for (5)_____ as a source of bank funds.

Although there are many bank regulatory agencies, duplication of activities is significantly reduced by the segmentation of regulatory responsibilities and the willingness of the federal agencies to accept each others' examinations. (6)_____ _____ are unannounced visits to the bank. Examiners carefully study the bank's records to ascertain whether the bank is complying with regulations and to determine if the bank has sufficient capital. In recent years, these examinations have turned up more (7)_____ _____, some of which have been highly publicized because of their size. The importance of discovering problem banks early is to prevent problems from spreading to other banks and to remind bank management that their behavior is being monitored by regulatory authorities. The consequences of the failure of regulators to monitor these problems has been dramatically demonstrated by the thrift crisis, as is discussed in the next chapter.

There were more bank failures in the 1980s than in any decade since the Great Depression. Despite the problems facing banking today, few would trade today's conditions for those of the 1920s and early 1930s before the introduction of (8)_____ insurance.

Some economists, most notably, Milton Friedman, have called the creation of the FDIC the most important monetary legislation of the century. It is not hard to understand why. Prior to the establishment of the FDIC, the mere rumor that a bank might be having problems could touch off a (9)_____ on a bank as people attempted to withdraw their funds before the bank's cash reserves were depleted. Unfortunately, even sound banks could fail. This occurred when banks were unable to get the cash they needed to meet depositor's withdrawal demands. Much of the bank's assets are loans, which tend to be highly illiquid. Also, because banks hold only a fraction of their total assets in the form of cash, they are unable to (10)_____ all depositors in a short time period. Should all depositors wish to withdraw their funds, the bank will be forced to close its doors unless it can get cash loans from other banks or the central bank. The creation of the FDIC has greatly reduced the incidence of bank runs, since depositors are guaranteed of receiving payment for insured deposits in the event the bank fails.

The FDIC generally employs one of two methods for insuring deposits. The most common method, the (11)_____ and _____ method, involves the reorganization of the bank, usually through a (12)_____ with a healthy bank that accepts the deposit liabilities of the failed institution. The (13)_____ method, tends to be more costly to the insurance fund and is, therefore, used less frequently by the FDIC.

Although there is general agreement that the FDIC has proved extremely beneficial, its existence creates a need for greater (14)_____. Because bank managers know that depositors are protected, they have less incentive to hold (15)_____ as a cushion to protect against losses. Holding less capital will mean greater returns to stockholders and more generous rewards for bank managers. Regulators, recognizing that private and public interests may diverge when deposits are insured, must set and enforce minimum capital requirements if adverse selection and moral hazard problems are to be avoided.

In addition to the many regulatory agencies, the U.S. banking industry is characterized by a plethora of small banks. This structure is best explained by the restrictions of both the federal government and many state governments to (16)_____ _____. These restrictions are the result of public hostility for large banks.

Significantly, however, stringent banking restrictions are starting to break down due to improvements in electronics technology and the push by banks to remain more competitive vis-a-vis nonbank competitors that are not subject to the same types of restrictive regulations. Although the growth of (17)_____ _____ companies has provided a traditional loophole around the McFadden Act, the use of this traditional method may soon be unnecessary. A U.S. Treasury proposal to abolish restrictions on branching across state lines could become law as early as late 1991 or early 1992.

Since 1980, federally-chartered S&Ls have been permitted to branch statewide, and since 1981, mergers of troubled S&Ls with sound institutions, have led to branching of S&Ls across state lines. The impetus behind the more liberal branching laws came from the reluctance of thrift regulators to use the (18)_____ method at a time when so many thrift institutions were in financial trouble. (For more on the actions of thrift regulators in the 1980s, see chapter 11.)

Significant changes have occurred in international banking, where the growth of (19)_____ _____ and the desire of domestic banks to obtain additional funds is evident by the rapid expansion of overseas offices. In the United States, foreign banks have traditionally enjoyed advantages not granted to domestic banks. In response to this disparity, Congress passed the (20)_____ _____ _____ of 1978, which prevented further interstate branching of foreign banks.

Current regulatory practices have been under increasing scrutiny in light of the great many bank and thrift failures. The next chapter presents an economic and political analysis of the crisis in the banking and thrift industries in the 1980s (with particular emphasis on the savings and loan crisis), the problems of the past and current regulatory structure in these industries, and the proposed reforms that are intended to prevent the reappearance of a similar debacle.

EXERCISES

Exercise 1: Definitions and Terminology

Match the terms on the right with the definition or description on the left. Place the letter of the term in the blank provided next to the appropriate definition.

_____ 1. Deposits in banks outside the United States yet denominated in dollars.

    a. International Banking Act of 1978

_____ 2. Bank subsidiary engaged primarily in international banking.

    b. dual banking

_____ 3. Legislation putting domestic and foreign banks on a more equal of the footing.

    c. Comptroller of the Currency

_____ 4. Limited service banks that either do not make commercial loans or alternatively do not acquire deposit liabilities.

d. Federal Reserve Act

_____ 5. System of bank regulation in which banks are supervised by both federal and state regulators.

e. Edge Act corporation

_____ 6. Legislation requiring that national banks join the Federal Reserve System.

f. Eurodollars

_____ 7. Regulatory body that charters national banks.

g. bank capital

_____ 8. Acts as a cushion against a drop in the value of bank assets.

h. nonbank banks

Exercise 2: Multiple Regulatory Agencies

A. In the left-hand column are listed types of financial institutions. In the right-hand column are the regulatory agencies that determine the extent of permissible activities of these institutions. Write the appropriate letter from the right-hand column after the financial institution on the left in the space provided. More than one letter may be used to indicate overlapping regulatory activities.

Financial Institution	Regulatory Agency
National banks _____	a. FDIC
State banks _____	b. Office of Thrift Supervision
Bank holding companies _____	c. Comptroller of the Currency
Savings and loan associations _____	d. Federal Reserve System
Mutual savings banks _____	e. NCUSIF
Credit Unions _____	f. NCUA
International banking facilities _____	g. State banking regulators

B. In February 1991, the U.S. Treasury called for a reform to rationalize the system of overlapping supervisory resposibilities of these different agencies. How would the Treasury proposal change the existing regulatory system?

_____

_____

_____

Exercise 3: FDIC Insurance

Critics of federal deposit insurance claim that it encourages banks to undertake riskier investments, since depositors have less incentive to monitor the activities and investments of banks. Propose some modifications to the current federal deposit insurance scheme that give banks less incentive to undertake excessive risks yet protect unwary depositors from bank failures. Compare your suggestions with those discussed in chapter 11.

_____

_____

_____

Exercise 4: Branch Banking

A. California law permits statewide branch banking. As a result, the California banking market is more concentrated than most other states. Despite the high level of concentration, many economists believe that the California banking market is highly competitive. Do these facts contradict one another? Explain.

_____

_____

_____

B. Nationwide branching is permitted in Canada, yet many economists suggest that competition is limited due to entry restrictions. Using the information from part A, suggest what this implies about competition in banking markets.

_____

_____

C. The savings and loan industry is more concentrated than the commercial banking industry (that is, there are a relatively smaller number of small savings and loans). What explains this fact?

_____

_____

SELF-TEST

Part A: True-False Questions

Circle whether the following statements are true (T) or false (F).

T   F   1.   As measured by the amount of deposits, savings and loans are by far the largest depository institutions.

T   F   2.   The existence of federal deposit insurance is just one indication of the government's desire to promote a sound banking system.

T   F   3.   Noting the lack of strong regulation, many economist argue that bank failures in the first half of the nineteenth century resulted from fraudulent practices.

T   F   4.   The willingness of people to accept checks in payment for goods or services was important to the preservation of state-chartered banks following the National Banking Act of 1863.

T   F   5.   The Comptroller of the Currency has been granted the sole responsibility for supervising bank holding companies.

T   F   6.   Regulations that restrict competition in the banking industry are often justified by the desire to prevent bank failures.

T   F   7.   Periodic examinations of banks help regulators identify problems at banks before they have a detrimental effect on the financial soundness of the economy.

T   F   8.   When a bank fails, the FDIC prefers to pay off insured depositors rather than merge the failed bank with a sound one.

T   F   9.   The ultimate advantage that the FDIC has over state deposit insurance schemes results from the federal government's ability to print money.

T F 10. Bank capital acts as a cushion in cases where the value of bank assets temporarily fall and might otherwise cause the bank to become insolvent.

T F 11. Bank managers have incentives to hold an insufficient amount of capital from a regulator's perspective.

T F 12. It has been argued that the large number of banking firms in the United States can be seen as an indication of the absence of competition rather than the presence of competition.

T F 13. An impetus leading to greater branching of savings and loans has been the merging of financially troubled S&Ls across state lines.

T F 14. Prior to 1978, foreign banks actually enjoyed an advantage over domestic banks in being able to branch across state lines.

T F 15. Some bank failures are a good thing.

Part B: Multiple-Choice Questions

Circle the appropriate answer.

1. Which of the following is a bank regulatory agency?

   a. Comptroller of the Currency
   b. Federal Reserve System
   c. Federal Deposit Insurance Corporation
   d. All of the above

2. The main purpose of federal deposit insurance is

   a. to drive state deposit insurance funds out of business.
   b. to drive private deposit insurance funds out of business.
   c. to help assure depositors that their deposits are safe, thereby preventing bank panics.
   d. none of the above.

3. Although bank regulations have been highly successful in preventing bank failures over the last 50 years, they have had the adverse side-effect of

   a. limiting competition.
   b. encouraging the growth of very large banks.
   c. significantly reducing the number of banks in our economy.
   d. doing each of the above.
   e. doing only (a) and (b) of the above.

4. Of the two primary methods the FDIC uses to handle a failed bank, which does the FDIC usually prefer?

   a. Payoff method
   b. Purchase and assumption method
   c. Bank acquisition method
   d. None of the above

5. Regulators would prefer that bank managers hold the level of capital that

   a. minimizes the probability of bank failure.
   b. maximizes the total revenues of the bank.
   c. maximizes net revenues of the bank.
   d. maximizes marginal revenues of the bank.

6. The large number of small banks that characterize the United States banking structure is probably best explained by

   a. the McFadden Act.
   b. restrictive state branching regulations.
   c. the National Bank Act of 1863.
   d. all of the above.
   e. only (a) and (b) of the above.

7. Savings and loans are regulated by

   a. the Office of Thrift Supervision.
   b. the FSLIC.
   c. the FHLBB.
   d. all of the above.
   e. only (b) and (c) of the above.

8. Which of the following factors explain the rapid growth in international banking in the past 25 years?

   a. Rapid growth of world trade in this period
   b. Decline in world trade since 1960
   c. Creation of the League of Nations
   d. None of the above

9. When economists argue that banking regulations have been a mixed blessing, they are referring to the fact that

   a. bank regulations foster competition at the expense of banking system safety.
   b. bank regulations foster banking system safety at the expense of competition.
   c. branch banking, while desired by consumers, leads to less competition.
   d. bank regulations foster competition by limiting branching.

10. The U.S. banking system has been labeled a dual system because

   a. banks offer both checking and savings accounts.
   b. it actually includes both banks and thrift institutions.
   c. it is regulated by both federal and state governments.
   d. it was established during the Civil War, thus making it necessary to create separate regulatory bodies for the North and South.

Chapter 11

The Crisis in Banking Regulation

CHAPTER SYNOPSIS/COMPLETIONS

As the United States entered into the last decade of this century, issues concerning the past performance, current adequacy, and future direction of banking regulation dominated much of the news coverage of financial affairs. In the wake of the savings and loan bailout, it is important to examine the role of regulation of financial institutions, and assess the behavior of regulators (particularly, as the projected cost to taxpayers continues to rise throughout the early 1990s). Why had the affairs of banking and the savings and loan industries moved from the financial pages to the front pages of America's newspapers and magazines? Where were the regulators in the 1980s as conditions deteriorated? These are important questions that need answers if the current crisis is not to be repeated in the future. Chapter 11 presents an economic analysis of banking regulation that helps one to understand why the banking and thrift industries entered the 1990s in such sorry condition, and offers suggestions so that future crises may be avoided.

In the United States, most depositors hold their funds in accounts insured by the (1)_____ _____ _____ _____ (FDIC). Federal deposit insurance has been a politically popular program since the Great Depression, and has become increasingly popular in the aftermath of disasters with private state-sponsored schemes in Ohio, Maryland, and Rhode Island. Unfortunately, deposit insurance makes it necessary that bank and thrift regulators be particularly diligent. Because deposits up to $100,000 are completely insured, depositors' lose their incentives to (2)_____ their funds when they suspect that the bank is taking on too much risk. The attenuation of depositors' incentives exacerbates (3)_____ _____ and (4)_____ _____ problems, encouraging bank and thrift managers to take on excessive risk.

Because deposit insurance gives financial institutions greater incentives to take on additional risk, regulators must devise methods to discipline managers of banks and thrifts to reduce excessive risk taking. For example, (5)_____ regulations reduce adverse selection problems by preventing undesirable people (e.g., crooks) from gaining control of financial institutions. Restrictions that prevent banks from holding risky assets such as common stocks and junk bonds, and requirements that banks hold minimum levels of (6)_____ reduce moral hazard problems by increasing the cost to owners of bank failures. Regular bank (7)_____ help to ensure that banks and thrifts comply with these requirements.

In recent years, the FDIC has come under criticism for its "too- big-to-fail" policy. Under this policy, the FDIC uses the purchase and assumption method to resolve the failure of a big bank, in effect guaranteeing all deposits. The rationale for this policy is that the failure of a large bank increases the likelihood that a major (8)_____ _____ will occur. This policy, however, reduces the incentives of depositors at big banks to monitor the riskiness of bank assets, thereby encouraging moral hazard. Moreover, critics complain that the policy discriminates against small banks as they find it more difficult to attract large depositors.

FDIC resolution policies generated little controversy before bank failures became increasingly common and the resolution costs soared. In the 1980s, banks failed at rates higher than at any time since the Great Depression. Legislation in the early 1980s afforded bank and thrift managers greater opportunities to take on risk, which many did with adverse consequences. Factors contributing to rising moral hazard and adverse selection problems included: raising deposit insurance coverage from $40,000 to $100,000 per account, phasing out (9)_____ _____ ceilings, the innovation and use of (10)_____ deposits, the sharp increase in (11)_____ _____ from 1979 until 1981, and the severe recession in 1981-82.

The untimely combination of these factors had devastating consequences: by early 1982 as many as one-half of the S&Ls in the U.S. had a negative net worth and were thus insolvent. Instead of closing the insolvent thrifts and stemming the flow of red ink, regulators (12)_____ capital requirements to keep ailing S&Ls open for business. This strategy, called (13)_____ _____, backfired as industry conditions worsened. In retrospect, regulators should have anticipated that regulatory forbearance would not have turned weak institutions into healthy ones. Regulatory forbearance increases (14)_____ _____ because an operating, but insolvent, thrift institution has nothing to lose by taking on greater risk. If the risky loans pay off, then the thrift's owners capture the benefits; if, however, the risky loans turn sour, it is the deposit insurance fund that bears the additional cost.

By 1989, conditions of the nation's savings and loans had deteriorated so dramatically that the government was forced to enact legislation to bail out the (15)_____, which had gone broke paying off the depositors of failed S&Ls. Under the legislation --the Financial Institutions Reform, Recovery and Enforcement Act (FIRREA)-- the Federal Home Loan Bank Board and the FSLIC were abolished. Thrift regulation was transferred to the Office of (16)_____ _____, a bureau within the U.S. Treasury Department, and the FDIC became the sole administrator of the federal deposit insurance system.

Other provisions in FIRREA (passed in August, 1989, at a time when losses at weak and failing thrifts were running at a rate of $1 billion per month) include: an increase in the deposit insurance premiums paid by S&Ls to replenish the reserves of the Savings Association Insurance Fund; the establishment of the (17)_____ _____ _____ to manage and resolve insolvent thrifts placed in conservatorship or receivership; and the imposition of new restrictions on thrift activities. Under these restrictions S&Ls can no longer purchase junk bonds, must limit their commercial real estate loans to four times capital, and must hold at least 70% of their assets in investments that are (18)_____ related.

Although an unfortunate set of economic factors combined to rock the thrift industry in the 1980s, fundamentally, the S&L crisis has its origins in a political structure that gave those individuals, who were responsible for monitoring industry affairs, incentives to pretend that thrifts were not in serious trouble and to pass blame to others. The thrift crisis is an example the moral hazard problem in politics, also known as the (19)_____-_____ problem. Neither regulators nor politicians (i.e., taxpayers' agents) faithfully served the taxpayers, who are ultimately responsible for covering the cost of the S&L bailout.

As conditions in the industry deteriorated, regulators adopted the policy of regulatory forbearance, refraining from closing insolvent thrifts. Perhaps regulators thought that thrifts would weather the adverse conditions and return to profitability. This behavior, described by professor Edward Kane as (20)_____ _____, was consistent with regulators' desire to escape blame for the industry's poor performance. Moreover, this regulatory behavior was tolerated, and even encouraged, by politicians who had received sizable campaign contributions from officers of insolvent thrifts.

EXERCISES

Exercise 1: Problems of Deposit Insurance

Ironically, the existence of deposit insurance increases the likelihood that depositors will require deposit protection, because the threat of withdrawls no longer constrains the managers of banks and thrifts from taking on too much risk. List some of the problems that deposit insurance create or make worse.

1. _____

   _____

2. _____

   _____

3. _____

Exercise 2: Bank Regulation: Reducing Adverse Selection and Moral Hazard

A. List the several ways that bank regulations reduce the adverse selection and moral hazard problems in banking.

1. _____

   _____

2. _____

   _____

3. _____

   _____

4. _____

   _____

B. Explain how regulations specifically designed to reduce moral hazard produce the additional benefit of reducing adverse selection.

_____

_____

_____

_____

Exercise 3: The "Too-Big-To-Fail" Policy

A. Justification of the Policy

1. Describe the intended purpose of the "too-big-to-fail" policy.

_____

_____

B. Implications of the Policy

1. When Continental Illinois became insolvent in 1984, the FDIC guaranteed all deposits, even those exceeding $100,000. The Comptroller of the Currency defended this action, arguing that the largest eleven banks were too big to fail. In 1990, however, the FDIC argued that the Bank of New England was too-big-to-fail, though it was only the thirty- third largest bank in the United States. What are some of the implications of this regulatory policy?

_____

_____

_____

_____

2. Of the 169 banks that failed in 1990, 149 were resolved through "purchase and assumption" transactions, whereby all deposits --including those in excess of the $100,000 limit-- were assumed by the healthy banks. How were the other 20 banks handled?

_____

_____

3. How are uninsured deposits handled in these type of transactions?

_____

_____

Exercise 4: The 1980s--A Rocky Decade for Thrifts and Regulators

A. In the thrift industry, moral hazard and adverse selection problems increased in prominence the 1980s. List the factors that contributed to worsening conditions in the thrift industry in the early 1980s.

1. _____

_____

2. _____

_____

3. _____

_____

4. _____

_____

B. How did regulators respond to worsening thrift performance in the 1980s?

_____

_____

C. Explain why regulators pursued this course of action.

1. _____

2. _____

3. _____

Exercise 5: FIRREA of 1989

A. List the major provisions of the Financial Institutions Reform, Recovery and Enforcement Act of 1989.

1. _____

_____

2. _____

_____

3. _____

4. _____

_____

5. _____

_____

6. _____

_____

Exercise 6: The Political Economy of the S&L Crisis

That taxpayers were poorly served by thrift regulators in the 1980s is now quite clear. An analysis of the political economy of the savings and loan crisis helps one to understand this poor performance, and explains why elected agents of the taxpayers failed to faithfully serve their constituents by directing regulators to do their job. Explain why both politicians and thrift regulators shirked their responsibilities to the taxpayers in the 1980s.

_____

_____

_____

_____

Exercise 7: Regulatory Reforms

The central issue in preventing another saving and loan debacle is the reform of the bank regulatory system to reduce the adverse selection and moral hazard problems created by deposit insurance. List the nine proposed reforms to the bank regulatory system intended to prevent another savings and loan debacle.

1. _____

2. _____

3. _____

4. _____

5. _____

6. _____

7. _____

8. _____

9. _____

SELF-TEST

Part A: True-False Questions

Circle whether the following statements are true (T) or false (F).

T F 1. When a bank is well-capitalized (i.e., has a large amount of equity capital), the bank has less to lose if it fails and is thus more likely to pursue more risky activities.

T F 2. Actions taken by regulators to reduce moral hazard by preventing banks from taking on too much risk (such as regular bank examinations) also help to reduce adverse selection problems by discouraging risk-prone entrepreneurs from entering the banking industry.

T F 3. The FDIC argues that the too-big-to-fail policy protects the soundness of the banking system, since the failure of a very large bank makes it more likely that a major financial disruption will occur.

T F 4. One problem with the too-big-to-fail policy is that it increases the incentives for moral hazard by big banks.

T F 5. Large banks are actually put at a competitive disadvantage relative to small banks as a result of the FDIC's too-big-to-fail policy.

T F 6. A financial innovation that made it easier for high-rolling banks to raise funds was brokered deposits.

T F 7. Part of the policy of regulatory forbearance pursued by thrift regulators in the 1980s included allowing S&Ls to include in their capital calculations a high value for tangible capital called "goodwill".

T F 8. In the 1980s, regulators pursued a policy of regulatory forebearance in hopes that the problems of thrifts would go away.

T F 9. The policy of regulatory forbearance was effective in reducing the risks that thrift institutions took on in the 1980s.

T F 10. The "Texas premium" refers to relatively high quality of Texas thrift institutions due to strict state regulation.

T F 11. The Competitive Equality Banking Act of 1987 transferred regulatory responsibilities of the FSLIC to the FDIC.

T F 12. The agency established to manage and resolve insolvent thrifts placed in conservatorship or receivership, and has the responsibility for selling the assets owned by failed institutions, is the Resolution Trust Corporation.

T F 13. In the 1980s, Congress provided inadequate appropriations to S&L regulators, hampering their ability to monitor thrifts properly.

T F 14. The problem with historical-cost accounting is that changes in the value of assets and liabilities because of changes in interest rates or default risk are not reflected in the calculation of the firm's equity capital.

T F 15. The legislation eliminating the Federal Home Loan Bank Board and transferring its regulatory role to the Office of Thrift Supervision was the Financial Institutions Reform, Recovery and Enforcement Act of 1989.

Part B: Multiple-Choice Questions

1. Moral hazard is an important feature of insurance arrangements because the existence of insurance

   a. reduces the incentives for risk taking.
   b. is a hinderance to efficient risk taking.
   c. causes the private cost of the insured activity to increase.
   d. does all of the above.
   e. does none of the above.

2. Deposit insurance

   a. attracts risk-prone entrepreneurs to the banking industry.

b. encourages bank managers to take on greater risks than they otherwise would.
c. increases the incentives of depositors to monitor the riskiness of their banks' asset portfolios.
d. does all of the above.
e. does only (a) and (b) of the above.

3. Regular bank examinations help to reduce the _____ problem, but also help to indirectly reduce the _____ problem because, given fewer opportunities to take on risk, risk- prone entrepreneurs will be discouraged from entering the banking industry.

a. adverse selection; adverse selection
b. adverse selection; moral hazard
c. moral hazard; adverse selection
d. moral hazard; moral hazard

4. If the FDIC decides that a bank is too big to fail, it will use the

a. payoff method, effectively covering all deposits--even those that exceed the $100,000 ceiling.
b. payoff method, covering only those deposits that do not exceed the $100,000 ceiling.
c. purchase and assumption method, effectively covering all deposits--even those that exceed the $100,000 ceiling.
d. purchase and assumption method, covering only those deposits that do not exceed the $100,000 ceiling.

5. The too-big-to-fail policy

a. puts small banks at a competitive disadvantage relative to large banks in attracting large depositors.
b. treats large depositors of small banks inequitably when compared to depositors of large banks.
c. ameliorates moral hazard problems.
d. does all of the above.
e. does only (a) and (b) of the above.

6. The policy of regulatory forbearance

a. meant delaying the closing of "zombie S&Ls" as their losses mounted during the 1980s.
b. had the advantage of benefiting healthy S&Ls at the expense of "zombie S&Ls", as insolvent institutions lost deposits to healthy institutions.
c. had the advantage of permitting many insolvent S&Ls the opportunity to return to profitability, saving the FSLIC billions of dollars.
d. meant all of the above.

7. The major provisions of the Financial Institutions Reform, Recovery and Enforcement Act of 1989 include

   a. transferring the regulatory role of the Office of Thrift Supervision to the Federal Home Loan Bank Board.
   b. significantly reducing the responsibilities of the FDIC, which no longer administers the federal deposit insurance system.
   c. the establishment of the Resolution Trust Corporation to manage and resolve insolvent thrifts placed in conservatorship or receivership.
   d. all of the above.
   e. only (a) and (b) of the above.

8. That taxpayers were poorly served by thrift regulators in the 1980s is now quite clear. This poor performance is explained by

   a. regulators' desire to escape blame for poor performance, leading to a perverse strategy of "regulatory gambling".
   b. regulators' incentives to accede to pressures imposed by politicians, who sought to keep regulators from imposing tough regulations on institutions that were major campaign contributors.
   c. Congress's dogged determination to protect taxpayers from the unsound banking practices of managers at many of the nations savings and loans.
   d. all of the above.
   e. only (a) and (b) of the above.

9. The bailout of the savings and loan industry was much delayed and, therefore, much more costly to taxpayers because

   a. of regulators' initial attempts to downplay the seriousness of problems within the thrift industry.
   b. politicians who received generous campaign contributions from the savings and loan industry, like regulators, hoped that the problems in the industry would ease over time.
   c. Congress encouraged, and thrift regulators acceded to, a policy of regulatory forbearance.
   d. of fraudulent practices in the S&L industry that went undetected because of weak monitoring efforts by thrift regulators.
   e. of all of the above.

10. Eliminating deposit insurance has the disadvantage of

    a. reducing the stability of the banking system due to an increase in the likelihood of bank runs.

    b. not being a politically feasible strategy.

    c. encouraging banks to engage in excessive risk taking.

    d. all of the above.

    e. only (a) and (b) of the above.

Chapter 12

Nonbank Financial Institutions

CHAPTER SYNOPSIS/COMPLETIONS

This chapter introduces the student to a wide array of nonbank financial institutions. Not long ago this group of institutions was more appropriately studied in a course on financial institutions and of little importance to students of money and banking. Recent financial innovation, however, has erased many of the barriers that once separated banks and nonbank financial institutions, and has blurred the distinction between courses in financial institutions and money and banking. For this reason, a brief overview of the types and activities of these institutions provides the student with a better understanding of the functioning and structure of financial markets.

Financial institutions are all alike in one respect--they all facilitate the movement of funds from savers to (1)_____. The existence of these institutions provides strong evidence of just how highly (2)_____ _____ is valued. Yet each institution is unique, indicating that the diversity of services offered by nonbank financial institutions is the result of specialization in the market for financial services.

(3)_____ _____ companies provide convenient savings plans and insure against the loss of life. Because life insurance companies are exempt from federal income tax, and since payouts can be predicted fairly accurately, they tend to invest in (4)_____-term securities such as corporate bonds.

(5)_____ and (6)_____ insurance companies protect against almost any type of event, such as medical malpractice, fire, automobile accidents, earthquakes, floods, and so on. Without the availability of this insurance, many activities would be too costly to engage in. For example, if physicians were forced to self-insure, many would either quit the profession or specialize in low-risk procedures, not wanting to risk the loss of everything they own due to a malpractice suit. Indeed, rising malpractice premiums for high-risk operations has led some doctors to change specialties or avoid high-risk cases.

The past 10 years has been a decade of change for property and casualty insurance companies. Declining interest rates, and growth in both the number of lawsuits and the size of damage awards in case disputes involving property and casualty insurance have caused the returns to providing this coverage to fall. In response, insurance companies have raised rates dramatically and have, at times, even refused to provide coverage against certain types of losses. Moreover, in the search for profits, insurance companies have begun to enter new markets by insuring the payment of interest on corporate and municipal bonds, and even mortgage-backed securities.

Pension funds also act as financial intermediaries. By providing individuals with (7)_____ _____, these funds help reduce the uncertainty that individuals have adequately provided for their retirement. For some, pension funds are a very convenient savings plan because they may otherwise find it difficult to save or costly to make investment decisions.

Recently, there has been more attention focused on the (8)_____ of pension funds, most notably Social Security. Anticipated liabilities (future payouts) currently exceed contributions to these plans, raising a difficult question of who will be required to pay for the shortfall. Congress has acted to restore confidence in pension funds and to encourage their continued growth with the establishment of the (9)_____ _____ _____Corporation (or Penny Benny), which is designed to function like the FDIC, guaranteeing minimum payments in the event a pension fund should fail to meet its obligations.

Finance companies are financial intermediaries that specialize in the types of loans they issue. (10)_____ _____ and (11)_____ _____ companies provide small loans for consumer purchases. Often these companies make loans to people who cannot obtain (12)_____ from other sources, such as a commercial bank. Business finance companies specialize in (13)_____ , that is, purchasing accounts receivable.

A type of financial intermediary that owes its existence primarily to financial regulations that prohibited interest payments on checking accounts is the (14)_____ _____ _____ _____. Money market mutual funds invest in short-term liquid securities. Other types of mutual funds invest in tax-exempt securities and stocks. These funds allow diversification to be purchased at a small price, especially if the fund is a (15)_____-_____ fund.

Securities (16)_____ are pure middlemen who act as agents for investors wishing to purchase or sell securities. Securities (17)_____, on the other hand, hold inventories of securities and stand ready to buy or sell securities to complete a trade. Dealers make their money on the spread between the bid and ask prices. A (18)_____ trades securities on the floor of organized exchanges. Because the specialist stands ready to buy stocks or sell them from his or her inventory when buy and sell orders do not match, he or she acts as both a broker and a dealer. Clearly, brokers, dealers, and specialists all facilitate exchange in the secondary financial markets.

(19)_____ _____ specialize in providing investment advice to corporations and underwriting their securities issues. (20)_____

shifts the risk to investment banks. Interestingly, it was this type of risk that led to the separation of investment and commercial banking in the 1930s with the passage of the (21)_____-_____ Act. In recent years, more economists have come to question the desirability of this separation, arguing that the act prevents entry and limits the (22)_____ forces that would make underwriting services less costly to business firms. This debate promises to be of special importance over the coming years as financial innovations continue to redefine the barriers that separate commercial and investment banking.

EXERCISES

Exercise 1: Terminology

Match the following terms from the left column with the closely related term from the right. Place the letter of the term from right column in the blank provided next to the appropriate term on the left.

____ 1. Mutual companies   a. Property and casualty insurance

____ 2. Term insurance   b. Regulator

____ 3. Earthquake insurance   c. No cash value

____ 4. ERISA   d. Owned by policyholders

____ 5. Social Security   e. Underwriting

____ 6. Investment banking   f. Underfunded

____ 7. Mutual funds   g. "Penny Benny"

____ 8. SEC   h. Load and no-load

____ 9. Corporate takeovers   i. Specialist

____10. Organized exchange   j. Junk bond financing

Exercise 2: Definitions and Terminology

Match the following terms from the left column with the closely related term from the right. Place the letter of the term from right column in the blank provided next to the appropriate term on the left.

_____ 1. Condition where those most likely to produce the adverse outcome insured against are the ones who purchase insurance.

    a. Coinsurance

_____ 2. Occurs when the existence of insurance encourages insured parties to take increased risks.

    b. Deductible

_____ 3. Premiums based on risk classifications.

    c. Moral hazard

_____ 4. Insurance clause requiring the insured to do certain actions in order for the policy to be in effect.

    d. Adverse selection

_____ 5. In the event of an accident the portion of loss that insured must pay before the insurance company pays anything.

    e. Risk-based premiums

_____ 6. In the event of an accident the portion of loss that insured must pay once the deductible has been paid.

    f. Sallie Mae

_____ 7. Purchases student loans granted by private financial institutions.

    g. Ginnie Mae

_____ 8. Federal agency that buys mortgages.

    h. Restrictive provision

110

Exercise 3: Nonbank Financial Intermediaries

For the following table of financial intermediaries place an X in the appropriate column for each intermediary if they are more likely to hold short- term or long-term assets. Put two Xs under the appropriate column if the intermediary holds tax-exempt securities.

Financial Intermediary	Long-Term Assets	Short-Term Assets
Life insurance companies		
Property and casualty insurance companies		
Private pension funds		
Finance companies		
Money market mutual funds		
Tax-exempt money market mutual funds		

Exercise 4: Property and Casualty Insurance

Assume that juries become more sympathetic to individuals who claim to have been negligently treated by their doctors, and as a result, payments by insurance companies to these individuals increase significantly. Further assume that state regulations prevent insurance companies from raising premiums to reflect the increase in cost. How would you react if you were an owner of a property and casualty insurance company that currently issues medical malpractice policies? How will your decision affect physicians.

_____

_____

_____

Exercise 5: Financial Intermediation

Match the following financial intermediaries with their descriptions. Terms may be used once, more than once, or not at all.

_____ 1. Acquire funds by issuing commercial paper.

    a. Life insurance companies

_____ 2. Municipal bonds represent a significant percentage of assets.

    b. Property and casualty insurers

_____ 3. Underfunding problems have put pressure on Congress.

    c. Investment banks

_____ 4. Specialize in purchasing the securities of energy companies.

    d. Mutual funds

_____ 5. Holds short-term debt securities and permits shareholders to redeem shares by writing checks.

    e. Money market mutual funds

_____ 6. Assist corporations wanting to sell securities in the primary credit markets.

    f. Finance companies

_____ 7. Stand ready to buy and sell securities at given prices.

    g. Public pension funds

_____ 8. Widespread bank failures in the 1930s led to their separation from commercial banks.

    h. Private pension funds

_____ 9. Owe their existence in large part to interest rate ceilings on checking accounts until 1980s.

    i. Securities brokers

_____ 10. Underwrite security issues.

    j. Securities dealers

Exercise 6: Pension Funds

A. The Employee Retirement Income Security Act created the Pension Benefit Guarantee Corporation to serve a role similar to that of the FDIC. What happens to an individual's incentive to monitor the activities of the pension fund knowing that his or her pension is

112

insured by the federal government? Who does have an incentive to monitor the activities of private pension funds that are federally insured?

_____

_____

_____

B. The Wall Street Journal reported on May 20, 1985 that the California State Teachers Retirement System was expected to be underfunded by $ 10 billion over the next 40 years. Controversy arose over a proposal to raise the retirement age from 60 to 65 and to increase teachers' contributions to help make up the shortfall. Naturally, teachers were opposed to increased contributions, preferring that California taxpayers make up the shortfall. Describe the similarities between this case and Social Security.

_____

_____

_____

SELF-TEST

Part A: True-False Questions

Circle whether the following statements are true (T) or false (F).

T F 1. Property and casualty insurance companies specialize in providing policies that pay for losses in the event of fire, accidents, or theft.

T F 2. Insurance companies are unproductive middlemen, since they pay out less than they take in, proving that they produce a service that is valued less than the resources given up.

T F 3. Life insurance companies are able to invest their funds in long-term assets because their payouts to policyholders can be predicted fairly accurately.

T F 4. Property and casualty insurance companies are more likely to hold tax-exempt securities than are life insurance companies.

T F 5. Many pension plans are underfunded, but this need not be a problem as long as companies have earnings sufficient to cover benefit obligations.

T F 6. Junk-bond financing is controversial because the capital raised is sometimes used to finance corporate takeovers.

T F 7. The Social Security system is a public pension plan for which benefits are determined by the contributions into the plan and their earnings.

T F 8. Finance companies, unlike commercial banks, tend to make very large loans.

T F 9. Factoring refers to the selling of accounts receivable at a discount in return for cash.

T F 10. Mutual funds specialize in the pooling of funds that are used to purchase a diversified portfolio of financial securities.

T F 11. Money market mutual funds allow shareholders to withdraw funds simply by writing a check.

T F 12. The chief executive officer of a large firm would likely seek the help of an investment banker if he or she wanted to issue more stock.

T F 13. Underwriters assume the risk of issuing new stock in the hope of earning a profit on its sale.

T F 14. When commercial and investment banking activities are combined under one firm, there is a potential for the risk inherent in investment banking to be transferred to the commercial bank.

T F 15. Commercial and investment banking activities were separated under the National Banking Act of 1863.

Part B: Multiple-Choice Questions

Circle the appropriate answer.

1. Which of the following are financial intermediaries?

   a. Commercial banks
   b. Insurance companies
   c. Pension funds
   d. Mutual funds
   e. all of the above

2. Life insurance policies typically contain a clause stating that the company will not be required to pay death benefits in the event that the insured commits suicide. Life insurance companies include such clauses in insurance contracts to protect against the _____ problem.

    a. moral hazard
    b. adverse selection
    c. restrictive covenant
    d. defined contribution

3. Social Security is an example of

    a. a private pension fund.
    b. an overfunded public pension fund.
    c. an underfunded public pension fund.
    d. a defined contribution plan.
    e. none of the above.

4. General Motors Acceptance Corporation (GMAC) is an example of a

    a. sales finance company.
    b. consumer finance company.
    c. business finance company.
    d. public finance company.

5. Mariann wants to add a new room to her house. What type of finance company will she deal with in getting the loan to finance the room addition?

    a. Sales finance company
    b. Consumer finance company
    c. Business finance company
    d. Public finance company

6. Mutual funds that charge a sales commission when shares are purchased are called

    a. no-load funds.
    b. loaded funds.
    c. sinking funds.
    d. sink-charge funds.
    e. none of the above.

7. When an investment bank purchases a new issue of securities in the hopes of making a profit, it is said to _____ the issue.

   a. pawn
   b. backstock
   c. underwrite
   d. syndicate

8. The agency that helps ensure that potential security purchasers are well-informed is the

   a. FCC.
   b. FTC.
   c. NRC.
   d. SEC.

9. Brokers are distinguished from the dealers in that brokers do not

   a. hold inventories of securities.
   b. make profits.
   c. incur losses.
   d. deal directly with the public.

10. The legislation separating investment and commercial banking is known as the

   a. Humphrey-Hawkins Act of 1978.
   b. Monetary Control Act of 1980.
   c. Federal Reserve Act of 1913.
   d. Glass-Steagall Act of 1933.

Chapter 13

Financial Innovation

CHAPTER SYNOPSIS/COMPLETIONS

Financial innovation was little discussed only 20 years ago. Since then it has received increasing attention from economists as they have come to realize that the financial structure of the economy and its institutions respond in ways that may nullify the intended effects of regulations and blur the distinctions among financial institutions. Over the past three decades, changing demands and costs have influenced the rate of financial innovation. Chapter 13 reviews these factors and offers insight into the course of future financial innovation.

In order to understand the process of financial innovation, always keep in mind that it is decisions by individuals that affect the pace of financial innovation. As a starting point, economists assume that individuals are motivated by the desire to make (1)_____. Since this motive is assumed not to change, any alteration in financial innovation must be explained by a change in the economic environment.

One such change occurred in the 1960s and 1970s as (2)_____ rates rose and became more (3)_____. These fluctuations in interest rates increased what is called (4)_____-_____ risk and led to a demand for financial instruments that would reduce this risk. The responses to these demands took several forms.

As a way of improving the attractiveness of CDs, the Morgan Guaranty Bank in 1977 developed the first (5)_____-_____ certificate of deposit. The motive was clear. By offering a variable-rate CD, Morgan Guaranty Bank became able to attract funds at a (6)_____ interest- rate cost, as many investors preferred the reduction of interest-rate risk.

Lenders discovered that adjustable-rate (7)_____ reduced interest-rate risk to the benefit of both lender and borrower. Borrowers were able to get adjustable-rate mortgages at lower interest rates than fixed-rate mortgages, and lenders preferred them because they reduced their exposure to interest-rate risk.

Another major financial innovation created in response to interest-rate risk was the development of the (8)_____ _____ market. This market enables participants to (9)_____ against adverse movements in the interest rate by locking in a guaranteed rate. A similar type of instrument that provides a form of insurance against adverse interest-rate movements is the (10)_____ contract.

In addition to the impetus toward financial innovation on the demand side, changes in computer technology have stimulated innovations by lowering the (11)_____ of supplying financial services. Three examples include the expansion of credit cards, the rapid growth in (12)_____, and the internationalization of financial markets. The development of new computer technology has lowered the cost of providing these services, making it profitable to offer them to the public.

Ironically, government financial (13)_____ spurred financial innovations designed to avoid the regulations, a process Edward Kane calls (14)_____ _____. For example, nonuniform reserve requirements and Regulation Q ceilings gave banks a strong incentive to create new accounts free of the requirements and ceilings in order to prevent (15)_____ when market interest rates rose above regulated ceilings. Eurodollars, bank commercial paper, overnight repurchase agreements, and NOW accounts are some of the innovations either created or expanded in response to regulations that prevented an orderly adjustment to rising interest rates.

A new financial institution, (16)_____ _____ _____ _____, grew by leaps and bounds in the latter 1970s as depositors sought higher interest rates on their savings. Even tax- exempt money market mutual funds were created for those depositors in high tax brackets.

Regulators respond to financial innovations by devising new regulations that constrain the scope of new services and instruments. This process can lead to a "cat and mouse" game between the financial institutions and the (17)_____ in which both parties adapt continually to each others' moves. In the past, regulators tended to respond both to fears that these innovations reduced the (18)_____ of the financial system and to complaints voiced by representatives of the housing industry concerning the availability of mortgage funds. Because regulatory measures failed to prevent continuing disintermediation, Congress responded with legislation designed to slow the process of financial innovation by removing many of the restrictions giving rise to the innovations. Known as the Depository Institutions Deregulation and Monetary Control Act of 1980, this legislation mandated the gradual phasing out of (19)_____ Q ceilings, and removed prohibitions on the nationwide expansion of (20)_____ accounts.

Given the analysis in Chapter 13, one can infer that the pace of future financial innovation will be in large part determined by the behavior of interest rates, changes in technology, and changes in regulations. In fact, the drop in (21)_____ and interest rates since the early 1980s has slowed, somewhat, the pace of financial innovation. Further changes of banking and financial market regulations, such as those proposed by the Treasury Department in early 1991, could further slow the pace of innovation.

EXERCISES

Exercise 1: Terminology and Definitions

Match the term on the right to the most closely related definition or description on the left by placing the appropriate letter in the blank provided. This exercise will help you become more familiar with the terminology of financial services and instruments presented in Chapter 13.

_____ 1. The process of transforming illiquid financial assets into marketable capital market instruments.

a. Money market mutual funds

_____ 2. Experienced rapid growth between 1978 and 1982.

b. Reserve requirements

_____ 3. 1975 innovation designed to reduce interest-rate risk faced by S&Ls.

c. Securitization

_____ 4. 1977 innovation designed to lower interest-rate cost of acquiring funds.

d. Hedge

_____ 5. Financial futures contract.

e. Call option

_____ 6. Option contracts providing holder with the right to sell a security at the strike price.

f. Adjustable-rate mortgage

_____ 7. Option contract giving holder the right to purchase a security at the exercise price.

g. Variable-rate CDs

_____ 8. Deposit rate ceilings.

h. Put option

_____ 9. Period of heavy stock trading volume due toprogram trading.

i. "Triple Witching Hour"

_____ 10. "Tax" on deposits.

j. Regulation Q

Exercise 2: Financial Innovation

We see in Chapter 11 that financial institutions have responded to changes in market conditions, improvements in technology, and changing regulatory constriants by modifying existing financial instruments and developing new financial instruments as part of ongoing efforts to remain profitable. Financial institutions innovate to: (1) avoid risk, (2) reduce costs by employing new technologies, and (3) evade regulatory constraints. The financial instruments listed below were specifically designed to satisfy these demands. Indicate the primary force behind the financial innovation or instrument. Let AR = avoid risk, RC = reduce cost, and ER = evade regulatory constraints.

_____ 1. Adjustable rate mortgages

_____ 2. Bank credit cards

_____ 3. Internationalization of financial markets

_____ 4. NOW accounts

_____ 5. Variable rate certificates of deposits

_____ 6. Financial futures contracts

_____ 7. Money market mutual funds

_____ 8. Overnight repurchase agreements

_____ 9. Securitization of mortgages

_____10. Options market for debt instruments

Exercise 3: Financial Innovation

Complete the following table. Use a + to indicate increase, 0 for no effect, or a - to indictae decrease. The first example is used to illustrate that an improvement in computer technology is a market disturbance that leads to an increase in financial innovation.

Source of the Disturbance	Effect on Financial Innovation
1. Improvement in computer technology	+
2. Federal Reserve decides to pay interest on required reserves held at district banks	
3. A rapid acceleration in inflation	
4. The reimposition of Regulation Q	
5. Law that reduces FDIC insurance to $10,000 per account	
6. A decline in inflation	
7. Federal Reserve raises the required reserve ratio on existing accounts	

120

SELF-TEST

Part A: True-False Questions

Circle whether the following statements are true (T) or false (F).

T F 1. Government financial regulation has significantly reduced the rate of financial innovation in the past.

T F 2. The underlying force that drives financial market innovation is the never-ending search for greater profits.

T F 3. It is reasonable to assume that when banks introduce variable-rate CDs, which sell very well, both the bankers and the savers are better off because of the innovation.

T F 4. One advantage of financial futures is that individuals can "lock in" a predetermined rate of interest, protecting themselves against movements in future interest rates.

T F 5. If everyone were risk-averse, there would be no demand for financial futures contracts.

T F 6. An option contract gives the individual the right to buy or sell a security at a specified price called the reservation price.

T F 7. Assume that Kristin buys a put option giving her the right to sell a U.S. Treasury bond for the current market price of $11,000. In the event of a significant drop in interest rates, Kristin is likely to exercise her option.

T F 8. The wider use of credit cards coincided with the decline in costs of computer technology.

T F 9. Economic analysis suggests that banks will devise ways around regulations which restrict certain banking activities.

T F 10. Banks look on reserve requirements as if they were a tax.

T F 11. Since Regulation Q could never eliminate competition, it just moved it to another arena. As a result, banks developed new types of securities to attract funds.

T F 12. NOW and share draft accounts are good examples of what Edward Kane calls "loophole mining."

T F 13. Money market mutual funds did not become popular until the Federal Reserve reduced the reserve requirement on them in 1977.

T F 14. Securitization is the process of transforming otherwise illiquid financial assets into marketable capital market instruments.

T F 15. The Monetary Control Act of 1980 (DIDMCA) permitted banks to issue money market deposit accounts (MMDAs) so that they could compete with money market mutual funds more effectively.

Part B: Multiple-Choice Questions

Circle the appropriate answer.

1. Which of the following factors led to financial innovation in the 1970s?

    a. Improvement in computer technology
    b. Increase in demand for securities with lower interest-rate risk
    c. Increase in the costs of financial innovation
    d. All of the above
    e. Only (a) and (b) of the above

2. An improvement in technology stimulates financial innovations by

    a. lowering the cost of providing new services.
    b. raising the demand of providing new services.
    c. reducing the competition from those providing financial services.
    d. doing all of the above.

3. The bundling of a portfolio of mortgage or auto loans into a marketable capital market instrument is known as

    a. "fastbacking."
    b. arbitrage.
    c. computerization.
    d. securitization.
    e. optioning the portfolio.

4. Financial intermediaries that were able to increase profits in the 1970s did so by offering financial services that

    a. appealed to only a small minority of the market.
    b. lowered interest-rate risk.

   c. did both (a) and (b) of the above.
   d. did neither (a) nor (b) of the above.

5. Examples of financial innovations of the 1970s that reduced interest-rate risk include

   a. variable-rate certificates of deposit.
   b. money market mutual funds.
   c. NOW accounts.
   d. all of the above.
   e. only (b) and (c) of the above.

6. Assume that Kayla purchases a call option giving her the right to buy a U.S. Treasury bond for the current market price of $98,000. Under what condition win Kayla want to exercise her option?

   a. U.S. Treasury bond prices fall.
   b. Interest rates fall.
   c. Interest rates rise.
   d. None of the above.

7. Financial futures markets are successful because they are beneficial to individuals who are

   a. risk-averse.
   b. risk-preferers.
   c. risk-seekers.
   d. none of the above.

8. Rather than purchase an insurance policy to protect against interest-rate risk, financial market participants purchase

   a. long-term government bonds.
   b. long-term corporate bonds.
   c. municipal bonds.
   d. options contracts.

9. Reserve requirements

   a. act as a tax on deposits
   b. reduce bank earnings.
   c. encourage banks to create new accounts to avoid reserve requirements.
   d. do all of the above.
   e. do only (a) and (b) of the above.

10. Suppose Federal Reserve policies help create relatively stable financial market conditions. Given this scenario, economic analysis predicts that

   a. people will be more likely to use financial futures.
   b. interest in financial futures will begin to wane.
   c. the pace of financial market innovation will accelerate.
   d. both (a) and (c) of the above will occur.
   e. none of the above will occur.

Chapter 14

Multiple Deposit Creation:
Introducing the Money Supply Process

CHAPTER SYNOPSIS/COMPLETIONS

Movements in the money supply influence all of us by affecting the health of the economy; thus it is important to understand how the money supply is determined. Since deposits at banks (and other depository institutions) comprise the largest component of the money supply, understanding how these deposits are created is the first step in understanding the money supply process. In this and the next two chapters we discover how the behavior of the four players in the money supply process --the (1) _____

_____ (2)_____, (3)_____ , and

(4)_____ from banks-- can lead to changes in the money supply. Of the

four players, the (5)_____ _____ _____,

the central bank of the United States, is the most important and therefore receives most of our attention. (The Federal Reserve System is described in greater detail in Chapter 17.)

The Federal Reserve System performs several important functions. It regulates the supply of money and credit by adjusting the level of reserves in the banking system. This function is referred to as (6)_____ _____. In addition, the Federal Reserve regulates the activities of banks and clears checks.

Examination of a simplified balance sheet of the Fed provides us with a better understanding of the money supply process. An increase in the Fed's monetary liabilities --(7)_____ _____ _____ and (8)_____-- leads to an increase in the money supply. The addition of Treasury currency in circulation (primarily coins) to the liabilities of the Fed is called the (9)_____

_____, or high-powered money. Increases in either

(10)_____ securities or (11)_____

_____, the two assets on the Fed's simplified balance sheet, lead to an increase in reserves and the money supply.

We see from its simplified balance sheet that the Fed can provide

(12)_____ to the banking system by extending loans to banks and/or purchasing government bonds. Reserves are drained from the banking system when the Fed

(13)_____ government bonds. The Fed's buying and selling of government bonds, which accounts for most of the changes in money supply, is called

(14)_____ _____ _____.

When a bank acquires additional excess reserves --total reserves less (15)_____ _____ -- either through the sale of a government bond or a discount loan from the Fed, it can lend the amount of its excess reserves, thereby expanding deposits by an amount equal to the increase in reserves. Since checkable deposits are part of the money supply, the bank's act of lending creates money.

Although an individual bank can lend and create deposits of an amount equal to its excess reserves, the banking system can generate a (16)_____ expansion of deposits when reserves in the system increase. When the Fed provides additional reserves to the banking system, checkable deposits and, therefore, the money supply increase by an amount that exceeds the initial change in reserves. This expansion occurs whether a bank chooses to use its excess reserves to purchase (17)_____ or make loans. The expression describing the multiple increase in deposits generated from an increase in reserves is called the (18)_____ _____ _____ and is equal to the reciprocal of the (19)_____ _____ _____.

A decline in the banking system's reserves will generate a multiple contraction of deposits, a process that is symmetrical to multiple deposit creation.

Although the simple deposit-expansion model indicates that the Fed is able to exercise complete control over the level of deposits by setting the required reserve ratio and the level of reserves, a realistic approach recognizes that the behavior of banks and depositors influences the level of deposits and hence the money supply. If depositors choose to hold more (20)_____ as deposits increase, or if banks choose to hold (21)_____ reserves, then the actual deposit expansion multiplier will be (22)_____ than the simple deposit expansion multiplier.

Chapters 15 and 16 present a more accurate picture of the deposit-expansion process; still, the main findings of Chapter 14 are retained: The Fed changes the money supply through its influence on the level of reserves, and a change in reserves leads to either a multiple expansion or contraction in deposits.

EXERCISES

Exercise 1: How the Fed Provides Reserves to the Banking System

A. Fill in the entries in the following T-accounts when the Fed sells $100,000 of T-bills to the First National Bank.

First National Bank		The Fed	
Assets	Liabilities	Assets	Liabilities

What has happened to reserves in the banking system? _____

_____

B. If, instead, the First National Bank pays off a $100,000 discount loan what will be the entries in the T-accounts below?

First National Bank		The Fed	
Assets	Liabilities	Assets	Liabilities

What has happened to reserves in the banking system? _____

_____

Exercise 2: Deposit Creation--The Single Bank

Suppose that the balance sheet of Pittsburg State Bank is currently as follows:

Pittsburg State Bank

Assets		Liabilities	
Vault cash	$ 100		
On deposit with the		Checkable deposits	$ 9,000
Federal Reserve	900		
Loans	8,000		

A. Calculate the level of excess reserves held by Pittsburg State Bank if the required reserve ratio is 10%.

_____

B. How much can Pittsburg State Bank lend? _____

C. Complete the following T-account when Pittsburg State Bank lends the amount you answered to Part B, assuming the deposits created by the bank are deposited with another bank.

Pittsburg State Bank

Assets	Liabilities

Exercise 3: Deposit Creation--The Banking System

A. Assume that the required reserve ratio is 0.20 and that the Fed purchases $1000 in government bonds from the First State Bank of Bozeman, which, in turn, lends the $1000 of reserves it has just acquired to a customer for the purchase of a used car. If the used car dealer deposits the proceeds from the sale in Bank A, how much in additional loans can Bank A make? What is the change in the money supply after Bank A lends this amount?

B. Assume a similar process occurs for Bank B, Bank C, and Bank D. Complete the following table for these banks (see Table 14.1 in the text for an example) and the totals for all banks.

Bank	Change in Deposits	Change in Loans	Change in Reserves
A	+ $1000.00	+ $800.00	+ $200.00
B	+ 800.00	+ 640.00	+ 160.00
C	_____	_____	_____
D	_____	_____	_____
.	.	.	.
.	.	.	.
.	.	.	.
Total All Banks	_____	_____	_____

Exercise 4: The Simple Deposit Multiplier

1. Write down the formula for the simple deposit multiplier.

_____

2. Assuming that the required reserve ratio is 0.20, what is the change in reserves when the Fed sells $10 billion of government bonds and extends discount loans of $5 billion to commercial banks?

_____

3. Using the simple deposit multiplier formula, calculate the resulting change in checkable deposits.

_____

SELF-TEST

Part A: True-False Questions

Circle whether the following statements are true (T) or false (F).

T F 1. Deposits in banks are the largest component of the money supply.

T F 2. The U.S. Treasury functions as the central bank of the United States.

T F 3. Currency held by depository institutions (banks) is added to currency circulating in the hands of the public to get total currency in circulation.

T F 4. The sum of required reserves and excess reserves is called total reserves.

T F 5. The sum of vault cash and currency in circulation is called the monetary base.

T F 6. The interest rate banks pay to borrow from their regional Federal Reserve bank is referred to as the discount rate.

T F 7. The Fed is limited solely to making loans to banks if it wishes to increase the money supply.

T F 8. The Fed's buying and selling of bonds in the open market is referred to as widening the market.

T F 9. If the First Security Bank of Belfry has $50 in excess reserves, it will be able to lend more than an additional $50 as long as the required reserve ratio is below 100%.

T F 10. An open market purchase of $1000 in government bonds by the Fed will cause the money supply to fall.

T F 11. Assuming that the required reserve ratio is 20%, and open market sale of $100 in government bonds by the Fed will cause the money supply to fail by $500 in the simple deposit expansion model.

T F 12. When a bank chooses to purchase securities instead of making loans, deposit expansion is diminished.

T F 13. Commercial banks (depository institutions) can increase their reserves by borrowing from the Federal Reserve.

T F 14. The Fed increases reserves to the banking system when it purchases government bonds.

T F 15. In the simple model, deposits in the banking system contract by a multiple of the loss in reserves caused by a Federal Reserve sale of government bonds.

Part B: Multiple-Choice Questions

Circle the appropriate answer.

1. The Federal Reserve, the central bank of the United States, performs several important functions. Which of the following are functions performed by the Fed?

   a. Regulation of banks
   b. Check clearing
   c. Supervision of monetary policy
   d. All of the above
   e. Only (a) and (b) of the above

2. The monetary base is comprised of

   a. currency in circulation and Federal Reserve notes.
   b. currency in circulation and government securities.
   c. currency in circulation and reserves.
   d. reserves and government securities.

3. The sum of vault cash and bank deposits with the Fed minus required reserves is called

   a. the monetary base.
   b. the money supply.
   c. excess reserves.
   d. total reserves.

4. When the Fed simultaneously purchases government bonds and extends discount loans to banks,

   a. the money supply unambiguously falls.
   b. the money supply unambiguously rises.
   c. the net effect on the money supply cannot be determined because the two Fed actions counteract each other.
   d. the Fed action has no effect on the money supply.

5. When the Fed simultaneously extends discount loans and sells government bonds,

   a. the money supply unambiguously increases.
   b. the money supply unambiguously falls.
   c. the net effect on the money supply cannot be determined without further information because the two Fed actions counteract each other.
   d. the Fed action has no effect on the money supply.

6. When the Fed wants to reduce reserves in the banking system, it will

   a. purchase government bonds.
   b. extend discount loans to banks.
   c. print more currency.
   d. sell government bonds.

7. The simple deposit multiplier is equal to 4 when the required reserve ratio is equal to

   a. 0.25.
   b. 0.40.
   c. 0.05.
   d. 0.15.

8. The First National Bank of Galata has $150 in excess reserves. If the required reserve ratio is 10%, how much extra can the First National Bank lend?

   a. $1500
   b. $750
   c. $150
   d. $0

9. If excess reserves in the banking system amount to $75 and the required reserve ratio is 0.20, checkable deposits could potentially expand by

   a. $75.
   b. $750.
   c. $37.50.
   d. $375.

10. If some proceeds from loans are used to raise the holdings of currency,

    a. checkable deposits will not increase by the amount indicated by the simple deposit multiplier.
    b. checkable deposits will increase by an amount exceeding that indicated by the simple deposit multiplier.
    c. checkable deposits will increase by an amount indicated by the simple deposit multiplier.
    d. none of the above will occur.

Chapter 15

Determinants of the Money Supply

CHAPTER SYNOPSIS/COMPLETIONS

In this chapter, depositor and bank behavior is incorporated into the monetary process, presenting a more realistic model of the money supply process. The analysis is separated into three steps. First, the focus is on the Fed's control of the monetary base. Second, factors determining the money multiplier are examined. Finally, the decisions of banks that affect the money supply are introduced.

The sum of currency in circulation and total reserves is called the monetary base or (1)_____-_____ _____. Because Federal Reserve actions have a more predictable effect on the monetary base than on (2)_____, money supply models typically focus on the Fed's control over high-powered money.

The primary method employed by the Fed for changing the monetary base is through an (3)_____ _____ _____, the purchase or sale of a government bond. Open-market purchases or sales may involve banks or the nonbank public. Open-market purchases from a bank increase reserves and the (4)_____ _____ by an identical amount. If the open-market purchase is from a member of the nonbank public who deposits the check in a bank, the purchase has an effect on reserves and the monetary base that is (5)_____ to the open-market purchase from a bank. Thus the distinction between reserves and the monetary base is not important for these two transactions. It is when a member of the nonbank public cashes the Fed's check (causing currency in circulation to increase) that a distinction between the effect on the monetary base and reserves needs to be made. The effect of an open-market purchase on the monetary base, however, is always the same, whether the proceeds from the sale are kept in deposits or (6)_____.

An open-market sale will have a predictable impact on the monetary base. The decline in reserves will equal the decline in the monetary base if the sale is to the bank or if a check is drawn to pay for the security. If the security is purchased with currency, reserves remain unchanged. Thus the Fed is much more (7)_____ about the effect of open-market operations on the monetary base than on reserves.

There is an additional reason why the Fed has greater control over the monetary base than over reserves. Shifts from (8)_____ to currency affect the volume of reserves in the banking system, but such shifts have no impact on the level of the monetary base, making it a more stable variable.

Although the preceding discussion indicates that the Fed has far better control over the monetary base than it does over reserves, it would be incorrect to assume that the Federal Reserve has complete control over the monetary base. The Fed cannot unilaterally determine, and thus predict perfectly, the amount of (9)_____ by banks from the Fed. As a reminder that the Fed does not have perfect control over the monetary base, it is useful to think of the monetary base as the sum of the (10)_____ monetary base and the (11)_____ base, which results from discount loans to banks. The (12)_____ base, which is tied directly to open-market operations, is under control of the Fed, but the (13)_____ base, and hence the monetary base, is not.

Inclusion of depositor behavior into the money supply model reveals that the money multiplier depends on depositor preferences for both currency relative to checkable deposits and time deposits relative to checkable deposits. A numerical example with realistic numbers reveals that the simple deposit multiplier greatly (14)_____ the expansion in deposits. Since an increase in the monetary base will mean an increase in (15)_____ _____ _____, only part of any increase in the monetary base will be available for deposit expansion. Also, the money multiplier is smaller because the (16)_____ _____- _____ _____ ratio is greater than zero. Because reserves needed to back time deposits are no longer available to support checkable deposits, the money supply will not increase (or decrease) as much for a given change in the monetary base.

Changes in the required reserve ratio for checkable deposits, the required reserve ratio on time deposits, the currency-checkable deposit ratio, and the time deposit-checkable deposit ratio alter the value of the (17)_____ _____. Increases in any of these ratios --because they reduce the reserves available for lending and deposit expansion-- (18)_____ the money multiplier.

The inclusion of bank behavior into the money supply model indicates that banks' decisions to hold excess reserves or to borrow reserves from the Fed affect the money supply. An increase (decrease) in the excess reserves- checkable deposit ratio reduces (increases) the value of the money multiplier. Thus, when banks hold greater levels of excess reserves, the money supply will (19)_____, all else constant. Alternatively, if banks choose to hold fewer excess reserves and/or increase their level of discount borrowing, the money supply will (20)_____, all else the same.

An examination of the 1980-1990 time period indicates that the behavior of players other than the Federal Reserve can lead to sharp changes in money supply growth in the short run.

Interestingly, the period also indicates that over periods of several years, actions of the Federal Reserve are the primary determinants of movements in the money supply.

EXERCISES

Exercise 1: Definitions

Match the following terms on the right with the definition or description on the left. Place the letter of the term in the blank provided next to the appropriate definition. Terms may be used more than once.

_____ 1. The ratio that relates the change in the money supply to a given change in the monetary base.

a. High-powered money

_____ 2. Federal reserve notes constitute the largest component.

b. Nonborrowed base

c. Monetary base

_____ 3. A purchase of bonds by the Fed.

d. Money multiplier

_____ 4. A sale of bonds by the Fed.

e. Total reserves

_____ 5. The sum of currency in circulation and total reserves.

f. Currency in circulation

_____ 6. The monetary base less discount from the Fed.

g. Open-market purchase loans

_____ 7. The sum of required reserves and excess reserves.

h. Open-market sale

Exercise 2: Open Market Operations, Reserves, and the Monetary Base

A. How will a Federal Reserve sale of $100 of government bonds to banks affect the monetary base and reserves? Fill in the following T-accounts in arriving at your answers:

Banking System

Assets	Liabilities

The Fed

Assets	Liabilities

Change in the monetary base = _____

Change in reserves = _____

B. How will a Federal Reserve sale of $100 of government bonds to the nonbank public affect the monetary base and reserves if the nonbank public pays for the bonds with checks? Fill in the following T-accounts in arriving at your answers:

Nonbank Public

Assets	Liabilities

Banking System

Assets	Liabilities

The Fed

Assets	Liabilities

Change in the monetary base = _____

Change in reserves = _____

C. How will a Federal Reserve sale of $100 of government bonds to the nonbank public affect the monetary base and reserves if the nonbank public pay for the bonds with currency? Fill in the following T-accounts in arriving at your answer:

Nonbank Public

Assets	Liabilities

The Fed

Assets	Liabilities

Change in the monetary base = _____

Change in reserves = _____

How do these answers differ from those in parts A and B? _____

_____

Exercise 3: The Money Multiplier

A. Write the formula for the money multiplier.

_____

B. Calculate the currency-checkable deposits ratio, the time deposit- checkable deposits ratio, the excess reserves ratio, and the money multiplier for the following numbers:

$$r_D = 0.11 \qquad C = \$280 \text{ billion} \qquad T = \$2400 \text{ billion}$$
$$r_T = 0.03 \qquad D = \$800 \text{ billion} \qquad ER = \$40 \text{ billion}$$

$\{C/D\}$ = _____

$\{T/D\}$ = _____

$\{ER/D\}$ = _____

m = _____

C. Calculate the monetary base (B) and total reserves (R).

B = $_____

R = $_____

D. Calculate the new money multiplier and money supply assuming that the Fed lowers the required reserve ratio on checkable deposits to 0.08 and does nothing to change the monetary base. Assume that the deposit ratios remain unchanged.

m = _____

M = $_____

E. Calculate the new level of deposits (D) and currency in circulation (C).

D = $_____

C = $_____

F. Calculate the new level of required reserves (RR) and excess reserves (ER).

RR = $_____

ER = $_____

Exercise 4: Adding Bank Behavior into the Money Supply Model

A. Given the following values, calculate the money multiplier and the money supply:

r_D = 0.10   {C/D} = 0.30 B_n = \$300billion
r_T = 0.02   {T/D} = 5.00   ER = DL = 0

m = _____

M = \$_____

B. Calculate the level of currency (C), the level of deposits (D), the level of required reserves (RR), and the level of total reserves (R) in the banking system.

C = \$_____   RR = \$_____

D = \$_____   R = \$_____

C. Suppose that bankers suddenly decide to hold a cushion of excess reserves equal to ten percent of their checkable deposits. Calculate the new money multiplier, the new money supply, the level of deposits, currency in circulation, and the amount of excess reserves that banks will now hold.

m = _____

M = \$_____

D = \$_____

C = \$_____

RR = \$_____

ER = \$_____

Exercise 5: Factors that Affect the Money Supply

Indicate how the money supply responds to the following changes by filling in the second column of the table below with either a (+) to indicate a rise in the money supply or a (-) to indicate a fall in the money supply.

Change in Variable	Money Supply Response
B	-
rD	-
{C/D}	-
rT	-
DL	-
{ER/D}	-
{T/D}	-

SELF-TEST

Part A: True-False Questions

Circle whether the following statements are true (T) or false (F).

T F 1. The ratio that relates the change in the money supply to a given change in the monetary base is called the money multiplier.

T F 2. Another name for the nonborrowed base is high-powered money.

T F 3. A Federal Reserve open-market purchase from a bank increases the monetary base by more than it increases reserves.

T F 4. When a member of the nonbank public buys a government bond from the Fed with currency, the level of bank reserves is unaffected.

T F 5. Open market purchases and sales have a more predictable effect on reserves than the monetary base because the Fed is unable to prevent changes of currency in circulation.

T F 6. When individuals reduce their holdings of currency by depositing these funds in their bank accounts, the money multiplier increases.

T F   7. If the Fed purchases $10,000 in government securities from a bank and simultaneously extends $10,000 in discount loans to the same bank, then the Fed has kept the monetary base from changing.

T F   8. The Fed has better control over the nonborrowed base than the borrowed base.

T F   9. As the currency-checkable deposit ratio falls, fewer reserves are available to support checkable deposits causing a decrease in the money supply.

T F 10. Deposit rate ceilings that increase the attractiveness of both currency and time deposits relative to checkable deposits cause the money multiplier to fall, all else constant.

T F 11. For a given level of the monetary base, if the Fed began to pay interest on deposits that banks maintain at the Federal Reserve, banks would have greater incentive to hold excess reserves, which would lead to a decline in the money supply, all else constant.

T F 12. The money multiplier from the money supply model that includes depositor and bank behavior is larger than the simple deposit multiplier.

T F 13. An increase in the required reserve ratio for time deposits will have no effect on the level of checkable deposits.

T F 14. If the Fed lowers the required reserve ratio on checkable deposits at the same time the currency-checkable deposit ratio unexpectedly increases, the money supply will expand by more than that predicted by the Fed.

T F 15. An increase in the time deposit-checkable deposit ratio will cause the money multiplier and the money supply to fall, all else the same.

Part B: Multiple-Choice Questions

Circle the appropriate answer.

1. A sale of government bonds by the Fed

   a. is called an open-market sale.
   b. reduces the nonborrowed base, all else the same.
   c. reduces the borrowed base, all else the same.
   d. does all of the above.
   e. does only (a) and (b) of the above.
   f. does only (a) and (c) of the above.

2. If a member of the nonbank public purchases a government bond from the Federal Reserve with currency, then

    a. both the monetary base and reserves will fall.
    b. both the monetary base and reserves will rise.
    c. the monetary base will fall, but reserves will remain unchanged.
    d. the monetary base will fall, but currency in circulation will remain unchanged.
    e. none of the above will occur.

3. Depositors often withdraw more currency from their bank accounts during Christmastime. Therefore, one would predict that

    a. the money multiplier will tend to fall during Christmastime.
    b. the money multiplier will tend to rise during Christmastime.
    c. discount borrowing will tend to fall during Christmastime.
    d. none of the above will occur.

4. The Fed lacks complete control over the monetary base because

    a. it cannot set the required reserve ratio on checkable deposits.
    b. it cannot perfectly predict the amount of discount borrowing by banks.
    c. it cannot perfectly predict shifts from deposits to currency.
    d. of each of the above.
    e. of only (a) and (b) of the above.

5. The money multiplier is smaller than the simple deposit multiplier when

    a. the required reserve ratio on time deposits is greater than zero.
    b. the time deposit-checkable deposit ratio is greater than zero.
    c. the required reserve ratio on checkable deposits is greater than zero.
    d. both (a) and (b) of the above occur.
    e. both (a) and (c) of the above occur.

6. The money multiplier is negatively related to

    a. the time deposits-checkable deposits ratio.
    b. the currency-checkable deposit ratio.
    c. the reserve ratio on time deposits.
    d. all of the above.
    e. only (a) and (b) of the above.

7. For a given level of the monetary base, a drop in the time deposit-checkable deposits ratio win mean

   a. an increase in the money supply.
   b. an increase in the monetary base.
   c. an increase in the nonborrowed base.
   d. all of the above.
   e. only (b) and (c) of the above.

8. For a given level of the monetary base, a drop in the currency-checkable deposits ratio will mean

   a. an increase in the nonborrowed base, but a decrease in the borrowed base of equal magnitude.
   b. an increase in the borrowed base, but a decrease in the nonborrowed base of equal magnitude.
   c. an increase in the money supply.
   d. a decrease in the money supply.
   e. none of the above.

9. If banks reduce their holdings of excess reserves,

   a. the monetary base will increase.
   b. the money supply win increase.
   c. both (a) and (b) of the above will occur.
   d. neither (a) nor (b) of the above will occur.

10. An examination of the 1980-1987 period indicates that

    a. the primary determinant of movements in the money supply is the nonborrowed base.
    b. the shorter the time period, the better is the Fed's control over the money supply.
    c. both (a) and (b) of the above are true.
    d. neither (a) nor (b) of the above are true.

Chapter 16

Explaining Depositor and Bank Behavior: The Complete Money Supply Model

CHAPTER SYNOPSIS/COMPLETIONS

In Chapter 15 we discovered that the decisions of both banks and depositors influence the money supply. Depositors' decisions to hold more currency or time deposits relative to checkable deposits cause both the money multiplier and the money supply to decline. A bank's decision to hold more excess reserves also reduces both the money multiplier and the money supply. Although we now understand how the behavior of both banks and depositors influence the money supply, our analysis is incomplete, because it does not provide a framework for explaining this behavior or predicting future movements in the money multiplier and the money supply. Chapter 16 completes the development of the money supply model by explaining depositor and bank behavior.

Although simple in structure, the complete model is the basis of much of the money supply analysis performed by economists in both the private and public sectors of the economy. For example, the Federal Reserve uses the model to forecast future changes in the money supply. These forecasts allow the Federal Reserve to conduct operations that help counteract the monetary effects of depositor and bank behavior.

Of the deposit ratios, the (1)_____-_____ _____ ratio has had a greater impact on past money supply growth. Examination of the movements in the currency-checkable deposit ratio reveals that changes in (2)_____, (3)_____ _____, (4)_____, and (5)_____ all can affect the currency-checkable deposit ratio. Because risk and liquidity factors do not appear to have appreciable independent effects on the currency-checkable deposit ratio, this chapter concentrates on how factors affecting wealth and expected returns influence this ratio.

An increase in wealth or income causes the currency-checkable deposit ratio to fall, since the holdings of checkable deposits grow relative to the holdings of currency when income or wealth increase. Therefore, as the nation becomes more wealthy over time, one expects the currency-checkable deposit ratio to (6)_____, everything else the same.

Changes in (7)_____ _____ on checkable deposits, (8)_____ _____, and changes in the benefits and costs of engaging in illegal activities produce changes in the expected return on currency relative to checkable deposits. For example, an increase in the interest rate paid on checkable deposits will give people more incentive to shift currency holdings to deposits, thereby causing the currency-checkable deposit ratio to (9)_____

Bank panics were a significant factor causing sharp increases in the currency-checkable deposit ratio before the creation of the (10)_____. Then, bank failures could mean the loss of life savings. Not surprisingly, therefore, fears of bank failures caused dramatic shifts from deposits to currency that (11)_____ the currency-checkable deposit ratio.

Increases in marginal tax rates and the growth of illegal activity also can lead to a growing currency-checkable deposit ratio. Rising marginal tax rates cause the return from underreporting income to rise, giving individuals more incentive to conduct transactions in (12)_____. Persons engaging in illegal activity also have a strong incentive to conduct transactions in cash, since law enforcement agencies find cash transactions difficult to trace.

The historical record of the currency-checkable deposit ratio indicates that the theory of asset demand provides an excellent guide for interpreting movements in the ratio. Moreover, this analysis provides a framework for predicting future movements in the currency-checkable deposit ratio.

The theory of asset demand provides a way of analyzing the movements of the time deposit-checkable ratio as well. Over the period 1951-1978, this ratio exhibited a strong upward trend. Since time deposits grow relative to checkable deposits as wealth increases, wealth and income growth during this 28-year period accounts for much of the ratio's rise. The marked deviation from the upward trend that appears in periods such as 1966-1970 and 1978-1981 occurred when market (13)_____ rates rose above Regulation Q ceiling rates.

Finally, the growth slowdown in the time deposit-checkable ratio beginning in the early 1980s is explained by the new regulatory environment, which includes the introduction of the (14)_____ _____ _____ _____ (MMDA) in 1982.

To understand banks' impact on the money supply, we focus on the determinants of their excess reserve holdings and volume of discount borrowing from the Fed. The market interest rate is one important factor affecting excess reserves holdings and discount borrowing. An increase in market interest rates acts to increase the money supply in two ways. First, rising interest rates increase the cost of holding excess reserves. As interest rates rise, banks will reduce their holdings of excess reserves and increase their lending, thereby expanding the money supply. Second, higher market rates increase the attractiveness of borrowing from the Fed relative to other sources, while an increase in the discount rate makes borrowing in the market relatively more attractive.

Additionally, expectations about (15)_____ _____
influence holdings of excess reserves. Deposit outflows may threaten bank liquidity and
force banks to sell loans at a loss. Higher levels of excess reserves reduce the probability
that deposit outflows will force closure and thus act to insure against this occurrence. If
banks believe that concerns over the soundness of the banking system are likely to lead to
increasing deposit outflows, banks will be induced to hold more (16)_____
_____. Although such concerns are less common today, they were quite
common in the past and help explain why fears of financial chaos were at times self-fulfilling
prophecies.

The complete money supply analysis is structured so that the effects of the eight
variables that influence the money supply can be readily seen. The model breaks these eight
variables into two groups: those which affect the monetary base and those which affect the
(17)_____ _____.

Although the money supply model indicates that a number of factors influence money
growth, it is important to remember that the (18)_____
_____ _____ is the most influential of these factors.
Fluctuations in the nonborrowed monetary base over the long run explain the significant
proportion of the fluctuations in the money supply.

The money supply model--in addition to explaining the money supply process--also
provides valuable insight into past economic events. For example, many economists argue
that it was the failure of the Federal Reserve to appreciate its own importance in the money
supply process that turned an otherwise harsh recession into a full-fledged depression in the
1930s. Milton Friedman and Anna Schwartz contend that a wave of
(19)_____ failures caused the money supply to fall precipitously, driving the
economy into a depression.

The decline in money supply can be easily understood in the context of the complete
money supply model. As concerns over the soundness of banks began to rise, people began
to (20)_____ their deposits from banks, causing the currency-checkable
deposit ratio to (21)_____. Banks responded to these concerns by increasing
their holdings of excess reserves. As banks increased their excess reserve holdings, the
(22)_____ _____ ratio increased. This, combined with a
rise in the currency-checkable deposit ratio, reduced the (23)_____
_____. The result is that predicted by the money supply model: a
significant decline in the money supply.

Many economists argue that much of the hardship of the Great Depression could have
been avoided had the Federal Reserve acted to stem the tide of bank failures by serving as a
lender of last resort, satisfying the demand for liquidity that closed so many banks. Could it
happen again? The next three chapters can help you gain a better understanding of the
evolution of Federal Reserve policymaking since the lessons of the Great Depression.

146

EXERCISES

Exercise 1: Depositor and Bank Behavior

Complete the following statements indicating whether the two variables are positively or negatively related, holding an other factors constant.

1. The currency-checkable deposits ratio is _____ related to income or wealth.

2. The currency-checkable deposits ratio is _____ related to the interest rate paid on checkable deposits.

3. The currency-checkable deposits ratio is _____ related to the occurrence of bank panics.

4. There is a _____ association between illegal activity and the currency-checkable deposits ratio.

5. There is a _____ association between tax rates and the currency-checkable deposits ratio.

6. The time deposit-checkable deposit ratio is _____ related to wealth.

7. The time deposit-checkable deposit ratio is _____ related to the interest rate paid on checkable deposits.

8. The time deposit-checkable deposit ratio is _____ related to the interest rates paid on other assets.

9. The level of excess reserves is _____ related to expected deposit outflows.

10. Discount loan borrowing is _____ related to the market interest rate and _____ related to the discount rate.

Exercise 2: Depositor Behavior

The payments system in Great Britain today must seem to many an outside observer as archaic by U.S. standards.[1]   For example, a British government study revealed that in 1979, 54 percent of all British workers and 78 percent of manual workers were paid in cash, usually on a weekly basis. In the United States, about one percent of workers are paid in cash. Fully 60 percent of British low-paid weekly wage-earners do not even have bank checking accounts. Why the heavy reliance on cash payments? Several explanations have been offered.

Cash payments were first mandated by the British government in the early 1800s to protect laborers from employers who paid employees with tokens that could only be exchanged for goods in company stores. Over time, this payment system has become a tradition that workers are understandably reluctant to abandon. It seems that in Britain's class-conscious society, banks have never been keen on promoting the advantages of banking services to low-paid workers. More than this, however, has been the lack of demand for such services. Inconvenient banking hours, the reluctance of many merchants to accept checks, and high marginal tax rates all create a greater relative demand for cash.

Despite these and other factors, there has been a push by banks to reduce the use of weekly cash payments. Employers are being encouraged to pay workers with checks, while employees have been granted incentives, such as interest-free loans, to open checking accounts.

A. Should the efforts of the British banks in modernizing the payments system prove successful, predict what will happen to the currency-checkable deposits ratio in Britain.

_____

_____

B. Assume that these banks successfully encourage many workers to open checking accounts. What do you predict will happen to the money multiplier over time in Great Britain, holding everything else constant?

_____

_____

C. A rise in muggings and robberies also seems to be affecting the transition. Does the rise in crime speed the transition to checks or hinder it? Explain.

_____

_____

[1] Based on L. Wallace, British Banks Press Workers to Take Check or Credit Instead of Cash Wages, *The Wall Street Journal*, 21 July 1981, p. 31.

Exercise 3: The Money Supply Response in the Complete Model

The following table lists factors affecting the money supply. For decreases in the variables shown indicate whether the money supply increases (+) or decreases (-).

Variable	Change in in Variable	Effect on Money Supply
1. Time deposit-checkable deposits ratio	-	
2. Discount rate	-	
3. Required reserve ratio on time deposits	-	
4. Nonborrowed base	-	
5. Required reserve ratio on checkable deposits	-	
6. Expected deposit outflows	-	
7. Currency-checkable deposits ratio	-	
8. Market interest rates	-	

Exercise 4: The Complete Money Supply Model

A. Suppose that the following relationships hold for the U.S. economy:

$r_D = 0.10$ $\{C/D\} = 0.40$ $B_n = \$220$ billion

$r_T = 0.02$ $\{T/D\} = 1.50$ $DL = ER = 0$

Calculate the money multiplier. $m = \underline{\hspace{2in}}$

Calculate the money supply. $M = \underline{\hspace{2in}}$

B. Assume that owing to fears of bank failures, the currency-checkable deposits ratio increases to 0.50. What is the new value of the multiplier?

$m = \underline{\hspace{2in}}$

If the nonborrowed base in unchanged, then what will be the value of the money supply?

$M = \underline{\hspace{2in}}$

If the Fed uses open market operations to expand the nonborrowed base to keep the money supply constant at its original level, what is the new level of the monetary base?

$$B_n = \rule{3cm}{0.4pt}$$

Exercise 5: The Complete Money Supply Model

A. Assume for a few moments that you are a member of the Federal Open Market Committee (the committee that makes decisions about how fast to let the money supply grow or how much interest rates should fluctuate). Suppose economists at the Fed have determined that the following relationships are believed to hold at the beginning of the month:

$r_D = 0.10$ $\{C/D\} = 0.45$ $B_n = \$250$ billion
$r_T = 0.02$ $\{T/D\} = 2.00$ $DL = ER = 0$

What is the value of the money multiplier? $m = \rule{3cm}{0.4pt}$

What is the value of the money supply? $M = \rule{3cm}{0.4pt}$

If the Fed uses open market operations to cause the money supply to grow by one percent in the next month, what is the new level of the monetary base?

$$B_n = \rule{3cm}{0.4pt}$$

B. Assume that the currency-checkable deposit ratio drops to 0.40 at the beginning of the month, and the Fed--not anticipating this change--increases the monetary base by $2.5 billion. What will be the actual growth rate of the money supply for the month?

_____

_____

What does this example indicate about the control the Fed has over the money supply for short periods of time?

_____

_____

150

SELF-TEST

Part A: True-False Questions

Circle whether the following statements are true (T) or false (F).

T F 1. The sharp increase in the currency-checkable deposit ratio during the Great Depression in part explains why the money supply fell so drastically in the early 1930s.

T F 2. A dramatic increase in the number of robberies across the United States would probably cause people to shift part of their currency holdings to deposits, thereby reducing the currency-checkable deposit ratio.

T F 3. If, in an attempt to reduce borrowing costs, the U.S. Treasury succeeds in encouraging Congress to reimpose interest-rate ceilings on checkable deposits, it is likely that the currency-checkable deposit ratio would increase, everything else constant.

T F 4. Over the last century, increases in income and wealth have contributed to the upward trend in the currency-checkable deposit ratio.

T F 5. The currency-checkable deposit ratio is positively related to the interest rate paid on checkable deposits.

T F 6. Bank panics of the type that occurred in Ohio in 1985 have less impact on the currency-checkable deposit ratio since the creation of the FDIC.

T F 7. A rising currency-checkable deposit ratio may indicate that the underground economy is growing relative to the overall economy.

T F 8. A rise in market interest rates encourages banks to reduce their holdings of excess reserves.

T F 9. An increase in the discount rate relative to market interest rates increases bank incentives to borrow from the Fed.

T F 10. When the Federal Reserve purchases government securities, the nonborrowed base increases.

T F 11. The money supply is negatively related to the discount rate.

T F 12. The public's concern over the soundness of depository institutions in the past has caused banks to hold extra reserves in expectation of net deposit outflows. This behavior may prove self-fulfilling because it causes a contraction in the money supply, all else constant.

T F 13. The money supply is positively related to the interest rate, since at higher interest rates banks will hold fewer excess reserves and increase their borrowing at the Federal Reserve discount window.

T F 14. Ideally, a lender of last resort provides the necessary liquidity to restore depositor confidence, thereby averting bank panics.

T F 15. In the 1930s, banks attempted to protect themselves from deposit outflows by holding higher levels of excess reserves.

Part B: Multiple-Choice Questions

Circle the appropriate answer.

1. The growth in wealth and income during the period 1892 to 1917 helped produce a decline in

   a. the time deposit-checkable deposit ratio.
   b. the currency-checkable deposit ratio.
   c. the required reserve ratio for time deposits.
   d. all of the above.
   d. only (a) and (b) of the above.

2. If marginal tax rates are increased in an effort to reduce government budget deficits,

   a. banks will increase their holdings of excess reserves.
   b. banks will increase the discount borrowing from the Federal Reserve.
   c. the currency-checkable deposits ratio is likely to increase.
   d. the currency-checkable deposits ratio is likely to fall.

3. The theory of asset demand predicts that the currency-checkable deposits ratio will rise when

   a. a large number of banks fail.
   b. marginal tax rates rise due to inflation-induced "bracket creep."
   c. interest rates paid on checkable deposits rise.
   d. all of the above occur.

e. only (a) and (b) of the above occur.
f. only (a) and (c) of the above occur.

4. The decline in the currency-checkable deposits ratio in 1919 and its subsequent rise in the 1920-1921 period is probably best explained by

   a. a reduction in marginal tax rates following World War I.
   b. the decline in income and an increase in the number of bank failures that occurred during the recession of 1920-1921.
   c. both (a) and (b) of the above.
   d. neither (a) nor (b) of the above.

5. The cost to banks of holding excess reserves equals the market interest rate less the interest rate paid on excess reserves. If the Fed increases the interest rate, it pays banks on deposits held at the Fed (currently, the Fed pays a zero rate of interest on these deposits), then banks will _____ their holdings of excess reserves, causing the money supply to _____, all else constant.

   a. reduce; increase
   b. reduce; decline
   c. increase; decline
   d. increase;increase

6. If the Federal Reserve wants to prevent a decline in the money supply during the Christmas holiday season, it will

   a. offset the increase in the money multiplier by reducing the monetary base.
   b. offset the decrease in the money multiplier by expanding the monetary base.
   c. offset the decrease in the money multiplier by expanding excess reserves.
   d. increase the discount rate.

7. If marginal tax rates are significantly increased, people will have a greater incentive to avoid taxes and conduct more transactions in cash. We would predict that

   a. the money multiplier will fall.
   b. the money multiplier will rise.
   c. the currency-checkable deposit ratio will fall.
   d. the money supply will rise.
   e. none of the above will occur.

8. Which of the following explains why the money supply is positively related to the interest rate?

a. An increase in the interest rate induces banks to hold greater excess reserves.
b. An increase in the interest rate induces banks to hold fewer excess reserves.
c. An increase in the interest rate encourages banks to borrow at the Fed discount window.
d. Both (a) and (c) of the above.
e. Both (b) and (c) of the above.

9. If banks expect a high rate of deposit outflows in the near future, they will most likely

a. suspend convertability.
b. print more banknotes.
c. hold more excess reserves.
d. do all of the above.

10. Federal deposit insurance helps insure against bank panics by

a. assuring depositors that their funds are protected.
b. assuring banks that they can legally refuse withdrawal requests.
c. providing the banking system with needed liquidity.
d. doing all of the above.

Chapter 17

The Structure of the Federal Reserve System

CHAPTER SYNOPSIS/COMPLETIONS

Chapter 17 describes the unique structure of the Federal Reserve System and its evolution since 1913. Although the Federal Reserve has been granted a high degree of independence, a clearer understanding of its decisions requires that one acknowledge the political and bureaucratic forces influencing its behavior.

The formal structure of the Federal Reserve System reflects Americans' distrust of the concentration of power in banking. Although many feared the creation of a central bank, the (1)_____ _____ of 1907 convinced many others that a banking system without a (2)_____ _____ _____ _____ could be prone to failures, panics, and payment problems. Thus, the formal structure of the Federal Reserve reflects a compromise among these concerns.

Although responsibility is formally shared across separate, cooperating entities, the Federal Reserve is fundamentally a hierarchical organization. At the top is the (3)_____ _____ _____ --a group of seven members appointed to lengthy terms by the president of the United States and confirmed by the Senate. One member is chosen as (4)_____ -- currently, Alan Greenspan-- who serves a (5)_____ -year term and may be reappointed. Ronald Reagan appointed Mr. Greenspan as chairman in 1987 to succeed two-term chairman, Paul Volcker. The chairman of the Board of Governors wields great power in Washington, D.C., as evidenced by his frequent trips to Capitol Hill to testify on economic policy matters.

Monetary policy decisions are determined by a majority vote of the twelve-member (6)_____ _____ _____ _____ or FOMC. The committee consists of the seven members of the Board of Governors, the president of the Federal Reserve Bank of (7)_____ _____, and presidents from other Federal Reserve banks. The chairman of the Board of Governors also serves as the (8)_____ of the FOMC. Presidents from the other Federal Reserve banks also attend FOMC meetings, and their input is important although they have no formal vote. It is, however, the Board of Governors that dictates the future course of monetary policy (though the FOMC goes to some lengths to achieve consensus).

If we are to understand the decisions of the FOMC, we need to understand the factors that motivate its behavior. Identification of these factors can help economists predict the future course of economic activity and suggest modification in the Fed's structure to improve policy performance. Of particular interest to economists are the bureaucratic and political forces that limit the Fed's independence and shape its decisions.

On the surface, the Federal Reserve is a highly independent government agency. Indeed, perhaps no other federal government institution enjoys greater formal independence. Federal Reserve independence is afforded primarily through three channels. First, the Fed is not directly dependent on congressional (9)_____ to finance its operations. The bulk of the Fed's budget is financed through the interest it earns on its massive holdings of United States (10)_____ _____. These earnings are so significant that in 1985 the Fed returned over $17 billion to the Treasury. Thus the Fed has a degree of discretionary budgetary authority not granted to other agencies.

Second, the seven members of the Board of Governors of the Federal Reserve System are appointed to (11)_____ -year terms on a staggered biannual basis. Therefore, when appointees serve their entire terms, any individual president can at most appoint four members to the board in an 8-year period. Under this constraint, even a reelected president would be unable to appoint a majority of the board until the last year of his second term in office. The 14-year term affords greater autonomy to board members than is found almost anywhere else in government.

Third, the chairman of the Board of Governors presently serves a 4-year term that is not necessarily concurrent with the presidential term. For example, Ronald Reagan did not have the opportunity to appoint a Fed chairman until the summer of 1983, almost 3 full years into the president's term. Stuck with another's appointee for the first 3 years of his term, an incoming president is likely to feel strong pressure from the financial and banking community to retain the present chairman. The present chairman is a known quantity, and financial market participants often favor the known quantity to someone who may substantially change existing arrangements. Interestingly, some observers suggest that President Reagan succumbed to this pressure when in 1983 he re-appointed (12)_____ _____ who had been previously appointed in 1979 by then President Jimmy Carter. In 1991, President Bush felt this same pressure from the financial community to re-appoint Alan Greenspan.

While the Fed retains a relatively high degree of independence, it is not free from political pressure. Politicians need favorable economic conditions to help them win reelection, lenders and the housing industry want low (13)_____ rates, and still other groups --such as those who are retired on fixed incomes-- want low inflation. Given these pressures, the theory of (14)_____ behavior suggests that the Federal Reserve will do best for itself by avoiding conflict with these groups.

In addition, the Fed's desire to hold as much power as possible explains why it lobbies to gain greater regulatory control over (15)_____ . In the past, the Fed has been able to effectively mobilize the banking lobby to kill legislation that would have limited the Fed's power.

Good arguments have been made both for retaining the Fed's independence and for restricting it. The strongest argument to be made for an independent Federal Reserve rests on the belief that subjecting the Fed to more political pressure would impart an (16)_____ bias to monetary policy. However, critics of an independent central bank contend that it is (17)_____ to have monetary policy controlled by a group that is not directly responsive to the electorate. The jury is still out on how best to improve monetary policy, but recognition that the Fed is subject to political and bureaucratic forces helps one to better understand current and past monetary policy (see Chapter 20) and helps one to predict how the Fed will respond to future events.

EXERCISES

Exercise 1: Structure of the Federal Reserve System

The authors of the Federal Reserve Act of 1913 designed a decentralized central banking system that reflected their fears of centralized financial power. Today, this decentralization is still evident in the allocation of responsibilities and duties among the various Federal Reserve entities. Match the Federal Reserve entity to its responsibilities and duties given on the left by placing the appropriate letter in the space provided.

Responsibilities and Duties	Federal Reserve Entity
_____ 1. Clears checks	a. Board of Governors
_____ 2. "Establishes" discount rate	
_____ 3. Reviews discount rate	
_____ 4. Appointed by the president of the United States	
_____ 5. Serve 14-year terms	b. Federal Open Market Committee
_____ 6. Decides discount rate	
_____ 7. Decides monetary policy	
_____ 8. Evaluates bank merger applications	
_____ 9. Determines margin requirements	c. District Federal Reserve Banks
_____ 10. Sets discount rate in practice	

Exercise 2: What Motivates the Fed?

The Board of Governors had the power to set Regulation Q interest-rate ceilings until 1986. In 1966, the Fed may have feared losing control over interest-rate ceilings when some members of Congress discussed passing a bill lowering the ceiling below the rate set by the Board of Governors. In response to the threatened action by Congress, the Fed lowered Regulation Q ceilings in 1966, despite a recognition among some of the board members that such action would create undesirable side effects.[1] Explain why the Fed wanted to act to lower Regulation Q ceilings before Congress did, despite its recognition of undesirable side effects.

_____

_____

_____

_____

Exercise 3: The Theory of Bureaucratic Behavior

According to the theory of bureaucratic behavior the Fed has incentives to employ operating procedures that obscure the actual direction of monetary policy so as to avoid criticism for unpopular policies. Congress has responded on at least two occasions to limit the Fed's ability to disguise monetary policy actions by mandating certain reporting requirements. Still, some critics contend that Congress has not gone far enough in constraining Fed actions. They believe that bureaucratic forces impair monetary policymaking to such a degree that anything short of eliminating independence will be ineffectual in eliminating the Fed's inflationary tendencies.

These critics depict the Fed as an active promoter of, rather than a more passive responder to, inflationary pressures. When the Fed expands the money supply through open-market purchases of government securities, Fed earnings increase as additional interest payments are collected from the U.S. Treasury. Hence critics contend that the Fed has a self-interest incentive to overly expand the money supply to increase its earnings. The additional revenues can then be used to boost employment at the Fed and increase purchases of new office furniture and computers.

_____

[1] See T. Mayer, A Case Study of Federal Reserve Policy-making: Regulation Q in 1966, *Journal of Monetary Economics* 10(1982) pp. 259-271.

Opponents of Fed independence--most notably Milton Friedman--argue that making the Federal Reserve a branch of the U.S. Treasury would eliminate this self-interest incentive. If expansions in the money supply result from the Fed's desire to increase expenditures and expand employment at the Reserve banks, how would making the Fed a branch of the Treasury control this source of inflationary monetary expansion?

_____

_____

_____

Exercise 4: The Independence of The Federal Reserve

The Senate, on July 27, 1983, confirmed the nomination of Paul A. Volcker to a second 4-year term as chairman of the Federal Reserve. The 84 to 16 vote was generally regarded as a strong vote of confidence in Volcker's efforts to bring inflation under control. Volcker, however, was not without his detractors. For example, Senator DeConcini (D-Ariz.) complained that the Fed chairman had "almost single-handedly caused one of the worst economic crises" in U.S. history by not checking the rise in interest rates. "We should be telling Mr. Volcker that in a democracy, we do not combat inflation by placing 12 million citizens on the rolls of the unemployed," DeConcini added.

Although congressional criticism of Fed policies, such as the remarks made by Senator DeConcini, is often intended for the representative's constituents, it does not go unnoticed at the Federal Reserve. After all, the independence of the Federal Reserve was created by congressional legislation, not Constitutional guarantee. Members of Congress have, at times, shown their displeasure of Fed policies by introducing bills threatening the removal of independence. Observers complain that members of the Federal Open Market Committee are so mindful of these threats that political pressures affect monetary policy decisions by constricting the set of feasible policy options considered by the FOMC.

A. How do statements such as those made by Senator DeConcini constrain Federal Reserve policymaking?

_____

_____

_____

_____

B. Many proposals for reforming the Fed have been motivated by concerns that it has not been independent enough and has accommodated too much inflation. Defenders of Federal Reserve independence note that inflation in Germany, Switzerland, and the United States was lower than that in France, Italy, and Great Britain over the period 1960-1984. Speculate as to which countries have the relatively more independent central banks.[2]

_____

_____

Exercise 5: Should the Fed be Independent?

A. List three arguments made by those who support a Federal Reserve that is independent of direct control from either the executive or legislative branches of government.

1. _____

2. _____

3. _____

B. List four arguments that favor a Federal Reserve that is brought under the control of Congress or the president.

1. _____

2. _____

3. _____

4. _____

_____

[2] See King Banaian et al., Central Bank Independence: An International Comparison, Federal Reserve Bank of Dallas *Economic Review*, March 1983, 1-13.

160

SELF-TEST

Part A: True-False Questions

Circle whether the following statements are true (T) or false (F).

T F 1. The Federal Reserve Act, which created a central banking system with regional banks, reflected a compromise between traditional distrust of monied interests and a concern for eliminating bank panics.

T F 2. The three largest Federal Reserve banks in terms of assets--New York, Chicago, and San Francisco--hold approximately 50 percent of the assets in the Federal Reserve System.

T F 3. In practice, each of the 12 Federal Reserve banks sets the discount rate.

T F 4. Membership in the Federal Reserve has continued to rise since a low in 1947.

T F 5. Rising interest rates in the 1970s made Fed membership more costly, accelerating the withdrawal of banks from the system.

T F 6. The Monetary Control Act of 1980 has reduced the distinction between member and nonmember banks.

T F 7. District Federal Reserve Banks essentially have no input regarding monetary policy decisions, since the Board of Governors has sole responsibility for monetary policy.

T F 8. Open-market operations, believe it or not, were not envisioned as a monetary policy tool when the Federal Reserve was created.

T F 9. Past chairmen of the Board of Governors have typically had strong personalities and have tended to dominate policy decisions of the board and the FOMC.

T F 10. The theory of bureaucratic behavior may explain why the Fed seems to be so preoccupied with the level of short-term interest rates.

T F 11. The Fed continues to defend its current discount policy, although economic theory suggests that alternatives would improve monetary control. This apparent paradox is possibly explained by the theory of bureaucratic behavior.

T F 12. The Fed's policy of delaying release of the FOMC directives is consistent with the theory of bureaucratic behavior.

T F 13. The theory of bureaucratic behavior suggests that monetary policy reflects only political and bureaucratic concerns.

T F 14. Placing the Fed under the control of the executive branch may lead to a monetary policy that is more responsive to political pressures.

T F 15. Supporters of placing the Fed under control of the executive branch believe that the electorate should have more control over monetary policy.

Part B: Multiple-Choice Questions

Circle the appropriate answer.

1. The primary motivation behind the creation of the Federal Reserve System was the desire to

    a. lessen the occurrence of bank panics.
    b. stabilize short-term interest rates.
    c. eliminate state regulated banks.
    d. finance World War I.

2. The theory of bureaucratic behavior indicates that

    a. government agencies attempt to increase their power and prestige.
    b. government agencies attempt to avoid conflicts with the legislative and executive branches of government.
    c. both (a) and (b) of the above are true.
    d. neither (a) nor (b) of the above are true.

3. The regional Federal Reserve banks

    a. "establish" the discount rate.
    b. ration discount loans to banks.
    c. clear checks.
    d. do all of the above.
    e. do only (a) and (b) of the above.

4. While the regional Federal Reserve banks "establish" the discount rate, in truth, the discount rate is determined by

    a. Congress.
    b. the president of the United States.
    c. the Board of Governors.
    d. the Federal Reserve Advisory CouncH.

5. A majority of the Federal Open Market Committee is comprised of

   a. the 12 Federal Reserve bank presidents.
   b. the five voting Federal Reserve bank presidents.
   c. the seven members of the Board of Governors.
   d. none of the above.

6. Monetary policy is determined by

   a. the Board of Governors.
   b. the Federal Reserve banks from each district.
   c. the Federal Open Market Committee.
   d. the Federal Reserve Advisory Council.

7. Power within the Federal Reserve is essentially located in

   a. New York.
   b. Washington, D.C.
   c. Boston.
   d. San Francisco.

8. While the Fed enjoys a relatively high degree of independence for a government agency, it feels political pressure from the president and Congress because

   a. Fed members desire reappointment every 3 years.
   b. the Fed must go to Congress each year for operating revenues.
   c. Congress could limit Fed power through legislation.
   d. of all of the above.
   e. of only (b) and (c) of the above.

9. The theory of bureaucratic behavior may help explain why the Fed

   a. remains concerned about short-term interest rates.
   b. reports more than one monetary aggregate.
   c. lobbied for the Monetary Control Act of 1980.
   d. does all of the above.

10. Supporters of keeping the Federal Reserve independent from both the executive and legislative branches of government believe that a less independent Fed would

    a. pursue overly expansionary monetary policies.
    b. be more likely to pursue policies consistent with the political business cycle.
    c. ignore short-run problems in favor of longer-run concerns.
    d. do only (a) and (b) of the above.

Chapter 18

Understanding Movements in the Monetary Base

CHAPTER SYNOPSIS/COMPLETIONS

Chapter 16 examines the factors that affect the monetary base. We discover that while actions of the Federal Reserve are the primary determinants of the monetary base, other factors also affect it.

Examining the Feds balance sheet is a useful way of identifying the factors that affect the monetary base. Factors that add to the monetary base include the following:

1. **Securities.** When the Fed purchases securities, the monetary base increases. If the check the Fed writes to pay for these securities is deposited in a bank, (1)_____ increase by an amount equal to the value of the check. Alternatively, if the check is cashed, currency in circulation rises. In either instance, the monetary base increases by an amount equal to the value of the securities purchased by the Fed.

2. **Discount loans.** Both reserves and the (2) _____ base rise when the Fed extends a discount loan to a bank.

3. **Gold, SDR accounts, and other Federal Reserve assets.** A Fed purchase of gold, SDRs, or any other asset is just an (3)_____ _____ purchase of these assets. Not surprisingly, the effect on the monetary base is the same as an open-market (4)_____ of bonds. Thus the Fed's purchase of a physical asset, say, a new painting to decorate the conference room of the Board of Governors, has an effect on the monetary base that is identical to an open-market purchase of Treasury bills. The Fed acquires an asset, and when the artist deposits the check at her local bank, reserves and the monetary base increase. (If the artist cashes the check, (5)_____ increases instead of reserves, but the effect on the monetary base is the same).

4. **Float.** Because the Fed agrees to credit checks to banks' accounts within a certain time limit, bad weather or other delays in the (6)_____ of checks can result in a check being simultaneously credited to two banks. When this happens, reserves in the banking system increase until the check is processed and the Fed is able to debit the issuing bank's account. In banking language, float is the difference between (7)_____ _____ in the _____ of _____ (checks on which the Fed has not yet collected payment) and (8)_____ _____ _____ _____

(checks that have not yet been debited from the bank on which they are drawn). Hence an increase in float leads to an increase in bank reserves and an equal increase in the monetary base.

5. **Treasury currency outstanding.** An increase in Treasury currency outstanding leads to an (9)_____ in the monetary base.

Factors that subtract from the monetary base include the following:

1. **Treasury deposits with the Fed.** When the Treasury withdraws funds from its accounts at commercial banks (called (10)_____ _____ _____ accounts) and deposits the funds in its account at the Fed, the resulting loss in reserves causes the monetary base to (11)_____. This drop in the base is likely to be only temporary, however, since these funds will soon return to banks as the Treasury writes checks to pay federal employees and suppliers. Although such Treasury actions do not influence the monetary base over longer periods, short-run fluctuations in the base can often be attributed to Treasury payments or tax collections.

2. **Foreign and other deposits with the Fed.** Checks written on U.S. banks that are deposited in foreign or other accounts at the Federal Reserve (12)_____ reserves available to the U.S. banking system, leading to a drop in the monetary base.

3. **Other liabilities and capital accounts.** An increase in "other liabilities and capital" leads to a (13)_____ in the monetary base.

It is important to note that while all the preceding factors lead to changes in the monetary base, the Federal Reserve's ability to affect the monetary base through discounting and (14)_____ _____ _____ gives it accurate control over the monetary base in all but the very short-run time period.

It is commonly thought that budget deficits are financed by printing money. This is true for some (mostly less developed) countries, but not for the United States. Budget deficits do need to be financed, however, and the Federal Reserve may at times feel pressure to finance these deficits in a way that causes the money supply to increase (see Chapter 17).

The (15)_____ _____ _____ indicates that an increase in the government budget deficit must lead to an increase in the sum of the monetary base and outstanding government bonds held by the public. If the government pays for additional spending with higher taxes, the deficit does not increase and the monetary base does not change. Should the government run a deficit, the Treasury must issue bonds to pay for the additional spending. If individuals buy these newly issued bonds, there will be no change in the monetary base. When the public purchases the bonds, the Treasury spends the proceeds returning the funds to the public. Hence the Treasury sale of bonds to the public has no effect on the (16)_____ _____.

When the Treasury issues a large volume of bonds, there may be upward pressure on
(17)_____ _____. Federal Reserve officials, concerned
about the effects rising interest rates have on the economy, may decide to
(18)_____ Treasury securities to ease deficit financing pressures. In
exchange for the securities, the Fed credits the Treasury's account by an amount equal to the
value of the securities. Importantly, when the Treasury spends these proceeds, reserves are
added to the banking system. Thus, unlike tax or bond financing, deficit financing through
Fed security purchases leads to an increase in the monetary base. This method of deficit
financing is often referred to as (19)_____ _____ because
high-powered money is created in the process (though money is not actually printed to
finance these purchases). The action is probably better referred to as
(20)_____ _____ _____ because the money
supply increases as a result of the increase in government debt.

EXERCISES

Exercise 1: The Fed's Balance Sheet

A. List the six items found on the asset side of the consolidated balance sheet of the Federal
Reserve System.

1. _____

2. _____

3. _____

4. _____

5. _____

6. _____

B. List the six items found on the liability side of the consolidated balance sheet of the
Federal Reserve System.

1. _____

2. _____

3. _____

4. _____

5. _____

6. _____

Exercise 2: Factors that Affect the Monetary Base

In the following table, factors affecting the monetary base are listed. For decreases in the factors shown, indicate in the second column whether the monetary base increases (+) or decreases (-).

	Change in Factor	Response of Monetary Base
Treasury Currency	-	
Gold and SDR accounts	-	
Other Fed assets	-	
Other Fed liabilities	-	
Securities	-	
Float	-	
Treasury deposits	-	
Discount loans	-	
Foreign deposits	-	

B. If the Fed wants to offset this change in the monetary base, what can it do?

_____

_____

_____

Exercise 5: Factors Affecting the Monetary Base

Data for bank reserves and the sources of changes in the monetary base (also the sources of changes in reserves) are published every Friday or Monday in *The Wall Street Journal*.

Reported in the following table are the changes in the selected items for the week ended October 21, 1987. Use the items listed in the table to calculate the change in the monetary base during the week.

**Changes in Weekly Averages of Reserves and Related Items
During the Week Ended October 21, 1987 (in millions of dollars)**

Purchases of U.S. government and agency securities and bankers' acceptances	+ 5416
Discount loans	+ 66
Float	+ 172
Gold and SDR accounts	0
Other Federal Reserve assets	+ 100
Treasury currency outstanding	+ 14
SUBTOTAL 1	_____
Treasury deposits at the Fed	+ 8910
Foreign and other deposits at the Fed	+ 78
Other Federal Reserve liabilities and capital accounts	+ 308
SUBTOTAL 2	_____
Change in monetary base = Subtotal 1 - Subtotal 2 =	_____

Source: *The Wall Street Journal*, 23 October 1987.

Exercise 6: The Budget Deficit and the Monetary Base

A. List the three methods that can be used to finance government spending.

1. _____

2. _____

3. _____

168

B. Which of the three methods has an affect on the monetary base?

_____

C. When the government borrows from the Fed, the monetary base increases. This method of finance is referred to as

_____

D. Does a large government deficit necessarily lead to a rapid growth in the monetary base? Why or why not?

_____

_____

SELF-TEST

Part A: True-False Questions

Circle whether the following statements are true (T) or false (F).

T F 1. If the Fed purchases foreign currencies (other Federal Reserve assets) from domestic banks, the monetary base will increase.

T F 2. Federal Reserve notes--paper money in the United States--are liabilities of the Federal Reserve System.

T F 3. When the Treasury writes a check to pay for refurbishing a World War II battleship, bank reserves fall.

T F 4. A Treasury purchase of office supplies leads to an increase in the monetary base no matter how the purchase is financed.

T F 5. A rise in Treasury deposits at the Fed increases the monetary base.

T F 6. When the Treasury sells gold coins, the sale causes the money supply to rise, since currency in circulation rises.

T F 7. The Federal Reserve can offset an increase in float by purchasing government securities.

T F 8. The Federal Reserve can offset a large Treasury purchase of gold by selling government securities.

T F 9. The Federal Reserve can offset an increase in Treasury deposits by extending discount loans to banks.

T F 10. When the government increases expenditures that it finances with a tax increase, the monetary base remains unchanged.

T F 11. Deficits financed by bond sales to the public reduce currency in circulation and the monetary base.

T F 12. The Fed may feel pressure to finance government budget deficits to keep interest rates from rising.

T F 13. When the Fed purchases securities issued to finance a deficit, the monetary base expands. This method of deficit finance is often called monetizing the debt.

T F 14. Although budget deficits do not have to affect the monetary base, they might because of Federal Reserve concerns over interest rates.

T F 15. Because many factors beyond the direct control of the Fed affect the monetary base, it is unreasonable to expect the Fed to have any meaningful control over the monetary base.

Part B: Multiple-Choice Questions

Circle the appropriate answer.

1. Which of the following are found on the asset side of the Federal Reserve's balance sheet?

   a. Treasury securities
   b. Treasury deposits
   c. Discount loans
   d. Both (a) and (b) of the above
   e. Only (a) and (c) of the above

2. Which of the following are found on the liability side of the Federal Reserve's balance sheet?

   a. Cash items in the process of collection
   b. Deferred availability cash items
   c. Gold
   d. All of the above
   e. only (b) and (c) of the above

3. When float increases,

    a. currency in circulation falls.
    b. the monetary base falls.
    c. the monetary base rises.
    d. the monetary supply falls.
    e. none of the above occurs.

4. A reduction in which of the following leads to an increase in the monetary base?

    a. U.S. Treasury deposits
    b. Float
    c. Discount loans
    d. All of the above

5. When the Treasury withdraws funds from tax and loan accounts at banks and deposits them at the Federal Reserve,

    a. the monetary base rises permanently.
    b. the monetary base rises temporarily.
    c. the monetary base falls temporarily.
    d. the monetary base falls permanently.

6. When the Federal Reserve purchases a copy of Milton Friedman's book *A Program for Monetary Stability*,

    a. the money supply will fall.
    b. the money supply will rise.
    c. the monetary base will fall.
    d. the monetary base will remain unchanged.

7. Factors that are beyond the control of the Fed yet influence the monetary base, such as float and Treasury deposits,

    a. make control of the monetary base impossible, explaining why the Fed targets interest rates.
    b. make control of interest rates impossible, explaining why the Fed targets nonborrowed reserves.
    c. make control of the monetary base somewhat more difficult.
    d. do none of the above.

8. Which of the following are methods used to finance government expenditures in the United States?

    a. Selling bonds to the public
    b. Taxes
    c. Selling bonds to the Fed
    d. `All of the above

9. The U.S. Treasury's sales of bonds add to the money supply whenever

    a. the government runs a deficit.
    b. the government has outstanding debt.
    c. the bonds are purchased by banks.
    d. the bonds are purchased by the Fed.

10. The Fed may feel pressure to purchase Treasury securities to prevent

    a. the money supply from rising.
    b. interest rates from rising.
    c. the monetary base from rising.
    d. inflation from rising.

Chapter 19

The Tools of Monetary Policy

CHAPTER SYNOPSIS/COMPLETIONS

Chapter 19 examines how the Federal Reserve uses its three policy tools --
(1)_____ _____ _____, changes in the
(2)_____ _____, and changes in (3)_____
_____ -- to manipulate the money supply. Proposed modifications of the
Fed's policy tools are also discussed.

By far the most important monetary policy tool at the Fed's disposal is its ability to buy
and sell government securities. (4)_____ _____
_____ is the Fed's most important monetary policy tool because it is the
primary determinant of changes in the monetary base. Recalling from Chapter 15 that the
main source of fluctuations in the money supply is the monetary base, it is easy to
understand the attention open market operations receive.

There are two types of open market operations. Open market operations designed to
change the level of reserves and the monetary base in an effort to influence economic activity
are called (5)_____ open market operations. (6)_____ open
market operations are intended to offset movements in other factors that affect the monetary
base, such as changes in Treasury deposits with the Fed and float.

Open market operations are conducted at the Federal Reserve Bank of New York and are
supervised by the Manager for Domestic Operations. The manager collects information from
several sources providing him with a barometer of current money market conditions. After
collecting this information, the manager devises a "game plan" for open market operations
--both dynamic and defensive-- that satisfies the FOMC directive. The manager purchases
(or sells) securities from dealers who have offered the best prices; actual trading takes less
than an hour.

Most of the time, the trading desk engages in repurchase agreements (repos) or reverse
repurchase agreements (reverse repos). A repo is actually a temporary open market
(7)_____ that will be reversed within a few days, and it is often argued to
be an especially effective way of conducting defensive open market operations. Matched
sale-purchase transaction or (8)_____ _____ are used when
the Federal Reserve wants to temporarily drain reserves from the banking system.

Open market operations have several advantages over the other tools of the Federal

Reserve that make them particularly desirable:

1. Open market operations occur at the initiative of the Fed. The Fed has complete control over the volume of open market operations, giving it control over the nonborrowed base.

2. Open market operations can be varied in any degree. Thus open market operations are said to be (9)_____.

3. Open market operations are easily reversed.

4. Open market operations can be implemented quickly.

The Fed can affect the size of the borrowed base through discount policy. Discount loan volume can be influenced by changing the (10)_____ _____ on the loans (the discount rate) or by changing the (11)_____ of loans administered through the discount window.

Discount loans to banks are of three types. Adjustment credit loans are intended to help banks with short-term (12)_____ problems. (13)_____ _____ is given to meet the needs of banks in vacation and agricultural areas that experience seasonal demands for funds. (14)_____ _____ is given to banks that are experiencing severe liquidity problems due to net deposit outflows; the $5 billion discount loan to Continental Illinois in 1984 provides a recent example.

Because the discount rate is usually kept below the federal funds interest rate, the Fed limits how often a bank can come to the discount window. At the time of its creation, the Fed's most important role was intended to be as a (15)_____ _____ _____ _____ so that the country might avoid financial panics as had occurred in 1893 and 1907. Unfortunately, the Fed failed in its role as lender of last resort during the Great Depression.

Some critics of the Federal Reserve now contend that discount borrowing ought to be eliminated. They argue that since the creation of the FDIC, the Fed's role of lender of last resort provides no useful purpose. Supporters counter that the Fed's role of lender of last resort complements the function of the FDIC and is not limited to the banking system, as when the Fed announced its intention to provide liquidity to the financial markets following the stock market crash in October 1987.

While discount rate changes can be used to change expectations that may reinforce the direction of monetary policy, the most important advantage of discount policy is that the Fed can use it to perform its role of lender of last resort.

Two problems arise under the current method of discount policy administration. First, since the discount rate is an administered rate, fluctuations in market rates lead to fluctuations in (16)_____ _____ and the monetary base. Second, changes in the discount rate may be misinterpreted by financial market participants and lead to greater uncertainty in financial markets.

Discounting's disadvantages as a tool of monetary policy have prompted economists to suggest various reforms. A long-time Fed critic, Milton Friedman, contends that better monetary control could be achieved if the Fed would terminate its discount facilities. Abolishing discounting would reduce fluctuations in the monetary base, but Friedman's critics believe that the Fed's role of lender of last resort is too important to sacrifice for improved monetary control.

An alternative proposal, favored by many economists, would tie the discount rate to a (17)_____ _____ of interest such as the 3-month Treasury bill rate or the federal funds rate.

While open market operations and discount policy influence the money supply by altering the monetary base, a change in reserve requirements changes the value of the (18)_____ _____. Because changes in reserve requirements are so powerful and costly to administer they are rarely used.

Two interesting reforms of reserve requirements have been proposed which supporters contend would improve monetary control. Some economists believe that reserve requirements should be eliminated because they act as a tax on banks. Abolishment of reserve requirements, however, could potentially make the money multiplier less stable, hampering monetary policy. Other economists suggest setting reserve requirements equal to (19)_____ of deposits. The desirability of this proposal rests on the assumption that financial institutions would develop no new liabilities to compete with checks. The discussion in Chapter 13 suggests that 100 percent reserve banking --should it foster new financial innovations-- might actually hamper the Fed's ability to control the (20)_____ _____.

EXERCISES

Exercise 1: Definitions and Terminology

Match the following terms on the right with the definition or description on the left. Place the letter of the term in the blank provided next to the appropriate definition.

_____ 1. Intended role of the Federal Reserve System at its inception

a. adjustment credit

_____ 2. Discount loan to meet short-term liquidity problems.

b. extended credit

_____ 3. Intended to offset temporary changes in factors affecting the monetary base.

c. dynamic open market operations

_____ 4. The FOMC directive is interpreted and implemented here.

d. defensive open market operations

_____ 5. Intended to affect economic activity by changing the monetary base.

e. matched sale purchase agreement (reverse repo)

_____ 6. Discount loan to meet the more serious problem of large deposit outflows.

f. repurchase agreement (repo)

_____ 7. Employed when the Fed wishes to temporarily absorb reserves.

g. lender of last resort

_____ 8. A change in this monetary policy tool causes the money multiplier to change.

h. Trading Desk

_____ 9. This monetary policy tool complements the Fed's role as lender of last resort.

i. reserve requirements

_____ 10. Employed when the Fed wishes to temporarily inject reserves into the system.

j. discount lending

Exercise 2: Open Market Operations

A. Why are open market operations the most important monetary tool?

_____

_____

B. What are the two types of open market operations?

   1. _____

   2. _____

C. List the advantages of open market operations.

   1. _____

   2. _____

   3. _____

   4. _____

Exercise 3: Discount Policy

A. List the three types of discount loans.

   1. _____

   2. _____

   3. _____

B. Why might it be important to have a lender of last resort even with the existence of deposit insurance?

_____

_____

Exercise 4: Discount Policy: Advantages and Disadvantages

Listed below are advantages and disadvantages of discount policy. Check the appropriate column.

	Advantage	Disadvantage
A. The discount policy creates confusion about the Federal Reserve's intentions.	_____	_____
B. Discount policy can lead to greater fluctuations in the money supply.	_____	_____
C. Discounting can be used by the Fed in its role as lender of last resort.	_____	_____

Exercise 5: Reserve Requirements

A. List two reasons why changes in reserve requirements are rarely used as a policy tool to conduct monetary policy.

1. _____

_____

2. _____

_____

B. Because of the disadvantages of using reserve requirements as a policy tool, some economists have suggested fixing reserve requirements at 100%. What is the main advantage of this proposal?

_____

What is the main disadvantage of this proposal?

_____

SELF-TEST

Part A: True-False Questions

Circle whether the following statements are true (T) or false (F).

T F 1. Open market operations are the most important monetary policy tool because they are the most important determinant of changes in the money multiplier, the main source of fluctuations in the money supply.

T F 2. Defensive open market operations are intended to change the level of reserves and the monetary base in an effort to influence economic activity.

T F 3. When the Fed purchases or sells a security in the open market, it is most likely trading in U.S. Treasury bills.

T F 4. The Manager for Domestic Operations is responsible for executing the directive issued by the Federal Open Market Committee.

T F 5. When the Fed engages in a matched sale-purchase agreement, it sells securities which the buyer agrees to sell back to the Fed within a few days.

T F 6. When the Fed wants to conduct a temporary open market sale, it engages in a reverse repo.

T F 7. The Fed has less than complete control over the volume of open market operations because banks can refuse to buy Treasury securities.

T F 8. Because banks in agricultural areas experience greater demands for funds in the spring, the Federal Reserve issues adjustment credit to these banks when they have deficient reserves.

T F 9. The Fed extends adjustment credit to banks that are expecting chronic deposit outflows.

T F 10. Evidence from the past 15 years suggests that Fed discount policy has approximated to some degree the variable discount rate proposal.

T F 11. The Fed's role of lender of last resort may still be useful even though deposit insurance has reduced the probability of bank panics.

T F 12. Changes in the discount rate may signal a change in monetary policy or may be an adjustment to a change in market interest rates, making it difficult to decipher the Fed's intentions regarding monetary policy.

T F 13. Abolishing discounting would reduce fluctuations in the borrowed base.

T F 14. The DIDMCA of 1980 simplified the structure of reserve requirements and eliminated all Fed discretion in setting reserve requirements.

T F 15. Assume that the required reserve ratio set by the Fed exceeds that desired by banks, which tends to be volatile. Then eliminating reserve requirements may tend to increase the instability in the money multiplier.

Part B: Multiple-Choice Questions

Circle the appropriate answer.

1. Open market operations are of two types:

   a. defensive and offensive.
   b. dynamic and reactionary.
   c. actionary and passive.
   d. dynamic and defensive.

2. If the Federal Reserve wants to inject reserves into the banking system, it will usually

   a. purchase government securities.
   b. raise the discount rate.
   c. sell government securities.
   d. lower reserve requirements.
   e. do either (a) or (b) of the above.

3. When the Fed wants to temporarily raise reserves in the banking system, it will engage in

   a. a repurchase agreement.
   b. a reverse repo.
   c. a matched sale-purchase transaction.
   d. none of the above.

4. When float increases, causing a temporary increase in reserves in the banking system, the Fed can offset the effects of float by engaging in

   a. a repurchase agreement.
   b. an interest rate swap.
   c. a matched sale-purchase transaction.
   d. none of the above.

5. The type of discount loan extended by the Fed in its role of lender of last resort is called

    a. adjustment credit.
    b. seasonal credit.
    c. extended credit.
    d. installment credit.

6. Which of the following proposed policies would tend to reduce instability in the monetary base?

    a. Penalty discount rate
    b. Discount rate that is tied to market interest rates
    c. Elimination of discounting
    d. All of the above
    e. Only (a) and (c) of the above

7. Changes in the reserve requirements are infrequently used for changing the money supply because

    a. reserve requirement changes tend to be powerful and are costly for banks to adjust to.
    b. reserve requirement changes tend to be ineffective.
    c. reserve requirement changes must be approved by the president.
    d. of only (a) and (c) of the above.
    e. of none of the above.

8. A reduction in reserve requirements causes the money supply to rise, since the change causes

    a. the money multiplier to fall.
    b. the money multiplier to rise.
    c. reserves to fall.
    d. reserves to rise.

9. Because the discount rate is frequently kept below the federal funds interest rate,

    a. the Fed must ration discount loans on a first-come, first-serve basis.
    b. the Fed limits how often a bank can come to the discount window.
    c. the Fed refuses to extend discount credit to banks that are not members of the Federal Reserve system.
    d. none of the above occurs.

10. Under 100% reserve banking, the money multiplier will be

    a. 0.
    b. 1.
    c. 10.
    d. 100.

Chapter 20

The Conduct of Monetary
Policy: Targets and Goals

CHAPTER SYNOPSIS/COMPLETIONS

This chapter discusses the important goals that the Federal Reserve attempts to achieve through its conduct of monetary policy and regulatory duties. The general operating strategy employed by the Federal Reserve to achieve these goals is presented in the second part of the chapter. The third section ties together the first two sections by examining the Fed's past policy procedures. This historical perspective provides important insights when it comes to assessing current and future monetary policy actions. Concluding this chapter is a brief section that discusses the Fed's ability to control the money supply.

The chapter presents six basic goals that are most often mentioned as objectives of monetary policy:

(1)_____

(2)_____

(3)_____

(4)_____

(5)_____

(6)_____

The Employment Act of 1946 and the Humphrey-Hawkins Act of 1978 commit the government to promoting high employment. By high employment, economists mean a level of unemployment consistent with labor market equilibrium. This level of unemployment is the (7)_____ _____ of _____.

Of these goals, price stability has received more attention in recent years. Higher rates of inflation since the mid-1960s has focused greater attention on the costs of price volatility. An inflationary environment makes planning for the future difficult and may strain a country's social fabric due to its effect on the distribution of wealth. Post-World War I

German inflation destroyed the wealth of those who held nominal assets (primarily retired persons and those approaching retirement), and in the wake of this tremendous redistribution of wealth, Adolf Hitler rose to power.

In the mid-1980s --inflation having declined to an acceptable level-- the Fed began to pay more attention to stabilizing the value of the dollar. Because exchange rate fluctuations have a greater relative impact on the domestic economy now that international financial and goods markets have become more integrated, the Federal Reserve no longer treats the United States as a closed economy. Therefore, when deciding the course of monetary policy, the Fed pays careful attention to the expected change in the value of the dollar.

Although achieving all the above-mentioned goals would be highly desirable, conflicts arise between goals in the short run. Higher employment or interest rate stability may mean (8)_____ inflation in the short run. Since expansionary monetary policies initially tend to stimulate aggregate output and employment and lower interest rates, such policies appear attractive at first. But an expansionary monetary policy will lead to inflationary pressures if continued for long. Thus the Federal Reserve faces difficult trade-offs and must weigh the benefits and costs of each action if it is to promote economic well-being.

Since the Fed's control over policy goals is imprecise, the Fed employs an (9)_____ _____ strategy to guide monetary policy. The Fed judges its actions by observing the behavior of an intermediate target, such as a monetary aggregate. The intermediate target provides a readily available proxy (the Fed hopes that it does, anyway) for the Fed's goals which it manipulates through variations in its (10)_____ _____. In turn, the Fed changes its operating target, say, the monetary base, through use of its (11)_____ _____, primarily open-market operations.

In general, the Fed has a choice between targeting a monetary aggregate or an interest rate such as the federal funds interest rate. Here again, the Federal Reserve faces a trade-off; if it targets a monetary aggregate, interest rate volatility is likely to (12)_____ and if it targets the federal funds rate, it loses control over the (13)_____ _____.

The policy of intermediate targeting suggests three criteria for choosing between an interest rate and a monetary aggregate target. The target must be (14)_____, as well as (15)_____ by the Fed, and it must have a (16)_____ _____ on the goal.

An examination of past Federal Reserve policy procedures indicates that the Fed has made many policy mistakes that have led to severe contractions and rapid inflations. Unfortunately, the Fed has often been extremely slow to alter procedures despite the warnings of economists. History seems to indicate that nothing less than an economic

184

(17)_____ is necessary to convince the Fed of the inadequacy of its procedures.

Although the jury is still out, examination of Federal Reserve monetary policy from October of 1979 through October of 1982 suggests that Paul Volcker's statements regarding control of monetary aggregates provided a smokescreen that permitted the Fed to fight inflation. The announced change in operating procedures allowed the Fed to increase interest rates sharply and slow economic activity to combat the rapidly rising price level. This interpretation of events provides one explanation for the volatility in both interest rates and monetary aggregates during this period.

It has been argued that poor monetary performance is the result of the Fed's inability to control the (18)_____ _____. The behavior of the currency-checkable deposit ratio and excess reserves does pose problems for the Fed, yet most economists contend that over a period of six months to a year the Fed can control the money supply. Thus the Federal Reserve's unwillingness to adopt policy procedures that would ensure better monetary control leads one to question the Fed's sincerity in controlling the money supply.

EXERCISES

Exercise 1: Goals of Monetary Policy

A. While the Federal Reserve System tends to be intentionally vague about the exact policy goals it may be pursuing at any one time, Federal Reserve personnel stress six basic goals more often than any other. These goals include:

1. _____

2. _____

3. _____

4. _____

5. _____

6. _____

B. What do economists mean by "full" employment? Do they mean zero unemployment?

_____

_____

_____

Exercise 2: Intermediate and Operating Targets

Although there is some ambiguity as to whether a particular variable is better categorized as an intermediate target or an operating target, list below those variables generally thought to be in each category.

A. Intermediate targets

   1. _____

   2. _____

B. Operating targets

   1. _____

   2. _____

Exercise 3: Criteria for Choosing Intermediate Targets

Selecting an intermediate target requires careful thought by members of the Federal Open Market Committee. The wrong choice can mean adverse consequences for the economy. Debate has tended to center around the choice between targeting a monetary aggregate or an interest rate. List the three criteria for choosing one variable as an intermediate target over another.

   1. _____

   2. _____

   3. _____

186

Exercise 4: Fed Control of the Money Supply

Many economists recommend two reforms that would improve the Fed's ability to control the money supply. What are these two reforms?

1. _____

   _____

2. _____

   _____

SELF-TEST

Part A: True-False Questions

Circle whether the following statements are true (T) or false (F).

T F 1. The Federal Reserve desires interest rate stability because it reduces the uncertainty of future planning.

T F 2. The Federal Reserve attempts to get the unemployment rate to zero, since any unemployment is wasteful and inefficient.

T F 3. The natural rate of unemployment is zero.

T F 4. The discount rate is the Fed's preferred operating target.

T F 5. An advantage of an intermediate targeting strategy is that it provides the Fed with more timely information regarding the effect of monetary policy.

T F 6. If the Fed targets a monetary aggregate, it is likely to lose control over the interest rate because of fluctuations in the money demand function.

T F 7. A monetary aggregate, such as M1, is often referred to as an operating target.

T F 8. The most important characteristic a variable must have to be useful as an intermediate target is that it must have a predictable impact on a goal.

T F 9. The real bills doctrine proved to be inflationary during and after World War I.

T F 10. Open market operations did not play an important policy role in the Federal Reserve System until about the 1960s.

T F 11. The passage of the Banking Act of 1935 limited the Fed's ability to alter reserve requirements by requiring it to secure presidential approval.

T F 12. Treasury influence over the Fed was reduced when the Fed and Treasury came to an agreement known as the "Accord."

T F 13. The difference between excess reserves and discount loans is known as free reserves.

T F 14. The Fed's use of free reserves as a guide to monetary policy in the 1960s proved a failure since it lead to procyclical monetary growth.

T F 15. While the Fed professed an interest in stabilizing interest rates, its actions during the 1960s and 1970s indicates that the Fed seemed to be preoccupied with stabilizing money growth.

Part B: Multiple-Choice Questions

Circle the appropriate answer.

1. Even if the Fed could completely control the money supply, not everyone would be happy with monetary policy, since

   a. the Fed is asked to achieve many goals, some of which are incompatible with one another.
   b. the goals that are stressed by the Fed do not include high employment, making labor unions a vocal critic of Fed policies.
   c. the Fed places primary emphasis on exchange rate stability, often to the detriment of domestic conditions.
   d. its mandate requires it to keep Treasury security prices high.

2. Because timely information on the price level and economic growth is frequently unavailable, the Fed has adopted a strategy of

   a. targeting the exchange rate, since the Fed has the ability to control this variable.
   b. targeting the price of gold, since it is closely related to economic activity.
   c. using an intermediate target such as a monetary aggregate.
   d. stabilizing the consumer price index, since the Fed has a high degree of control over the CPI.

3. Which of the following are potential operating targets?

   a. Monetary base
   b. Nonborrowed reserves
   c. Federal funds interest rate
   d. Nonborrowed monetary base
   e. All of the above

4. Fluctuations in money demand will cause the Fed to lose control over a monetary aggregate if the Fed emphasizes

   a. a monetary aggregate target.
   b. an interest-rate target.
   c. a nominal GNP target.
   d. all of the above.

5. While the Fed professed to target monetary aggregates in the 1970s, its behavior indicates that it actually targeted

   a. exchange rates.
   b. nominal GNP.
   c. nominal interest rates.
   d. the monetary base.

6. Most economists question the desirability of targeting real interest rates by pointing out that

   a. the Fed does not have direct control over real interest rates.
   b. changes in real interest rates have little effect on economic activity.
   c. real interest rates are extremely difficult to measure.
   d. all of the above are correct.
   e. only (a) and (c) of the above are correct.

7. The Fed's policy of keeping interest rates low to help the Treasury finance World War I by rediscounting eligible paper caused

   a. inflation to accelerate.
   b. aggregate output to decline sharply.
   c. the Fed to rethink the efficacy of the real bills doctrine.
   d. both (a) and (b) of the above.
   e. both (a) and (c) of the above.

8. The Fed added to the problems it helped create in the early 1930s by

   a. raising the discount rate in 1936-1937.
   b. raising reserve requirements in 1936-1937.
   c. contracting the monetary base in 1936-1937.
   d. expanding the monetary base in 1936-1937.

9. The March 1951 Accord gave the Fed greater freedom to let

   a. interest rates rise.
   b. unemployment rise.
   c. interest rates fall.
   d. inflation accelerate.

10. The Fed's policy of "leaning against the wind" through targeting free reserves and the federal funds interest rate actually proved to be

   a. anticipated.
   b. procyclical.
   c. neutral.
   d. stabilizing.

Chapter 21

The Foreign Exchange Market

CHAPTER SYNOPSIS/COMPLETIONS

Exchange rate movements are extremely important to our economy. Chapter 21 develops a modern analysis of exchange rate determination that explains both recent behavior in the foreign exchange market, and why exchange rates are so volatile from day to day.

The exchange rate is the price of one country's (1)_____ in terms of another's. Trades in the foreign exchange market typically involve the exchange of bank (2)_____ denominated in different currencies. Spot exchange rates involve the immediate exchange of bank deposits, while (3)_____ exchange rates involve the exchange of deposits at some specified future date. When a currency increases in value, it has (4)_____; when a currency falls in value and is worth fewer U.S. dollars, it has depreciated. Exchange rates are important because when a country's currency appreciates, its exports become (5)_____ expensive and foreign imports become (6)_____ expensive. Conversely, when a country's currency depreciates its goods become less expensive for foreigners, but foreign goods become more expensive (implying that net exports decline, all else constant).

The starting point for undertaking an investigation of how exchange rates are determined is the law of one price, which states the following: If two countries produce an identical good, the price of the good should be the (7)_____ throughout the world no matter which country produces it. Applying the law of one price to countries' price levels produces the theory of (8)_____ _____ _____, which suggests that if one country's price level rises relative to another's, its currency should (9)_____.

The theory of purchasing power parity cannot fully explain exchange rate changes because goods produced in different countries are not (10)_____, and because many goods and services (whose prices are included in a measure of a country's price level) are not (11)_____ across borders. Other factors also affect the exchange rate in the long run, including trade barriers such as (12)_____ and _____, the demand for imports and exports, and relative (13)_____.

The key to understanding the short-run behavior of exchange rates is to recognize that an

(14) _____ _____ is the price of domestic bank deposits in terms of foreign bank deposits. Because the exchange rate is the price of one asset in terms of another, the natural way to investigate the short-run determination of exchange rates is through an asset-market approach using the theory of asset demand.

The theory of asset demand indicates that the most important factor affecting the demand for both domestic (dollar) and foreign deposits is the (15) _____ _____ on these assets relative to one another. According to the (16) _____ _____ condition, however, the expected return on both domestic and foreign deposits is identical in a world in which there is (17) _____ _____. Because the interest parity condition is an equilibrium condition, it provides a framework for understanding short-run movements in exchange rates as a result of factors that cause the expected return on either domestic or foreign deposits to change temporarily.

Therefore, changes in either the foreign or domestic (18)_____ _____, or a change in the expected future exchange rate will cause the exchange rate to change in the short run. Because long-run determinants of the exchange rate influence the expected future exchange rate, the five determinants of long-run exchange rates affect short-run exchange rates. For example, any factor that raises the expected return on domestic deposits relative to foreign deposits causes the domestic currency to appreciate. These factors include a rise in the domestic interest rate, a (19)_____ in the foreign interest rate, or any factor affecting exchange rates in the long-run that cause the expected future exchange rate to be (20)_____.

A rise in domestic interest rates relative to foreign interest rates can result in either an appreciation or a depreciation of the domestic currency. If the rise in the domestic interest rate is due to a rise in expected inflation, then the domestic currency depreciates. If the rise in the domestic interest rate, however, is due to a rise in the real interest rate, then the domestic currency (21)_____, as happened to the dollar in the early 1980s. Higher domestic money growth leads to a (22)_____ of the domestic currency.

Exchange rates have been very volatile in recent years. The theory of asset demand model explains this volatility as a consequence of changing (23)_____ , which are also volatile, and play an important role in determining the demand for domestic assets (which, in turn, affects the value of the exchange rate).

The current international environment in which exchange rates fluctuate from day to day is called a managed-float regime or a (24)_____ float. In a managed-float regime, central banks allow rates to fluctuate but intervene in the foreign exchange market in order to influence exchange rates. Interventions are of two types. An unsterilized central bank intervention in which the domestic currency is sold to purchase foreign assets leads to: a gain in international reserves, an (25)_____ in the money supply, and a

192

(26)_____ of the domestic currency. Sterilized central bank interventions have little effect on the exchange rate.

EXERCISES

Exercise 1: Definitions and Terminology

Match the following terms on the right with the definition or description on the left. Place the letter of the term in the blank provided next to the appropriate definition. Terms may be used once, more than once, or not all.

_____ 1. The price of one country's
currency in terms of another's.

a. law of one price

_____ 2. Condition in which exchange rate falls
more in short run than long run when
the money supply increases.

b. interest parity condition

_____ 3. The current exchange rate regime in which
exchange rates fluctuate from day to
day, but central banks intervene to
influence exchange rate movements.

c. capital mobility

d. devaluation

_____ 4. States that the domestic interest rate
equals the foreign interest rate plus
the expected depreciation of the
domestic currency.

e. exchange rate

f. quota

_____ 5. Value of the domestic currency
increases relative to one or
more foreign currencies.

g. managed float regime
(dirty float)

_____ 6. Value of foreign currency increases
relative to the domestic currency.

h. tariff

_____ 7. When two countries produce an
identical good, the price of the
good should be the same throughout
the world, no matter which country
produces it.

i. exchange rate
overshooting

_____ 8. Theory that exchange rates between
any two countries will adjust to
reflect changes in the price levels
of the two countries.

j. spot exchange
transaction

_____ 9. Barrier to trade involving a restriction
on quantity of foreign goods that can
be imported.

k. forward exchange
transaction

_____10. The predominant type of exchange rate
transaction that involves the immediate
exchange of bank deposits denominated
in different currencies.

l. purchasing power
parity

_____11. Americans can easily purchase foreign
assets; foreigners can easily purchase
American assets.

m. appreciation

_____12. An exchange rate transaction that
involves the exchange of bank deposits
denominated in different currencies
at some specified future date.

n. depreciation

Exercise 2: Foreign Exchange Rates and Goods Prices

1. Suppose the exchange rate between the Swiss franc and the dollar is $0.50 per franc.
What would be the exchange rate if it is quoted as francs per dollar? _____

2. If you are contemplating buying a fancy Swiss watch that costs 1000 francs, how much
will it cost you in dollars? _____

3. If a Swiss is contemplating buying an American pocket calculator that costs $100, how
much will it cost him in francs? _____

4. If the exchange rate changes to $.25 per Swiss franc, has there been an appreciation or
depreciation of the Swiss franc? _____ Of the dollar? _____

5. Now if you buy the Swiss watch that costs 1000 francs, how much will it cost you in
dollars? _____ Does the Swiss watch cost you more or less than before? _____

6. Now how much will it cost the Swiss in francs for the $100 pocket calculator? _____
Does it cost more or less than before? _____

194

7. What does the example here indicate about the effect on prices of foreign goods in a country and domestic goods sold abroad when the exchange rate appreciates? _____

Exercise 3: Law of One Price and Purchasing Power Parity

A. Suppose that Argentinian wheat costs 3000 pesos per bushel and that American wheat costs $6 per bushel. In addition, assume that American wheat and Argentinian wheat are identical goods.

1. If the exchange rate is 300 Argentinian pesos per U.S. dollar, what is the price of Argentinian wheat in dollars? _____

2. What is the price of American wheat in pesos? _____

3. What will be the demand for Argentinian wheat? _____

    Why? _____

    _____

4. If the exchange rate is 600 Argentinian pesos per U.S. dollar, what is the price of Argentinian wheat in dollars? _____

5. What is the price of American wheat in pesos? _____

6. What will be the demand for American wheat? _____

    Why? _____

    _____

7. What does the law of one price indicate will be the exchange rate between the Argentinian peso and the U.S. dollar? _____

    Why? _____

    _____

8. If the price of American wheat rises to $10 per bushel, what does the law of one price suggest will be the new exchange rate? _____

    Is this an appreciation or depreciation of the U.S. dollar? _____

B.

1. If the American price level doubles while that in Argentina remains unchanged, what does the theory of purchasing power parity suggest will happen to the exchange rate which initially is at 500 pesos to the dollar?

_____

2. If the American inflation rate is 5% and the Argentinian inflation rate is 7%, then what does the theory of purchasing power parity predict will happen to the value of the dollar in terms of pesos in one year's time?

_____

Exercise 4: Factors that Affect Exchange Rates

In the second column of the following table indicate with an arrow whether the exchange rate will rise (+) or fall (-) as a result of the change in the factor. (Recall that a rise in the exchange rate is viewed as an appreciation of the domestic currency.)

Change in Factor	Response of the Exchange Rate
Domestic interest rate	-
Foreign interest rate	-
Expected domestic price level	-
Expected tariffs and quotas	-
Expected import demand	-
Expected export demand	-
Expected productivity	-

SELF-TEST

Part A: True-False Questions

Circle whether the following statements are true (T) or false (F).

T F 1. Most trades in the foreign exchange market involve the buying and selling of bank deposits.

T F 2. Forward transactions in the foreign exchange market involve exchanges of bank deposits more than two days into the future.

T F 3. One reason why the theory of purchasing power parity might not fully explain exchange rate movements is that monetary policy differs across countries.

T F 4. If the interest rate on franc-denominated assets is 5% and is 8% on dollar-denominated assets, then the expected return on dollar-denominated assets is higher than that on franc-denominated assets if the dollar is expected to depreciate at a 5% rate.

T F 5. When a country's currency appreciates, its goods abroad become more expensive, and foreign goods in that country become cheaper, all else constant.

T F 6. If the interest rate on dollar deposits is 10 percent, and the dollar is expected to appreciate by seven percent over the coming year, then the expected return on the dollar deposit in terms of foreign currency is three percent.

T F 7. An expected rise in foreign productivity relative to domestic productivity (holding everything else constant) causes the domestic currency to depreciate.

T F 8. The interest parity condition does not hold if there is perfect capital mobility in international finance.

T F 9. The model of foreign exchange rate behavior indicates that whenever the domestic interest rate rises relative to the foreign interest rate, the exchange rate appreciates.

T F 10. If a central bank lowers the growth rate of the money supply, then its currency will appreciate.

T F 11. If expected inflation in the U.S. rises from 5 to 8% and the interest rate rises from 7 to 9%, the dollar will appreciate.

T F 12. Under the current exchange rate regime, central banks rarely intervene in the foreign exchange market.

T F 13. The phenomenon in which the exchange rate falls by more in the short run than it does in the long run when the money supply increase is called exchange rate overshooting.

T F 14. The high volatility of exchange rate movements indicates that participants in the foreign exchange market do not behave in a rational manner.

T F 15. Whenever a central bank buys domestic currency in the foreign exchange market, it loses international reserves.

Part B: Multiple-Choice Questions

Circle the appropriate answer.

1. When the Swiss franc appreciates (holding everything else constant), then

    a. Swiss watches sold in the United States become more expensive.
    b. American computers sold in Switzerland become more expensive.
    c. Swiss army knives sold in the United States become cheaper.
    d. American toothpaste sold in Switzerland becomes cheaper.
    e. Both (a) and (d) of the above are true.

2. The theory of purchasing-power parity indicates that if the price level in the United States rises by 5% while the price level in Italy rises by 6%, then

    a. the dollar appreciates by 1% relative to the lira.
    b. the dollar depreciates by 1% relative to the lira.
    c. the exchange rate between the dollar and the lira remains unchanged.
    d. the dollar appreciates by 5% relative to the lira.
    e. the dollar depreciates by 5% relative to the lira.

3. If, in retaliation for "unfair" trade practices, Congress imposes a quota on Japanese cars, but at the same time Japanese demand for American goods increases, then in the long run

    a. the Japanese yen should appreciate relative to the dollar.
    b. the Japanese yen should depreciate relative to the dollar.
    c. the dollar should depreciate relative to the yen.
    d. it is not clear whether the dollar should appreciate or depreciate relative to the yen.

4. If the interest rate on dollar-denominated assets is 10% and it is 8% on franc-denominated assets, then if the franc is expected to appreciate at a 5% rate,

   a. dollar-denominated assets have a lower expected return than franc-denominated assets.
   b. the expected return on dollar-denominated assets in francs is 2%.
   c. the expected return on franc-denominated assets in dollars is 3%.
   d. none of the above will occur.

5. Of the following factors, which will not cause the expected return schedule for foreign deposits to shift?

   a. A change in the expected future exchange rate.
   b. A change in the foreign interest rate.
   c. A change in the current exchange rate.
   d. A change in the productivity of American workers.

6. A rise in the expected future exchange rate shifts the expected return shedule on foreign deposits to the _____ and causes the exchange rate to _____.

   a. right; appreciate
   b. right; depreciate
   c. left; appreciate
   d. left; depreciate

7. A rise in the domestic interest rate is associated with

   a. a shift in the expected return schedule for domestic deposits to the right.
   b. a shift in the expected return schedule for domestic deposits to the left.
   c. a shift in the expected return schedule for foreign deposits to the right.
   e. a shift in the expected return schedule for foreign deposits to the left.

8. If the foreign interest rate rises and people expect domestic productivity to rise relative to foreign productivity, then (holding everything else constant)

   a. the expected return schedule for domestic deposits shifts to the left and the domestic currency appreciates.
   b. the expected return schedule for domestic deposits shifts to the right and the domestic currency appreciates.
   c. the expected return schedule for foreign deposits shifts to the left and the domestic currency depreciates.
   d. the expected return schedule for foreign deposits shifts to the right and the domestic currency depreciates.
   e. the effect on the exchange rate is uncertain.

9. When domestic real interest rates rise, the

    a. the expected return schedule for dollar deposits shifts to the right, and the dollar appreciates.
    b. the expected return schedule for dollar deposits shifts to the left, and the dollar appreciates.
    c. the expected return schedule for dollar deposits shifts to the right, and the dollar depreciates.
    d. the expected return schedule for dollar deposits shifts to the left, and the dollar depreciates.

10. A central bank's international reserves rise when

    a. it sells domestic currency to purchase foreign assets in the foreign exchange market.
    b. it sells foreign currency to purchase domestic assets in the foreign exchange market.
    c. it buys domestic currency with the sale of foreign assets in the foreign exchange market.
    d. it buys gold with the sale of foreign assets in the foreign exchange market.

Chapter 22
The International Finance System
and Monetary Policy

CHAPTER SYNOPSIS/COMPLETIONS

The growing interdependence of the United States with other economies of the world means that our monetary policy is influenced by international financial transactions. Chapter 22 examines the international financial system and explores how it affects the way our monetary policy is conducted.

The (1)_____ _____ _____ is a bookkeeping system for recording all payments that have a direct bearing on the movement of funds between countries. All payments from foreigners are entered as (2)_____ while all payments to foreigners are entered as debits. The (3)_____ _____ shows international transactions that involve currently produced goods and services. The difference between merchandise exports and imports is called the (4)_____ _____. The capital account describes the flow of capital between the United States and other countries. The (5)_____ _____ _____ balance is the sum of the current account balance plus the items in the capital account. It indicates the amount of international reserves that must move between countries to finance international transactions.

A change in a country's holdings of international reserves leads to an equal change in its (6)_____ _____, which, in turn, affects the money supply. A currency like the U.S. dollar, which is used by other countries to denominate the assets they hold as international reserves, is called a (7)_____ _____. A reserve currency country (the United States) has the advantage over other countries that balance of payments deficits or surpluses do not lead to changes in holdings of international reserves and the monetary base.

Before World War I, the world economy operated under a gold standard, under which the currencies of most countries were convertible directly into gold, thereby fixing exchange rates between countries. After World War II, the Bretton Woods system was established in order to promote a (8)_____ exchange rate system in which the U.S. dollar was convertible into gold. The Bretton Woods agreement created the International Monetary Fund (IMF), which was given the task of promoting the growth of world trade by setting rules for the maintenance of fixed exchange rates and by making loans to countries that were experiencing (9)_____ _____ _____ difficulties. The

Bretton Woods agreement also set up the World Bank in order to provide
(10)_____-_____ _____ loans to assist developing countries
to build dams, roads, and other physical capital.

The Bretton Woods system --because it did not allow for smooth and gradual adjustments
in exchange rates when they became necessary-- was often characterized by destabilizing
international financial crises, in which adjustment occurred through a
(11)_____ _____ on a currency, that is, a massive sale of a
weak currency (or purchases of a strong currency) that would hasten the change in exchange
rates. After a series of such attacks culminated in a massive intervention in the foreign
exchange market by the German central bank in the first half of 1971, the Bretton Woods
system finally collapsed. The international financial system then evolved into the current
(12)_____ _____ regime, in which central banks intervene
in the foreign exchange market, but exchange rates fluctuate from day to day.

Three international considerations affect the conduct of monetary policy: direct effects of
the foreign exchange market on the money supply, balance of payments considerations, and
(13)_____ _____ considerations. If a central bank
intervenes in the foreign exchange market to keep its strong currency from appreciating, as
did the German central bank in the early 1970s, it will (14)_____
international reserves, and the monetary base and the money supply will
(15)_____. To prevent this, the central bank might engage in
(16)_____, which involves offsetting any increase in international reserves
with equal open-market sales of domestic securities in order to prevent the monetary base
from rising. In order to prevent balance of payments deficits, a country's central bank (such
as the Bank of England in the 1960s) might pursue (17)_____ monetary
policy. Monetary policy is also affected by exchange rate considerations. Because an
appreciation of the currency causes domestic businesses to suffer from increased foreign
competition, a central bank might (18)_____ the rate of money growth in
order to lower the exchange rate. Similarly, because a (19)_____ of the
currency hurts consumers and stimulates inflation, a central bank might slow the rate of
money growth in order to prop up the exchange rate.

Because the United States has been a (20)_____ _____ country
in the post-World War II period, U.S. monetary policy has been less affected by
developments in the foreign exchange market and its balance of payments than is true for
other countries. In addition, there seems to be less political pressure in the United States
regarding exchange rate changes than in other countries. Nonetheless, the balance of
payments and exchange rates have had some effect on U.S. monetary policy.

Some critics of the current international financial system contend that it is inherently
(21)_____. They advocate a return to the (22)_____
_____, in which all currencies are convertible into gold. They believe that
a gold standard would impose more (23)_____ _____ on

central banks and would have the added benefit of preventing fluctuations in exchange rates. Critics of the gold standard point out that the price of gold has fluctuated dramatically in recent years and that the gold standard period of the late nineteenth and early twentieth centuries was not a period of (24)_____ prices and high employment. In addition, since South Africa and the Soviet Union would have an increased ability to affect world monetary policy, critics do not believe that a gold standard would necessarily promote a more stable world economy, including a more stable price level.

EXERCISES

Exercise 1: Definitions and Terminology

Match the following terms on the right with the definition or description on the left. Place the letter of the term in the blank provided next to the appropriate definition. Terms may be used once, more than once, or not at all.

_____ 1. A bookkeeping system for recording all payments that have a direct bearing on the movement of funds between a country and foreign countries.

a. Speculative attack

_____ 2. Account that shows international transactions that involve currently produced goods and services.

b. Balance of payments

_____ 3. Merchandise exports less imports.

c. Gold standard

_____ 4. Account that describes the flow of capital between the United States and other countries.

d. Trade balance

_____ 5. Massive sales of a weak currency or purchases of a strong currency that hasten a change in the exchange rate.

e. Current account

_____ 6. The current account balance plus items in the capital account.

f. Reserve currency

_____ 7. A situation in which the par value of a currency is reset at a lower level.

g. Capital account

_____ 8. A currency (like the U.S. dollar) that is used by other countries to denominate the assets they hold as international reserves.

h. Bretton Woods

_____ 9. A regime under which the currency of most countries is directly convertible into gold.

i. Devalue

_____ 10. The international monetary system in use from use from 1945 to 1971 in which exchange rates were fixed and the U.S. dollar was freely convertible into gold (by foreign governments and central banks only).

j. Official Reserve Transactions Balance

Exercise 2: The Balance of Payments

Suppose that the U.S. economy in 1994 has generated the following data (in billions of dollars) for items in the balance of payments:

Merchandise exports	500	Capital outflows	50
Merchandise imports	600	Capital inflows	100
Net investment income	-40	Increase in U.S. official	
Net services	20	reserve assets	5
Net unilateral transfers	-15	Increase in foreign official assets	25

Fill in the figures for all the numbered items in the balance of payments table below. (Hint: The Statistical Discrepancy item is deduced from the fact that the balance of payments must balance.)

U.S. Balance of Payments in 1994 (billions of dollars)

	Receipts (+)	Payments (-)	Balance
Current account:			
1. Merchandise exports			
2. Merchandise imports			
3. Trade balance			
4. Net investment income			
5. Net services			
6. Net unilateral transfers			
7. Current account balance			
Capital account:			
8. Capital outflows			
9. Capital inflows			
10. Statistical discrepancy			
11. Official reserves transactions balance			
Method of financing:			
12. Increase in U.S. official reserve assets			
13. Increase in foreign official assets			
14. Total financing of surplus			

204

Exercise 3: How a Fixed Exchange Rate Regime Works

The most important feature of the Bretton Woods system was that it established a fixed exchange rate regime. Figure 22A describes a situation in which the domestic currency is initially overvalued: the expected return on the foreign deposits schedule (Ret^f_1) intersects the expected return on domestic deposits schedule (Ret^d_1) at an exchange rate that is below the fixed par rate, E_{par}.

FIGURE 22A

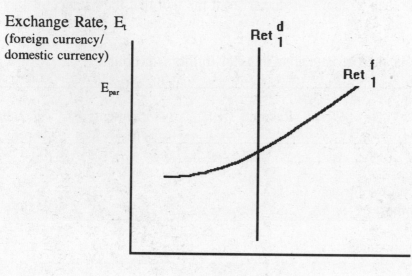

A. Complete the following statements:

1. In order to return the exchange rate to equilibrium at E_{par}, the central bank must intervene in the foreign exchange market to _____ the domestic currency by _____ foreign assets.

2. The central bank's purchase of domestic currency has the effect of _____ the money supply, causes the interest rate on domestic deposits to _____, and shifts the expected return schedule on domestic deposits to the _____.

B. Illustrate the effect of a central bank's purchase of domestic currency in Figure 22A by shifting the Ret^d.

SELF-TEST

Part A: True-False Questions

Circle whether the following statements are true (T) or false (F).

T   F   1.   The capital account balance indicates whether the country is increasing or decreasing its claims on foreign wealth.

T   F   2.   The official reserves transactions balance equals the current account balance plus the items in the capital account.

T   F   3.   The current account balance equals the difference between exports and imports.

T   F   4.   Under the Bretton Woods system, the dollar was overvalued if the equilibrium exchange rate (expressed as units of foreign currency per dollar) was below the par (fixed) value of the exchange rate.

T   F   5.   When the domestic currency is undervalued in a fixed exchange rate regime, the country's central bank must intervene in the foreign exchange market to purchase the domestic currency by selling foreign assets.

T   F   6.   The gold standard of the late nineteenth century always prevented inflation from developing.

T   F   7.   A particular problem with a fixed exchange rate system (or regime) is that it is periodically subject to speculative attacks on currencies.

T   F   8.   Special drawing rights (SDRs) are IMF loans to member countries.

T   F   9.   The Bretton Woods international financial system was toppled by a series of international financial crises.

T   F   10.   The World Bank makes loans to countries suffering balance of payments difficulties.

T   F   11.   The current international financial system is perhaps best described as a hybrid of fixed and flexible exchange rate systems.

T   F   12.   The ECU is a paper currency issued by the European Common Market.

T   F   13.   Critics of a return to the gold standard claim that it would probably not produce the price stability desired by gold standard proponents.

T F 14. A central bank that wants to strengthen its currency is likely to adopt a more contractionary policy.

T F 15. Monetary policy in a reserve currency country is less influenced by balance of payments deficits because they will be financed by other countries' interventions in the foreign exchange market.

Part B: Multiple-Choice Questions

Circle the appropriate answer.

1. Which of the following appear as debits in the U.S. balance of payments?

    a. French purchases of American jeans
    b. Purchases by Japanese tourists in the United States
    c. American exports of Apple computers
    d. Income earned by Coca-Cola from its factories abroad
    e. None of the above

2. Which of the following appears in the current account part of the balance of payments?

    a. An Italian's purchase of IBM stock
    b. Income earned by Barclay's Bank of London, England, from subsidiaries in the United States
    c. A loan by a Swiss bank to an American corporation
    d. A purchase by the Federal Reserve System of an English Treasury bond
    e. None of the above

3. If Americans are buying $1 billion more English goods and assets than the English are willing to buy from the United States, and so the Bank of England therefore sells $1 billion worth of pounds in the foreign exchange market, then

    a. England gains $1 billion of international reserves and its monetary base rises by $1 billion.
    b. England loses $1 billion of international reserves and its monetary base falls by $1 billion.
    c. England gains $1 billion of international reserves and its monetary base falls by $1 billion.
    d. England loses $1 billion of international reserves and its monetary base rises by $1 billion.
    e. England's level of international reserves and monetary base remains unchanged.

4. An important advantage for a reserve currency country is that

   a. its balance of payments deficits are financed by other countries' interventions in the foreign exchange market.
   b. it has more control over its monetary policy than nonreserve currency countries.
   c. it has more control over its exchange rate than nonreserve currency countries.
   d. Both (a) and (b) of the above are true.

5. Under a gold standard in which one dollar could be turned into the U.S. Treasury and exchanged for 1/20th of an ounce of gold and one Swiss franc could be exchanged for 1/60th of an ounce of gold,

   a. at an exchange rate of 4 francs per dollar, gold would flow from the United States to Switzerland and the Swiss monetary base would fall.
   b. at an exchange rate of 4 francs per dollar, gold would flow from Switzerland to the United States and the Swiss monetary base would rise.
   c. at an exchange rate of 2 francs per dollar, gold would flow from the United States to Switzerland and the U.S. monetary base would fall.
   d. at an exchange rate of 2 francs per dollar, gold would flow from Switzerland to the United States and the U.S. monetary base would rise.

6. In a speculative attack against a weak currency under a fixed exchange rate system, the central bank for this country must shift the expected return schedule for domestic deposits further to the _____ through the _____ of international reserves.

   a. left; purchase
   b. right; sale
   c. left; sale
   d. right; purchase

7. Countries with deficits in their balance of payments often do not want to see their currencies depreciate because

   a. this would hurt consumers in their country by making foreign goods more expensive.
   b. this would stimulate inflation.
   c. this would hurt domestic businesses by making foreign goods cheaper in their country.
   d. this would hurt domestic businesses by making their goods more expensive abroad.
   e. of both (a) and (b) of the above.

8. The International Monetary Fund is an international organization that

   a. promotes the growth of trade by setting rules for how tariffs and quotas are set by countries.
   b. makes loans to countries to finance projects such as dams and roads.
   c. oversees the international financial system and makes loans to countries with balance of payments difficulties.
   d. does each of the above.

9. When a central bank buys its currency in the foreign exchange market,

   a. they acquire international reserves.
   b. they lose international reserves.
   c. the money supply will increase.
   d. both (a) and (b) of the above occur.
   e. both (b) and (c) of the above occur.

10. Advocates of the gold standard claim it acts as a check against inflation because

   a. the supply of gold is fixed.
   b. monetary discipline would be imposed on central banks because a country experiencing inflation relative to other countries would suffer a gold outflow.
   c. world trade would be promoted because there would be less uncertainty about the value of currencies.
   d. policies in one country could not affect inflation to another.

Chapter 23

The Demand for Money

CHAPTER SYNOPSIS/COMPLETIONS

Chapter 23 discusses in chronological order the major developments in the theory of the demand for money. These developments have attempted to explain the reasons people hold money while providing a rationale for the procyclical movement of velocity.

The earliest treatment of the demand for money was offered by the classical economists. The classical economists --most notably Irving Fisher-- argued that the demand for money was a function of nominal aggregate (1)_____. This followed from their assumptions regarding (2)_____ (the average number of times per year that a dollar is spent on final goods and services produced in the economy) and the equation of exchange.

The classical economists argued that the speed with which money is spent is a function of the institutional features of the economy. While these features changed over time (due to improvements in technology, for example), velocity could be regarded as (3)_____ in the short run.

Nothing more than an identity, the (4)_____ _____ _____ states that the quantity of money times velocity must equal nominal income. But when combined with Irving Fisher's assumption regarding the fixity of velocity, the equation of exchange is transformed into the (5)_____ _____ _____ _____. Given the assumption of constant velocity, the quantity theory of money implies that changes in nominal income are solely determined by changes in the quantity of money. The classical economists also assumed that prices and wages were completely (6)_____, meaning that the economy would always remain at full employment. This last assumption led to the conclusion that changes in the money supply had no effect on aggregate output and were therefore translated solely into changes in the (7)_____ _____.

If one divides both sides of the equation of exchange by the constant velocity, it becomes clear that the quantity of money people hold is a constant fraction of nominal income. Thus, the classical economists regarded the demand for money as a demand for a medium of exchange.

The Cambridge economists viewed the quantity theory of money as too mechanistic.

Instead, they focused on the factors influencing how much money individuals would want to hold. Like Fisher, they regarded the level of income as the most significant factor influencing people's holdings of money. But they also believed that changes in (8)_____ _____ could affect individuals' decisions about using money as a store of wealth.

John Maynard Keynes believed that a decline in velocity in part explained the Great Depression, and his efforts to explain this decline in velocity led to his theory of money demand, which he called (9)_____ _____ _____. Keynes contended that there were three separate and distinct motives for holding money: the (10)_____ motive, the (11)_____ motive, and the (12)_____ motive.

It was the speculative motive that distinguished Keynes's theory from the other theories. Keynes argued that (13)_____ _____ played an important role in determining the amount of wealth people desire to hold in the form of money. Though bonds pay interest, a rise in interest rates causes bond values to (14)_____, subjecting their holders to capital losses and even negative returns if bond values fall significantly. Thus at low rates of interest, people reduce their holdings of bonds and hold more money as they expect interest rates to rise, returning to their (15)_____ levels. Therefore, Keynes concluded that the demand for money was negatively related to the level of interest rates.

Since Keynes's early attempt, economists have improved on his analysis providing a better rationale for the (16)_____ relationship between interest rates and velocity. The works of Baumol and Tobin indicate that the (17)_____ component (and, by extension, the precautionary component) of the demand for money is negatively related to the level of interest rates.

Milton Friedman has offered an alternative explanation for the (18)_____ behavior of velocity. Rather than rely on the procyclical behavior of interest rates, Friedman argues that since changes in actual income exceed changes in permanent income, velocity will tend to move procyclically.

Friedman --noting that the interest rate paid on checking deposits tends to move with market rates so that the differential between market interest rates and the interest rate paid on (19)_____ remains relatively constant-- believes that changes in (20)_____ _____ will have little effect on the demand for money, This result does not require the absence of deposit rate ceilings, as banks pay implicit interest on deposits by providing "free" services such as branch offices, more tellers, or "free" checking. Friedman's modern quantity theory of money is consistent with the procyclical behavior of velocity, as are the other modern money demand stories. We will see in Chapter 27 that the distinctions suggest different implications of the effectiveness of fiscal policy.

EXERCISES

Exercise 1: The Quantity Theory of Money

A. Define velocity.

_____

_____

B. What is the equation of exchange?

_____

_____

C. The view that velocity is constant in the short run transforms the equation of exchange into the

_____

Exercise 2: Velocity and the Quantity Theory of Money

Complete the following table.

	M	V	P	Y
	200	5	1	1000
1.	200	6	2	____
2.	300	5	1.5	____
3.	400	6	____	1200
4.	400	____	1	1600
5.	____	5	2	2000

Exercise 3: The Keynesian Approach to Money Demand

A. What are the three motives behind the demand for money postulated by Keynes?

1. _____

2. _____

3. _____

B. What motive did Keynes believe was a function of the interest rate?

_____

C. Tobin's model of the speculative demand for money shows that people hold money as a store of wealth as a way of reducing

_____

Exercise 4: Theories of the Demand for Money

Indicate whether the following statements are associated with Fisher's quantity theory of money (Q), the Cambridge approach to money demand (C), Keynes's liquidity preference theory (K), or with Friedman's modern quantity theory of money (F). Place the appropriate letter in the blank to the left of the statement.

_____ 1. Interest rates have no effect on the demand for money.

_____ 2. Money has two properties explaining why people want to hold it: money functions as a medium of exchange and as a store of wealth.

_____ 3. The demand for money is proportional to income, but the effect of interest rates on the demand for money cannot be completely ignored.

_____ 4. There are three distinct motives for holding money: (a) a transactions motive, where money balances are held if there is imperfect synchronization between receipts and expenditures; (b) a precautionary motive, where money is held because of uncertainty of future expenditures; and (c) a speculative motive, where money is held if bonds are expected to fall in value.

_____ 5. Permanent income is the primary determinant of money demand, and changes in interest rates should have little effect on the demand for money.

_____ 6. The demand for money is insensitive to interest rates --not because the demand for money is insensitive to changes in the opportunity cost of holding money, but because changes in interest rates actually have little effect on the opportunity cost of holding money.

_____ 7. More recent developments in this approach suggest that interest rates are important to the transactions and precautionary components of money demand, as well as to the speculative component.

_____ 8. The transactions and precautionary components of the demand for money are proportional to income, while the speculative component is negatively related to the level of interest rates.

_____ 9. Movements in the price level result solely from changes in the quantity of money.

_____ 10. The demand for money is purely a function of income; interest rates have no effect on the demand for money.

_____ 11. Theory that offered an explanation for the decline in velocity during the Great Depression.

_____ 12. The demand for money is a function of both permanent income and the opportunity cost of holding money.

SELF-TEST

Part A: True-False Questions

Circle whether the following statements are true (T) or false (F).

T F 1. The most important feature of the classical quantity theory of money is that it implies that interest rates have a significant effect on the demand for money.

T F 2. The equation of exchange states that the product of the quantity of money and the average number of times that a dollar is spent on final goods and services in a given period must equal nominal income.

T F 3. Irving Fisher argued that velocity would be relatively constant in the short run, since institutional features of the economy, such as the speed at which checks were cleared, were likely to change only slowly over time.

T F 4. The classical economists' contention that velocity could be regarded as a constant transformed the equation of exchange (an identity) into the quantity theory of money.

T F 5. The Cambridge economists argued that the demand for money was unaffected by changes in interest rates.

T F 6. Evidence indicates that velocity has remained relatively constant since the mid-1950s.

T F 7. At relatively low interest rates, people might be reluctant to hold money due to a concern about capital losses should interest rates rise.

T F 8. Keynes's liquidity preference theory offered an explanation for why velocity had fallen during the Great Depression.

T F 9. The demand for money approach developed by Keynes is consistent with the procyclical movements in velocity observed in the United States.

T F 10. Studies by economists in the 1950s found evidence that even the transactions motive for holding money was sensitive to the level of interest rates.

T F 11. The interest rate can be viewed as the opportunity cost of holding money, implying that the demand for money is positively related to interest rates.

T F 12. James Tobin suggested that people might prefer to hold money to bonds as a store of wealth in an effort to reduce risk.

T F 13. Milton Friedman postulated that the demand for money is a function of both permanent income and the opportunity cost of holding money.

T F 14. The permanent income argument in Friedman's demand for money formulation suggests that velocity will fluctuate with business cycle movements.

T F 15. Friedman's theory of money demand suggests that changes in velocity are fairly predictable implying that changes in the money supply have a fairly predictable effect on economic activity.

Part 3: Multiple-Choice Questions

Circle the appropriate answer.

1. The quantity theory of money suggests that cutting the money supply by one- third will lead to

   a. a sharp decline in output by one-third in the short run and a decline in the price level by one-third in the long run.
   b. a decline in output by one-third.
   c. a decline in output by one-sixth and a decline in the price level by one-sixth.
   d. a decline in the price level by one-third.
   e. none of the above.

2. The classical economists believed that velocity could be regarded as constant in the short run, since

   a. institutional factors, such as the speed with which checks were cleared through the banking system, changed slowly over time.
   b. the opportunity cost of holding money was close to zero.
   c. financial innovation tended to offset changes in interest rates.
   d. none of the above are true.

3. Empirical evidence supports the contention that

   a. velocity tends to be procyclical; that is, velocity declines (increases) when economic activity contracts (expands).
   b. velocity tends to be countercyclical; that is, velocity declines (increases) when economic activity contracts (expands).
   c. velocity tends to be countercyclical; that is, velocity increases (declines) when economic activity contracts (expands).
   d. velocity is essentially a constant.

4. Keynes's liquidity preference theory explains why velocity can be expected to rise when

   a. income increases.
   b. wealth increases.
   c. brokerage commissions increase.
   d. interest rates increase.

5. Keynes argued that people were more likely to increase their money holdings if they believed that

   a. interest rates were about to fall.
   b. bond prices were about to rise.
   c. bond prices were about to fall.
   d. none of the above was true.

6. The Baumol-Tobin analysis suggests that

   a. velocity is relatively constant.
   b. the transactions component of money demand is negatively related to the level of interest rates.
   c. the speculative motive for money is nonexistent.
   d. both (a) and (c) of the above are true.
   e. both (b) and (c) of the above are true.

7. One possible implication of the elimination of deposit rate ceilings is that the implicit interest rate on money will more closely approach bond rates. This suggests that changes in interest rates will

   a. have a greater impact on money demand.
   b. have less effect on the demand for money.
   c. no longer affect the speculative demand for money.
   d. cause velocity to become more volatile.

8. Milton Friedman argues that the demand for money is relatively insensitive to interest rates because

   a. the demand for money is insensitive to changes in the opportunity cost of holding money.
   b. competition among banks keeps the opportunity cost of holding money relatively constant.
   c. people base their investment decisions on expected profits not interest rates.
   d. transactions are not subject to scale economics as wealth increases.

9. Friedman's belief regarding the interest insensitivity of the demand for money implies that

   a. the quantity of money is the primary determinant of aggregate spending.
   b. velocity is countercyclical.
   c. both (a) and (b) of the above are correct.
   d. neither (a) nor (b) of the above are correct.

10. In Friedman's view, because income tends to decline relative to permanent income during business cycle contractions, the demand for money with respect to actual income will increase, causing velocity to

   a. rise.
   b. decline.
   c. remain unchanged, since velocity is only sensitive to changes in interest rates.
   d. decline, provided that interest rates increase when the economy contracts.

Chapter 24

The Keynesian Framework
and the ISLM Model

CHAPTER SYNOPSIS/COMPLETIONS

Chapter 24 presents the simple Keynesian model and introduces the ISLM model of simultaneous money and goods markets equilibrium. These models allow us to better understand the functioning of the economy and better assess the effects of fiscal and monetary policy actions. In addition, the ISLM model is used to derive the aggregate demand curve that is used in aggregate demand and supply analysis (Chapter 26).

The Keynesian model arose from John Maynard Keynes's concern with explaining the cause of the Great Depression. Keynes came to the conclusion that the dramatic decline in economic activity was the result of insufficient (1)_____
_____. Aggregate demand in an open economy is the sum of four components of spending: (2)_____ _____,
(3)_____ _____, (4)_____
_____, and net exports. A decline in any one of these components causes output to decline, potentially leading to recession and rising unemployment.

The Keynesian model, though highly simplified, provides a framework that is very useful for understanding fluctuations in aggregate output. This is more easily accomplished by examining the individual spending components separately.

Keynes argued that consumer expenditures were primarily determined by the level of (5)_____ _____. As income increases, consumers will increase their expenditures. The change in consumer expenditures that results from an additional dollar of disposable income is referred to as the (6)_____
_____ _____ _____, or simply mpc. At low levels of income it is likely that individuals consume more than their disposable income. Thus some amount of consumer expenditure is (7)_____ , that is, independent of disposable income. This description of consumption behavior is summarized by the consumption function, where autonomous consumption is represented by a constant term, a, and the positive slope of the function is given by the mpc.

Investment spending includes fixed investment --spending by business on equipment and structures, and by households on residential houses-- and planned inventory investment. (8)_____ _____ is the spending by business on additional holdings of raw materials, parts, and finished goods.

Keynes believed that managers' expectations of future conditions, as well as interest rates, explained the level of planned investment. If actual investment, the sum of fixed investment and (unplanned) inventory investment, differs from desired investment, fixed investment plus (9)_____ inventory investment, the actions of business firms will move the economy toward a new equilibrium. Consider a situation where business firms' inventories have risen above desired levels. Because firms find inventories costly to hold, they will (10)_____ production in an attempt to sell the excess inventories. Aggregate output will fall and the desired level of inventories will eventually be restored.

After this equilibrium is achieved, business firms may become more optimistic about the future health of the economy. As business firms spend more, inventory levels will fall below desired levels, inducing a further expansion in aggregate output. Hence, the initial increase in investment spending is likely to cause a multifold increase in aggregate output. The ratio of the change in aggregate output to the change in investment spending is called the (11)_____ _____.

An increase in investment spending causes aggregate output to expand by an amount greater than the initial change because (12)_____ _____ also increases. As firms expand output, they hire more factor inputs such as labor, raising households' disposable incomes. Consumers respond by spending more, leading to a further expansion in output and creating a multifold increase. Since this multifold increase is dependent on additional consumer expenditure, it is not surprising that the value of the (13)_____ is used to determine the value of the multiplier.

Once government spending and taxes are added to the simple Keynesian model, policy decisions can be evaluated. Although the tax multiplier is (14)_____ than the government expenditure multiplier, changes in either taxes or government spending can be effective in returning the economy to a (15)_____ _____ equilibrium.

The ISLM model allows one to determine the influence monetary policy has on the economy in the Keynesian framework. The (16)_____ curve illustrates that at lower interest rates the level of (17)_____ _____ and therefore, aggregate output, is greater. Because the IS curve represents goods market equilibrium, the economy must be on the IS curve to be in general equilibrium. Goods market equilibrium is not, however, sufficient to guarantee general equilibrium; the economy must also be on the LM curve.

The LM curve slopes up, indicating that as income rises, (18)_____ interest rates are required to maintain money market equilibrium. The increase in money demand due to an increase in (19)_____ must be exactly offset by the decrease in money demand due to the increase in (20)_____ _____.

The ISLM model determines both the level of aggregate output and interest rates when the price level is fixed. Therefore, the ISLM model can be used to illustrate the effect on aggregate output and interest rates of monetary or fiscal policy actions, a topic extensively discussed in the next chapter.

EXERCISES

Exercise 1: Definitions and Terminology

Match the following terms on the right with definition or description on the left. Place the letter of the term in the blank provided next to the appropriate definition.

_____ 1. Spending by business firms on equipment and structures, and planned spending on residential houses.

a. Planned investment spending

_____ 2. Spending by business firms on additional holdings of raw materials, parts, and finished goods, calculated as the change in holdings in a given time period.

b. Consumer expenditure

_____ 3. Used by economic forecasters, this model explains how interest rates and aggregate output are determined for a fixed price level.

c. "Animal spirits"

_____ 4. Total demand for consumer goods and services.

d. IS Curve

_____ 5. Planned spending by business firms on equipment, structures, raw materials, parts, and finished good and planned spending on residential houses.

e. Expenditure multiplier

_____ 6. Total quantity demanded of output produced in the economy.

f. LM Curve

_____ 7. Aggregate income less taxes, or the total income available for spending.

g. Fixed investment

_____ 8. Consumer expenditure that is independent of disposable income.

h. Inventory investment

_____ 9. The change in consumer expenditure that results from an additional dollar of disposable income.

i. ISLM model

_____10. Spending by all levels of government on goods and services.

j. Disposable income

_____11. The relationship that describes the combinations of aggregate output and interest rates for which the goods market is in equilibrium.

k. Marginal propensity to consume

_____12. The relationship that describes the combination of interest rates and aggregate output for which the money market is in equilibrium.

l. Aggregate demand

_____13. Emotional waves of business optimism and pessimism that Keynes believed dominated fluctuations in planned investment spending.

m. Government spending

_____14. The ratio of the change in aggregate output to the change in planned investment spending.

n. Aggregate demand function

_____15. The relationship between aggregate output and aggregate demand that shows the quantity of aggregate output demanded for each level of aggregate output.

o. Autonomous consumer expenditure

Exercise 2: The Consumption Function

This exercise examines the relationship between the level of disposable income and consumer expenditures known as the consumption function.

A. Assume that the consumption function is given by $C = 50 + 0.75DI$. Complete the following table:

Point	Disposable Income (DI)	Change in DI	Change in C	Autonomous Consumption	Total Consumption
A	0	_____	_____	50	_____
B	100	_____	_____	_____	_____
C	200	_____	_____	_____	_____
D	300	_____	_____	_____	_____
E	400	_____	_____	_____	_____
F	500	_____	_____	_____	_____

B. In Figure 24A, plot the points on the consumption function you derived in the table.

FIGURE 24A

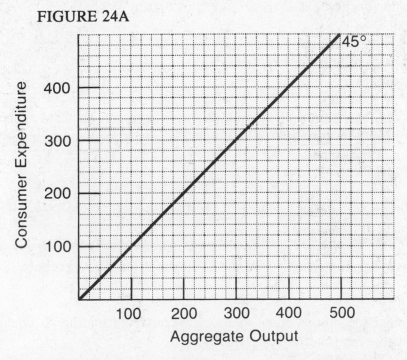

Exercise 3: Determination of Equilibrium Aggregate Output

Suppose that for a particular economy, planned investment spending is 10, government spending is 10, taxes are zero, and consumer expenditure is given by the consumption function:

$$C = 20 + 0.8DI$$

which is plotted in Figure 24B.

FIGURE 24B

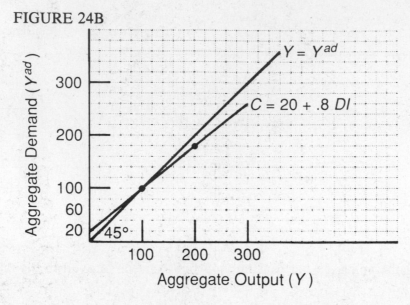

A. Plot the aggregate demand function and mark it as Y^{ad}_1 in Figure 24B.

B. What is the equilibrium level of aggregate output? Y_1 = _____

C. If planned investment spending rises to 30, draw in the new aggregate demand function, Y^{ad}_2. What is the new equilibrium level of aggregate output?

   Y_2 = _____

D. What is the value of the expenditure multiplier? _____

Exercise 4: Unplanned Inventory Investment and the Determination of Aggregate Output

Assume that planned investment spending is equal to 100, government spending is equal to 200, taxes are zero, and consumer expenditure is given by:

   C = 100 + 0.9DI

A. Write down the equation describing the aggregate demand function.

B. If current aggregate output is 3000, what is the level of unplanned inventory investment?

_____

C. What will happen to the level of aggregate output in the next time period?

_____

D. At what level of aggregate output will unplanned inventory disinvestment be zero?

_____

E. At what level will aggregate output eventually settle? _____

Exercise 5: The Response of Aggregate Output

In the following matrix there is noted at the top of each column Autonomous Consumer Expenditure, Induced Consumer Expenditure, Planned Investment Spending, Government Spending, and Equilibrium Aggregate Income. At the beginning of each row there is a hypothetical change in some variable in the model. In each cell of the matrix indicate by a, +, -, or 0 whether the assumed change will increase, decrease, or cause no change in the variables in each column for the model in the text.

	Consumer Expenditure		Planned Investment Spending	Government Spending	Equilibrium Aggregate Income
	Autonomous	Induced			
Decrease in rate of interest					
Decrease in MPC					
Decrease in tax rate					
Increase in planned investment spending					
Increase in autonomous consumer expenditure					
Decrease in MPS					
Decrease in government spending					

224

Exercise 6: The Expenditure Multiplier

Assume that the equilibrium level of income is 4000 and the mpc = 0.8.

A. Calculate the value of the government expenditure multiplier. _____

B. Calculate the value of the tax multiplier. _____

C. Suppose that the government knows that the full-employment level of income is 4200. Calculate the increase in government spending or the size of the tax cut necessary to raise equilibrium income to the full employment level.

Change in government spending = _____

Change in taxes = _____

Exercise 7: Deriving the LM Curve

The LM curve is the relationship that describes combinations of interest rates and aggregate output for which the quantity of money demanded equals the quantity of money supplied. Panel (a) of Figure 24C shows the equilibrium values of interest rates in the money market for aggregate income levels of $400 billion, $600 billion, and $800 billion. Complete panel (b) by plotting the level of equilibrium output corresponding to each of the three interest rates. Connect the three points with straight-line segments. Compare your results with Figure 24.8 in the text.

FIGURE 24C

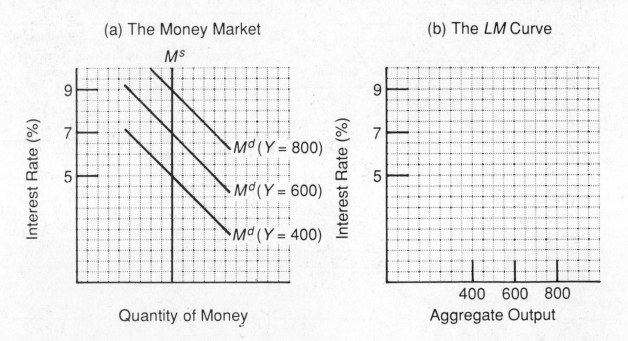

(a) The Money Market   (b) The LM Curve

Exercise 8: Deriving the IS Curve

The IS curve is the relationship that describes the combinations of aggregate output and interest rates for which the total quantity of goods produced equals the total quantity demanded. The investment schedule in panel (a) of Figure 24D shows that as the interest rate rises from 5 to 7 to 9 percent, planned investment spending falls from $150 billion to $100 billion to $50 billion. Panel (b) of Figure 24D indicates the levels of equilibrium output $400 billion, $600 billion, and $800 billion that correspond to those three levels of planned investment. Complete panel (c) by plotting the level of equilibrium output corresponding to each of the three interest rates. Then connect the points with straight-line segments. Compare your results with Figure 24.7 in the text.

FIGURE 24D

(a) Interest Rates and Planned Investment Spending

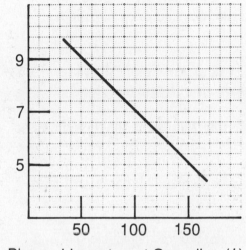

(b) The Keynesian Cross Diagram

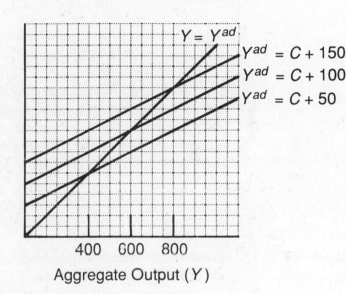

(c) The *IS* Curve

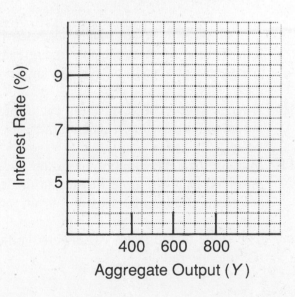

SELF-TEST

Part A: True-False Questions

Circle whether following statements are true (T) or false (F).

T   F   1.   The Keynesian model of consumer expenditures implies that the interest rate is the most important factor affecting a person's demand for consumer items.

T   F   2.   Suppose that after taxes you take home $10,000 per year. If you spend $8,500 of your disposable income on consumer goods and services, your mpc is equal to 0.85.

T   F   3.   The investment spending component of aggregate demand does not include unplanned inventory investment.

T   F   4.   Jean purchases 1000 shares of Exxon common stock through her broker. This transaction is included in the investment component of aggregate demand.

T   F   5.   The 45-degree line in the Keynesian cross diagram represents all possible or potential equilibrium points.

T   F   6.   If the level of aggregate output exceeds aggregate demand, income will rise, causing the level of output to expand.

T   F   7.   Unplanned inventory investment occurs when the level of aggregate demand exceeds aggregate output.

T   F   8.   Business firms are likely to cut production in the face of rising unplanned inventory levels.

T   F   9.   The simple Keynesian model suggests that an increase in planned investment will actually lead to an expansion in aggregate output that exceeds the initial change in investment spending. This is known as the multiplier effect.

T   F   10.   Keynes believed that business cycle fluctuations were dominated by changes in autonomous consumer expenditure.

T   F   11.   Suppose that the economy is in the midst of a deep recession. The analysis provided by the simple Keynesian model indicates that appropriate government action should include a tax cut or an increase in government spending or both.

T   F   12.   The slope of the IS curve reflects the fact that investment is negatively related to the interest rate.

T F 13. At any point along an IS curve the level of unplanned inventory investment is zero.

T F 14. The demand for money is negatively related to the level of income.

T F 15. At points to the left of the LM curve there is an excess supply of money which will cause interest rates to fall.

Part B: Multiple-Choice Questions

Circle the appropriate answer.

1. Which of the following describes the equilibrium condition in the simple Keynesian model?

    a. Aggregate output equals aggregate demand.
    b. Unplanned inventory investment is zero.
    c. Actual investment equals planned investment.
    d. All of the above.
    e. Only (a) and (b) of the above.

2. Keynes believed that the economy could achieve an equilibrium level of output

    a. only at the full-employment level of output.
    b. below the full-employment level of output.
    c. only if the government took a "hands off" approach.
    d. by doing none of the above.

3. Inventory investment is distinguished from fixed investment in that

    a. fixed investment is never unplanned.
    b. inventory investment is never planned.
    c. unplanned inventory investment is always zero.
    d. There is no distinction.

4. If one knows the value of the multiplier and the change in the level of autonomous investment, one can determine

    a. the change in the interest rate.
    b. the change in the money supply.
    c. the change in the aggregate output.
    d. all of the above.

5. Keynes believed that fluctuations in aggregate output were largely the result of fluctuations in

    a. the money supply.
    b. autonomous investment spending.
    c. autonomous consumer expenditure.
    d. government spending.

6. If the mpc is 0.75, the multiplier is

    a. 3.00
    b. 3.75.
    c. 0.25.
    d. 4.00

7. Assume that an economy characterized by the simple Keynesian model is in equilibrium at full employment but the government budget is in deficit. If the government raises taxes to balance the budget, then

    a. the rate of unemployment will increase.
    b. the level of aggregate output will increase.
    c. the price level will increase.
    d. all of the above will occur.

8. An increase in the interest rate will cause

    a. investment spending to fall.
    b. investment spending to rise.
    c. tax rates to rise.
    d. no change in aggregate spending.

9. Points to the left of the IS curve represent interest rate and output combinations characterized by reductions in

    a. unplanned inventory accumulations.
    b. unplanned inventory reductions.
    c. an excess demand for money.
    d. an excess supply of money.

10. The money market is in equilibrium

    a. at any point on the LM curve.
    b. at only one point on the IS curve.
    c. at any point on the IS curve.
    d. at only one point on the LM curve.
    e. when only (a) and (b) of the above occur.
    f. when only (c) and (d) of the above occur.

Chapter 25

Monetary and Fiscal
Policy in the ISLM Model

CHAPTER SYNOPSIS/COMPLETIONS

In this chapter we explore the mechanics of the ISLM model, discovering how
(1)_____ _____ --the control of the money supply and
interest rates-- and (2)_____ _____ --the control of
government spending and taxes-- affect the level of aggregate output and interest rates. Since
government policymakers have these two tools at their disposal, they will be interested in
knowing the effects each policy can be expected to have on the economy. The ISLM model
provides a convenient but powerful framework for comparing the relative effects of proposed
monetary and fiscal actions. By comparing these predicted effects, policymakers can better
decide which policy is most appropriate.

The ISLM model also provides a framework that allows one to compare the desirability
of interest-rate targeting against money-supply targeting. In addition, the aggregate demand
curve is derived using the ISLM model. It is for these three important reasons that we study
the ISLM model in the money and banking course.

As is true for any economic model, we can better comprehend the workings of the ISLM
model by first examining the behavior of the individual curves. Once this has been done, the
effects on interest rates and aggregate output of changes in fiscal and monetary variables can
be determined.

The (3)_____ curve shows the combinations of interest rates and aggregate output
that ensure equilibrium in the goods market. Therefore, changes in autonomous consumer
expenditures, autonomous (4)_____ spending, and government spending or
taxes are all factors that shift the IS curve. For example, if Congress enacts legislation to
spend $100 billion over the next 10 years to repair the decaying infrastructure (roads,
bridges, canals) of the economy, the added government spending will shift the IS curve to
the (5)_____. An example of a leftward shift in the IS curve is provided by
the precipitous drop in autonomous investment spending during the Great Depression. It is
important to distinguish between autonomous changes in investment and changes in
investment due to changes in interest rates. A change in investment that results from a
change in interest rates is shown as a movement along a given IS curve, not as a shift in the
IS curve.

Interest rate and aggregate output combinations that represent equilibrium in the money market define an (6)_____ curve. Therefore, changes in either money supply or money (7)_____ can cause the LM curve to shift.

Consider the effect an increase in money supply has on the LM curve. At the initial interest rate, an increase in the money supply creates an (8)_____ supply of money. Holding output constant, equilibrium is regained in the money market by a fall in the (9)_____ _____. Alternatively, the interest rate held constant, equilibrium is regained in the money market when the increase in (10)_____ _____ is sufficient to raise money demand to a level that eliminates the excess supply of money.

Changes in money demand also shift the LM curve. If more people come to expect a surge in the stock market, they will try to conserve on their holdings of money, filling their portfolios with more stocks (recall the analysis of Chapter 5 on asset demand). The drop in money demand creates an excess supply of money at the initial interest rate. Therefore, interest rates will (11)_____, holding output constant, and the LM curve will shift to the (12)_____. Conversely, an increase in the demand for money shifts the LM curve to the left.

Putting the IS and LM curves together allows us to consider the effects of autonomous spending and policy changes on the equilibrium levels of the interest rate and aggregate output. For example, an increase in taxes aimed at reducing the budget deficit shifts the IS curve (13)_____ due to the decline in spending by consumers. The decline in output causes the demand for money to fall, which in turn creates an excess supply of (14)_____, putting downward pressure on interest rates. Although the decline in interest rates will cause interest-sensitive investment to increase, the increase is not enough to offset the contractionary effects of the tax increase. No wonder tax increases are so unpopular among incumbent politicians: a tax increase may cause rising unemployment and a net loss of votes on election day.

Some economists contend that there is a tendency for the money supply to expand prior to elections. Since the ISLM model indicates that an increase in the money supply causes aggregate output to (15)_____ and interest rates to fall, and since both are likely to help the incumbent politician, such a contention has credibility.

The ISLM framework also has been employed to analyze the appropriateness of Federal Reserve operating procedures. While interest-rate targets can be shown to be more consistent with stable economic activity when the (16)_____ curve is unstable, a money supply target helps ensure greater stability when the (17)_____ curve is unstable. Since neither targeting procedure outperforms the other in every situation, it becomes an empirical question as to which curve is more stable and under which conditions. Thus it is not surprising that economists still debate over the appropriate targeting procedure the Fed should employ.

Another debate has centered around the slope of the LM curve. If the LM curve is very steep, approaching a vertical line, then an expansionary fiscal policy is likely to be an (18)_____ tool for expanding aggregate output since investment spending will be (19)_____ _____ by the rising interest rates.

Finally, the ISLM model is useful in deriving the aggregate demand curve used in aggregate demand and supply analysis. Since aggregate demand and supply analysis is so powerful, this function of the ISLM model is especially important. A decline in the price level raises the (20)_____ money supply, causing interest rates to fall and investment spending to (21)_____. Simultaneous goods and money market equilibrium will correspond to higher levels of aggregate output as the price level falls, indicating that the aggregate demand curve slopes (22)_____ to the right.

The aggregate demand curve shifts in the same direction as a shift in the IS or LM curves. Increases in the money supply and government spending or decreases in taxes all cause the aggregate demand curve to shift to the (23)_____. We see in the next chapter that the aggregate demand and supply model provides a powerful framework for understanding recent economic events.

EXERCISES

Exercise 1: Factors that Cause the IS and LM Curves to Shift

This exercise provides a summary of the factors that cause the IS and LM curves to shift.

A. List the factors that cause the IS curve to shift to the right.

1. _____

2. _____

3. _____

4. _____

B. List the factors that cause the IS curve to shift to the left.

1. _____

2. _____

3. _____

4. _____

C. List the factors that cause the LM curve to shift to the right.

1. _____

2. _____

D. List the factors that cause the LM curve to shift to the left.

1. _____

2. _____

Exercise 2: Monetary and Fiscal Policy

Indicate whether the following statements are a description of monetary policy (M), fiscal policy (F), or both (B). Place the appropriate letter in the blank next to the statement.

_____ 1. Changes in money supply and interest rates.

_____ 2. Shown as a shift in the IS curve.

_____ 3. Changes in government spending and taxing.

_____ 4. Shown as a shift in the LM curve.

_____ 5. Policy made by the Federal Reserve.

_____ 6. Policy made by the president and Congress.

_____ 7. Shown as a shift in the aggregate demand curve.

Exercise 3: Response to a Change in Both Monetary and Fiscal Policy

The United States experienced its deepest post-World War II recession in the years 1981 and 1982 despite the fiscal stimulus provided by the Reagan tax cut. The recession was somewhat unusual in that interest rates rose throughout 1981 and the first half of 1982. In Figure 25A the stimulus provided by the tax cut is shown as the rightward shift of the IS curve from IS_1 to IS_2, moving the economy from point 1 to point 2. Draw in the new LM curve in Figure 25A consistent with the decline in aggrete output and rise in interest rates.

FIGURE 25A

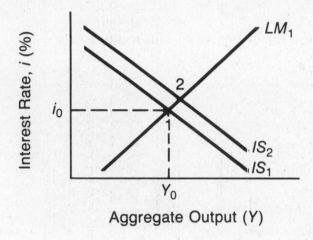

Explain why the LM curve might have shifted in the direction it did.

_____

_____

_____

Exercise 4: Expansionary Monetary and Fiscal Policy

When President Kennedy took office in 1961, he appointed Walter Heller as his chairman for the Council of Economic Advisors. Heller was concerned with the high rate of unemployment and suggested that Kennedy adopt an expansionary fiscal policy. Heller convinced Kennedy that a tax cut would lead to economic expansion, lowering unemployment and thereby fulfilling Kennedy's campaign promise to "get the economy moving again." As a consequence of these efforts, taxes were cut in 1964. The results were favorable as unemployment fell from 5.7% in 1963 to 4.5% in 1965. In addition, interest rates remained relatively stable over this period, suggesting that the Federal Reserve was pursuing an interest-rate targeting strategy, effectively accommodating the fiscal expansion. The position of the economy just prior to the tax cut provides the initial conditions in Figure 25B at point 1. Graph the position of the economy in 1965 in Figure 25B, showing the increase in aggregate output and stable interest rates.

FIGURE 25B

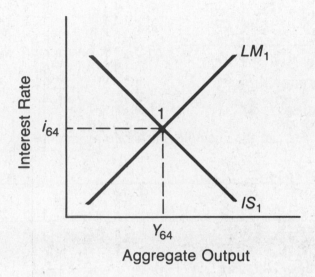

Exercise 5: Contractionary Monetary and Fiscal Policies

The combination of the tax cut in 1964 and the increase in government spending due to involvement in the Vietnam war significantly reduced unemployment by 1968, but this reduction had come at the cost of higher inflation. Response to the high inflation came on two fronts. First, Congress enacted a measure in 1968 that imposed a 10% surtax on personal income taxes and on corporate incomes. Then in 1969, Richard Nixon reduced federal spending growth. Thus fiscal policy became contractionary in 1968- 1969. Second, the Federal Reserve tightened monetary policy. While both fiscal and monetary policy turned contractionary, it appears that fiscal policy proved less contractionary than monetary policy. In Figure 25C, the condition of the economy in early 1968 is represented by the intersection of the IS curve (IS$_1$) and the LM curve (LM$_1$) at point 1. In Figure 25C, show the shifts in the IS and LM curves that took place in 1969.

236

FIGURE 25C

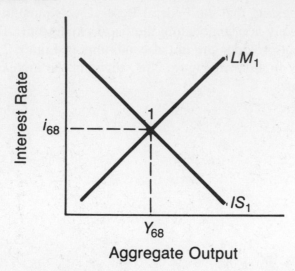

Predict what happened to interest rates and the unemployment rate by mid-1970.

_____

_____

Exercise 6: Effectiveness of Monetary Versus Fiscal Policy

Policymakers often must choose between monetary and fiscal policies. Under some circumstances, fiscal policies will be preferred to monetary policies, while the converse may be true under alternative conditions. For the given hypothetical conditions, indicate whether the policymaker would have a preference for fiscal policy (F) or monetary policy (M).

_____ 1. Investment is relatively responsive to changes in interest rates.

_____ 2. The demand for money is unaffected by the interest rate.

_____ 3. Investment is relatively responsive to changes in the interest rate, and the demand for money is unaffected by the interest rate.

_____ 4. The demand for money is relatively responsive to changes in the interest rate, and investment is relatively unresponsive to changes in the interest rate.

_____ 5. Investment is completely crowded out when taxes are cut or government spending is increased.

Exercise 7: Factors that Cause the Aggregate Demand Curve to Shift

In the following table, factors that cause the aggregate demand curve to shift are listed. For a decrease in the variable, indicate whether the aggregate demand shifts to the right (-->) or to the left (<--).

Factors that Cause the Aggregate Demand Curve to Shift

Change in Variable	Direction of Aggregate Demand Curve Shift
Taxes -	A. _____
Money Supply -	B. _____
Government spending -	C. _____
Autonomous consumption -	D. _____
Money demand -	E. _____
Business confidence -	F. _____

SELF-TEST

Part A: True-False Questions

Circle whether the following statements are true (T) or false (F).

T F 1. An increase in the interest rate causes the IS curve to shift to the left, since investment spending will fall.

T F 2. If businesses should suddenly become "bearish" (pessimistic) about the future profitability of investment, aggregate output will fall, all else constant. This is shown as a leftward shift of the IS curve.

T F 3. Assume that the Federal Reserve pursues a policy of pegging (preventing fluctuations in) the interest rate. If government policymakers increase government spending, the Fed will be forced to increase the money supply to keep interest rates from rising.

T F 4. Financial innovation--by increasing the liquidity of financial assets--has enabled some people to reduce their demand for money. The decline in the demand for money has the effect of shifting the LM curve to the left.

238

T F 5. Within the ISLM framework an expansionary fiscal policy win lead to an increase in aggregate output and cause interest rates to rise.

T F 6. An expansion of the money supply will lead to lower interest rates and an increase in investment spending as people attempt to rid themselves of excess money balances.

T F 7. Interest rates in the United States rose over the period 1965 through 1966. Since this coincided with the Vietnam war buildup, we can assume that the LM curve shifted to the left.

T F 8. The condition known as complete crowding out occurs when the demand for money is insensitive to the interest rate.

T F 9. The more responsive is money demand to the interest rate, the less effective is fiscal policy.

T F 10. The effect of an open market purchase is to shift the LM curve to the left.

T F 11. Assume that money demand is very unstable and the IS curve is stable. Such knowledge makes the case for monetary targeting stronger, since the IS curve will be stable relative to the LM curve.

T F 12. A decline in the price level, ceteris paribus, will mean lower interest rates and thus a higher level of investment.

T F 13. A decline in taxes, as occurred in 1964, causes the aggregate demand curve to shift to the left.

T F 14. Monetary policy changes have no effect on the aggregate demand curve, since it is only factors that shift the IS curve which affect aggregate demand.

T F 15. High unemployment leads the Federal Reserve to expand the money supply. Such a policy will shift both the LM and aggregate demand curves to the right.

Part B: Multiple-Choice Questions

Circle the appropriate answer.

1. Which of the following causes the IS curve to shift to the left?

    a. Increase in taxes

    b. Increase in government spending
    c. Increase in the money supply
    d. All of the above
    e. Only (b) and (c) of the above

2. An increase in government spending causes both interest rates and aggregate output to increase. In the ISLM framework, this is represented by a _____ shift of the _____ curve.

    a. leftward; LM
    b. rightward; LM
    c. leftward; IS
    d. rightward; IS

3. In the early 1930s there was a significant contraction in the money supply. In the ISLM framework, such a contraction is illustrated as a _____ shift of the _____ curve.

    a. rightward; IS
    b. rightward; LM
    c. leftward; IS
    d. leftward; LM

4. In 1981, President Reagan was able to get through Congress a fiscal package containing a tax cut and increased federal expenditures. Such a policy shifts the _____ curve to the _____.

    a. LM; left
    b. IS; right
    c. LM; right
    d. IS; left

5. Assume that an economy suffers a recession in spite of an expansionary monetary policy. The ISLM framework suggests that even if the LM curve shifts to the right, the level of aggregate output might fall if the

    a. IS curve shifts to the right.
    b. investment function shifts to the right.
    c. IS curve shifts to the left.
    d. taxes are cut.
    e. none of the above occurs.

6. Suppose that the economy is suffering from both high interest rates and high unemployment. Viewed from an ISLM framework, we can conclude that _____ policy has been too _____.

    a. fiscal; expansionary
    b. monetary; expansionary
    c. monetary; contractionary
    d. fiscal; contractionary

7. Assume that econometric studies indicate that the demand for money is highly sensitive to interest rate changes. Such evidence would tend to support the belief that

    a. fiscal policy has no aggregate output effects.
    b. fiscal policy is effective in increasing output.
    c. monetary policy is effective in increasing output.
    d. none of the above is true.

8. Investment spending in the country Curtonia is highly unstable, making the IS curve very unstable relative to the LM curve. Given the nature of the economy, the Central Bank of Curtonia will want to target the

    a. money supply.
    b. interest rate.
    c. exchange rate.
    d. discount rate.
    e. monetary base.

9. The aggregate demand curve slopes downward to the right, since

    a. a decline in the price level raises the real money supply, lowering interest rates.
    b. a decline in the price level raises the real money supply, causing output to fall.
    c. an increase in the price level raises the real money supply, causing output to rise.
    d. none of the above occurs.

10. A Federal Reserve purchase of government securities will shift the aggregate demand curve in which direction?

    a. Right
    b. Left
    c. A Fed purchase of securities does not shift the aggregate demand curve.
    d. All of the above are a possible result of an expansion in the money supply.

Chapter 26

Aggregate Demand and Supply Analysis

CHAPTER SYNOPSIS/COMPLETIONS

This chapter develops the basic tool of aggregate demand and supply analysis in order to study the effects of money on aggregate output and the price level. The model is very powerful in gaining insight into the workings of the economy, yet it is relatively simple and, with a little work, relatively easy to master.

We construct the aggregate demand and aggregate supply model by first examining the individual curves. The aggregate demand curve describes the relationship between the (1)_____ level and the quantity of aggregate output demanded. The (2)_____ derive the aggregate demand curve from the quantity theory of money. Holding the money supply and velocity constant, an increase in the price level reduces the quantity of aggregate output demanded. A falling price level implies an increase in the quantity of aggregate output demanded. Keynesians argue that a falling price level --because it causes the real (3)_____ _____ to increase which in turn lowers (4)_____ _____ -- causes investment spending and hence the quantity of aggregate output demanded to (5)_____ . Both explanations are consistent with a downward sloping aggregate demand curve.

Though both monetarists and Keynesians agree that the aggregate demand curve is downward sloping, they hold different views about the factors that cause the aggregate demand curve to shift. Monetarists contend that changes in the (6)_____ supply are the primary source of changes in aggregate demand. An increase in the money supply shifts the aggregate demand curve to the (7)_____ , while a decrease in the money supply shifts it to the left.

Keynesians do not dispute the effect a change in the money supply will have on aggregate demand, but they regard changes in fiscal policy and (8)_____ expenditure as additional factors that can explain shifts in the aggregate demand curve. For example, Keynesians believe that increased government expenditures or a cut in taxes will shift the aggregate demand curve to the (9)_____ , while a decrease in government expenditures or a tax increase shifts the aggregate demand curve to the left.

The other piece to aggregate demand and supply analysis is the aggregate supply curve. The aggregate supply curve is upward sloping, illustrating that an increase in the price level will lead to an increase in the quantity of output supplied, all else constant. Explaining why the aggregate supply curve slopes upward is fairly straightforward. Since the costs of many inputs (factors of production) tend to be (10)_____ in the short run, an increase in the price of the output will mean greater profits, encouraging firms to (11)_____ production, increasing the quantity of aggregate output supplied.

Note, however, that this increase in output cannot last. Eventually workers will demand higher wages, and resource suppliers will demand higher prices. As factor prices (12)_____, the aggregate supply curve shifts in, causing aggregate output supplied to fall back to its original level.

Combining the aggregate supply and the aggregate demand curves allows one to consider the effects on the price level and aggregate output when one of the factors affecting either aggregate demand or aggregate supply changes. For example, an increase in the money supply shifts the aggregate demand curve to the right. This implies that an increase in the money supply will cause both (13)_____ _____ and the (14)_____ _____ to increase in the short run. In the long run, the (15)_____ _____ curve will shift in as workers demand higher nominal wages to compensate for the increase in prices. Since the aggregate supply curve will shift when unemployment and aggregate output differ from their (16)_____ - _____ levels, the long-run equilibrium will coincide with the natural-rate level of output.

Therefore, changes in either monetary or fiscal policies can have only (17)_____ effects on unemployment and aggregate output. In the long run, monetary and fiscal expansions can do nothing more than raise the (18)_____ _____. This concept is illustrated by the long-run aggregate supply curve, a vertical line passing through the natural rate of aggregate output.

The aggregate supply curve will shift inward not only as workers come to expect higher inflation, but when negative supply (19)_____ hit the economy (as in the 1970s when OPEC dramatically increased the price of oil) or when workers push for higher real wages. Unfortunately, the economy experiences both rising prices and falling aggregate output in the short run, an outcome referred to as (20)_____. Eventually, the aggregate supply curve will shift outward returning the economy to the natural rate of output.

The aggregate demand and supply analysis indicates that aggregate output and unemployment can deviate from their natural-rate levels for two reasons: shifts in aggregate demand and shifts in aggregate supply. Whether these shifts cause aggregate output to fall or rise, the change will be (21)_____. Factor prices eventually adjust, moving the economy back to the vertical long-run aggregate supply curve. In the long run, shifts in aggregate demand merely change the price level, and shifts in short-run aggregate supply have no permanent effects.

EXERCISES

Exercise 1: The Monetarist View of Aggregate Demand

A. The equation of exchange tells us that aggregate spending will equal the product of the money supply and income velocity. Assume that the money supply is $600 billion and velocity is 6. Graph the aggregate demand function in Figure 26A.

FIGURE 26A

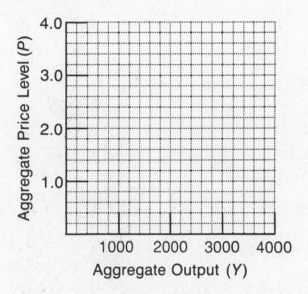

B. If the Fed lowers the money supply to $500 billion, what will happen to aggregate spending if velocity remains unchanged?

_____

C. Graph the new aggregate demand curve in Figure 26A representing the aggregate output price level combinations for the level of aggregate spending in part B.

Exercise 2: Factors that Shift the Aggregate Demand Curve

A. List the factors that cause the aggregate demand curve to shift to the right.

1. _____

2. _____

3. _____

4. _____

5. _____

6. _____

B. List the factors that cause the aggregate demand curve to shift to the left.

1. _____

2. _____

3. _____

4. _____

5. _____

6. _____

Exercise 3: Factors that Shift the Aggregate Supply Curve

In the following table, factors that cause the aggregate supply curve to shift are listed. For each factor indicate whether the aggregate supply curve shifts in ($\leftarrow$) or shifts out ($\rightarrow$).

Factors that Shift the Aggregate Supply Curve

Factor	Shift in Aggregate Supply
1. OPEC increases the price of oil	
2. "Tightening" up of the labor market	
3. A decline in the expected price level	
4. Drought conditions in the Midwest	
5. Citrus crops in Florida freeze	
6. Improved productivity	

Exercise 4: Shifts in Aggregate Supply

A. Using information provided in the following table and assuming that the aggregate demand curve remained at AD_1 in both periods, graph in Figure 26B the short-run aggregate supply curves for the two years.

Year	Real GNP (1972$)	GNP Deflator (1972 = 100)	Unemployment Rate	Natural Unemployment Rate
1974	1248.0	114.9	5.6	5.4
1975	1233.9	125.5	8.5	5.4

Source: R. Gordon, *Macroeconomics*, 3d Ed. (Boston: Little, Brown, 1984), Appendix B.

FIGURE 26B

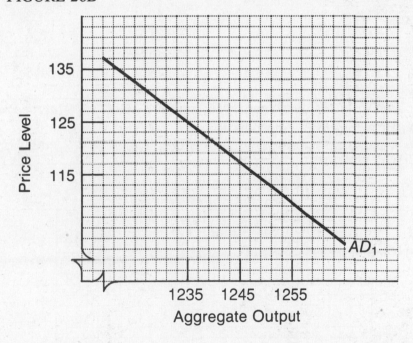

B. Is it likely that worker's expectations of higher wages were the force that shifted the aggregate supply curve in?

_____

_____

246

Exercise 5: Shifts in Aggregate Demand

Using the information given in the following table, plot the price level and real output combinations for the years 1929 to 1936 in Figure 26C. Also, in Figure 26C graph the decline in aggregate demand from 1929 to 1933 (assume that the aggregate supply curve does not shift during this period). Then graph the aggregate demand and supply curves for 1936. Explain the behavior of the shifts.

Year	GNP ($1958)	CPI (1958=100)	Money Supply	Expenditures ($1958)
1929	203.6	59.7	----	22.0
1930	183.3	58.2	25.8	24.3
1931	169.2	53.0	24.1	25.4
1932	144.1	47.6	21.1	24.2
1933	141.5	45.1	19.9	23.3
1934	154.3	46.6	21.9	26.6
1935	169.6	47.8	25.9	27.0
1936	193.0	48.3	29.9	31.8

Source: *Economic Report of the President*, 1966; and R. J. Gordon, *Macroeconomics*, 2d Ed. (Boston: Little, Brown, 1981), Appendix B.

FIGURE 26C

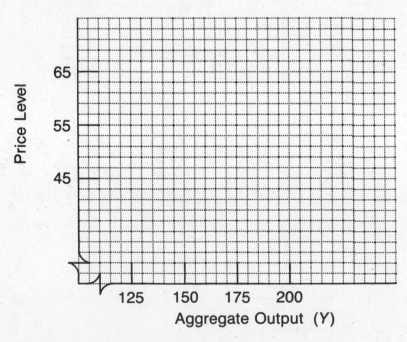

Exercise 6: Differences Between Monetarist and Keynesian Analyses

Indicate whether the following statements are consistent with monetarist aggregate demand and supply analysis (M), Keynesian aggregate demand and supply analysis (K), both (B), or neither (N).

_____ 1. The aggregate demand curve is downward sloping and shifts in response to changes in the money supply.

_____ 2. The short-run aggregate supply curve is vertical at the natural rate of output.

_____ 3. Movements in the price level and aggregate output are driven by changes in government spending and taxes in addition to changes in the money supply.

_____ 4. The economy will return to full employment in the face of shocks but active use of government intervention to stabilize the economy is to no avail.

_____ 5. An increase in government spending will not cause aggregate output to increase, since private spending will be "crowded out" by government spending.

_____ 6. Changes in consumer and business confidence, imports and exports, and government spending and taxes shift the aggregate demand curve.

_____ 7. Adjustments in wages and prices may be quite prolonged delaying the self-correction of the economy back to the natural-rate level.

_____ 8. Changes in aggregate spending are primarily determined by changes in the money supply.

_____ 9. The aggregate supply curve does not remain fixed over time. Rather, it shifts whenever aggregate output is either above or below the natural-rate level.

_____ 10. A rise in the expected price level causes the aggregate supply curve to shift inward.

SELF-TEST

Part A: True-False Questions

Circle whether the following statements are true (T) or false (F).

T F 1. Monetarists argue that a change in the money supply is the primary factor causing aggregate demand to shift.

T F 2. Income velocity is defined as the value of nominal gross national product divided by the money supply.

T F 3. Friedman argues that changes in the money supply affect output almost immediately as if it were injected directly into the bloodstream of the economy.

T F 4. Keynesians contend that at a lower price level the real quantity of money expands, encouraging higher spending.

T F 5. Along a given aggregate supply curve, input prices are assumed fixed.

T F 6. If workers come to expect higher inflation, the aggregate supply curve will shift out to reflect the expectation of lower real wages.

T F 7. Persistently high unemployment is likely to force wage concessions by workers, resulting in an eventual outward shift in the aggregate supply curve.

T F 8. Adverse supply shocks such as OPEC oil price increases or citrus fruit crop freezes are referred to as negative price shocks and cause the aggregate supply curve to shift inward.

T F 9. Suppose that the economy is currently producing an aggregate output above the natural level of aggregate output. We can expect price reductions in the future as firms lower prices to sell the excess output.

T F 10. The aggregate demand and supply framework indicates that in the long run the ultimate effect of an increase in the money supply is an increase in aggregate output.

T F 11. Aggregate demand and supply analysis indicates that if adverse weather causes major crop failures throughout the United States, aggregate output will fall and the price level will rise.

T F 12. In 1970 both inflation and unemployment increased. Such a condition is called "stagflation."

T F 13. Keynesians tend to question the effectiveness of fiscal policy in shifting aggregate demand, since they believe that crowding out of investment will be nearly complete.

T F 14. Monetarists, unlike Keynesians, believe that wages and prices adjust very slowly over time.

T F 15. The positive supply shock from declining oil prices in 1986 did not produce the business cycle boom that some had predicted, in part, because a decline in net exports that year caused a wekening in aggregate demand.

Part B. Multiple-Choice Questions

Circle the appropriate answer.

1. Keynesians and monetarists have different views regarding the factors that cause the aggregate demand curve to shift. This difference is best explained by which of the following statements?

   a. Monetarists place greater emphasis on the importance of money yet believe that fiscal actions can shift the aggregate demand curve, while Keynesians contend that money has no effect on aggregate demand.
   b. Keynesians believe that only fiscal policy can affect aggregate demand, while monetarists believe that fiscal policy is ineffective in altering the level of aggregate demand.
   c. Keynesians contend that both fiscal and monetary policy actions influence the level of aggregate demand, while monetarists claim that monetary policy is far more important than fiscal policy in affecting the level of aggregate demand.
   d. Keynesians place more significance on monetary actions than on fiscal actions, while monetarists believe that neither monetary nor fiscal actions influence the level of aggregate demand.

2. In Keynesian analysis, if investment is unresponsive to changes in the interest rate, the aggregate demand curve will be

   a. downward sloping.
   b. horizontal.
   c. downward sloping if consumer expenditures are sensitive to the interest rate.
   d. none of the above.

3. The upward slope of the short-run aggregate supply curve reflects the belief that

   a. factor prices are more flexible than output prices.
   b. output prices are more flexible than factor prices.
   c. factor prices are fixed in the long run.
   d. factor prices are completely flexible even in the short run.

4. Which of the following factors cause the aggregate supply curve to shift?

    a. Changes in the tightness of the labor market
    b. Changes in expectations of inflation
    c. Supply shocks such as commodity price changes
    d. Attempts by workers to push up their real wages
    e. All of the above

5. The aggregate demand and supply analysis suggests that the economy has a self-correcting mechanism which ensures that aggregate output and unemployment will move toward their natural-rate levels. However, Keynesians contend that this mechanism

    a. is unacceptably slow due to the stickiness of wages.
    b. cannot be improved on, even though the adjustment process is slow.
    c. while slow, can be improved through activist policy.
    d. does both (a) and (b) of the above.
    e. does both (a) and (c) of the above.

6. If the economy experiences a period of both a rising price level and rising unemployment, one can reasonably infer

    a. that the aggregate demand curve has shifted to the right.
    b. that the aggregate demand curve has shifted to the left.
    c. that the aggregate supply curve has shifted out.
    d. that the aggregate supply curve has shifted in.

7. Which of the following statements accurately describes the difference between monetarists and Keynesians?

    a. Monetarists believe that crowding out can be a major problem reducing the effectiveness of fiscal policy, while Keynesians contend that crowding out will not be complete.
    b. Keynesians regard wage stickiness as a factor that prevents quick adjustment back to the natural rate of unemployment, while monetarists believe that wages are sufficiently flexible to ensure relatively quick adjustment.
    c. Monetarists do not see a need for activist policies, while Keynesians argue that activist policies can prove highly beneficial.
    d. All of the above.
    e. Only (a) and (c) accurately represent differences between monetarists and Keynesians.

8. The long-run aggregate supply curve is a vertical line running through

    a. the natural rate of output.
    b. the natural-rate price level.
    c. the natural rate of unemployment.
    d. none of the above.

9. Which of the following statements is not one commonly associated with Keynesian analysis?

    a. "The economy is inherently unstable, and failure to take corrective action now could mean prolonged unemployment."
    b. "It would be foolish to tie the hands of government policymakers and prevent them from responding to a negative supply shock."
    c. "Wages and prices, while not perfectly flexible, do respond quickly, and in the correct direction, to economic disturbances."
    d. "Crowding out is unlikely to be a problem in the current economic recovery."

10. If policymakers accommodate supply shocks by increasing the money supply, unemployment will return to its natural level sooner, but

    a. even Keynesians, in general, will oppose such a policy.
    b. the price level will increase in the long run.
    c. prices will take much longer in returning to their original level.
    d. none of the above will occur.

Chapter 27

Money and Economic Activity: The Empirical Evidence

CHAPTER SYNOPSIS/COMPLETIONS

This chapter examines the connection between money and economic activity, focusing on the debate between the (1)_____ and the (2)_____ over the years since the Great Depression, and illustrates how the accumulation of evidence has led to greater (3)_____ regarding the importance of money on economic activity. Although views have converged, differences still exist, primarily because monetarists and Keynesians prefer different types of (4)_____.

Monetarists regard money's effect on economic activity as diverse and constantly changing; thus they prefer to model the impact of money supply changes directly. Evidence indicating a high correlation between changes in money growth and fluctuations in economic activity is referred to as (5)_____ _____ evidence. Reduced-form evidence merely indicates the existence of a relationship; it does not describe how money affects economic activity.

Keynesians tend to be skeptical of reduced-form evidence, preferring to model the (6)_____ by which money affects the economy. Keynesian models, therefore, are constructed using a system of equations, each equation describing part of the monetary transmission (7)_____. These models are called (8)_____ models because they attempt to describe the relationships among the various segments of the economy; that is, they attempt to describe how the pieces of the structure fit together.

The structural-model approach has three major advantages over the reduced-form approach:

1. Structural models allow us to evaluate each segment separately for its plausibility. This investigation improves our understanding of money's effect on economic activity.

2. Our improved understanding of the economy's workings may mean more accurate economic (9)_____.

3. Our ability to predict the consequences of institutional change may be improved from the knowledge of economic relationships provided by structural-model evidence.

The one disadvantage of the structural-model approach is that it must be correctly (10)_____ or it will tend to give poor predictions. For example, suppose that a change in money growth causes stock prices to change, which in turn causes consumer expenditures to change. If this transmission mechanism is not part of the model, then the model will provide inaccurate results. In weighing the advantages and disadvantages monetarists conclude that reduced-form models give more reliable results.

Although less sensitive to the correct specification, reduced-form models can prove to be misleading. Since reduced-form models focus on correlations, they may imply that movements in one variable cause the movements in another when causality actually runs in the other direction or is nonexistent. (11)_____ _____ refers to the condition where influence runs in the direction opposite that hypothesized. If two variables are highly correlated, it is possible that an independent (12)_____ _____ influences the behavior of both variables in a way that gives the appearance that one influences the other.

Early Keynesian models were poorly specified, leading to results indicating that money had little effect on economic activity. Had the early Keynesians specified relationships in terms of (13)_____ interest rates, rather than nominal interest rates, they would have been less likely to conclude that (14)_____ does not matter.

In the early 1960s, the monetarists presented evidence indicating that monetary policy had never been more contractionary than during the Great Depression. The implication was that monetary policy mattered a great deal in determining aggregate economic activity. Friedman and other monetarists emphasized three types of evidence when making their case about the importance of monetary growth: (15)_____ evidence, (16)_____ evidence, and (17)_____ evidence. Of the three types of evidence, most economists find (18)_____ evidence to be the most supportive of monetarist theory.

The impact of the monetarist attack on early Keynesian models led to improvements in these models to account for more channels of monetary influence on aggregate economic activity. One of the first improvements entailed the recognition that banks might (19)_____ credit rather than raise interest rates in response to restrictive monetary policy. This phenomenon is referred to as credit rationing, and helps to explain why the fall in investment spending, especially (20)_____ _____, can be more pronounced than expected given relatively small changes in interest rates.

Tobin's q theory indicates that (21)_____ prices can have an important effect on investment spending. Under this monetary channel, increasing stock prices stimulate investment as firms discover that the cost of replacement capital declines relative to the market value of business firms.

In addition, Keynesians have examined more closely the link between monetary policy and consumer expenditure. Research in this area has focused on three transmission mechanisms: (22)_____ _____ effects on consumer durable expenditures, (23)_____ effects on consumption, and (24)_____ effects on consumer durable expenditures.

These three monetary transmission mechanisms indicate that changes in interest rates and stock prices can have a significant effect on aggregate demand. Research findings from the Great Depression support the economic significance of these monetary channels. Declining stock prices and the increase in real consumer debt (due to falling prices) depressed consumer durable expenditures by over 50 percent from 1929 to 1933.

Although not all matters have been fully resolved, the comparison of the effects of monetary policy in the more sophisticated Keynesian structural models with that of new reduced-form models indicates a convergence of views since the 1950s. In the next chapter, the link between money and inflation is examined in much greater detail. Here, again, there is general consensus regarding money's role in the process of inflation, although disagreements on several issues--especially with regard to policy--remain.

EXERCISES

Exercise 1: Two Types of Empirical Evidence

For each of the following statements, indicate whether reduced-form evidence or structural-model evidence is being presented by writing in the space provided an R for reduced-form evidence and an S for structural-model evidence.

_____ 1. Dutch researchers report that eating fish is associated with a lower risk of heart attack.

_____ 2. Eating fish appears to be effective in reducing heart attack risk. Fish oil reduces fat and cholesterol in the blood thereby preventing heart disease, the underlying cause of heart attacks.

_____ 3. Medical research has found that men who take one aspirin per day following a coronary attack significantly reduced the probability of a second coronary.

_____ 4. Drinking 1 ounce of alcohol per day seems to reduce cholesterol levels in the bloodstream, reducing the likelihood of coronary heart disease and heart attack.

_____ 5. Canadian researchers report that beer drinkers are less likely to report illness than nondrinkers, although they could not directly link the beverage itself to better health.

_____ 6. A reduction in the money supply causes the volume of loans to fall, which causes investment to fall as banks ration credit. This in turn causes aggregate output to fall.

_____ 7. An increase in the money supply causes interest rates to fall. Consumer durable expenditures rise in response, leading to an increase in aggregate output.

_____ 8. An increase in the money supply increases the demand for stocks. Rising stock prices cause Tobin's q to increase, which induces firms to undertake more investment spending.

_____ 9. An increase in the money supply is followed by an increase in aggregate output.

Exercise 2: Monetarists Versus the Keynesians

Listed below are a number of statements. Indicate which of the following statements are associated with monetarists (M) and which are associated with Keynesians (K).

_____ 1. Structural-model evidence is superior to reduced-form evidence because it allows us to better understand how the economy works.

_____ 2. Reduced-form evidence allows for the luxury of not having to know all the many ways in which money might affect economic activity.

_____ 3. The channels through which changes in the money supply affect output and employment are numerous and ever changing.

_____ 4. The problem with looking at simple correlations is that it may be extremely difficult to determine the direction of causation. How can one be sure that aggregate output does not affect money growth rather than the reverse?

_____ 5. Changes in the money supply are the most important determinants of economic fluctuations in output, employment, and prices.

_____ 6. The main advantage of employing a monetary rule is that it would greatly diminish the use of discretionary stabilization policies.

_____ 7. The economy tends to be very unstable, making the use of discretionary monetary and fiscal policy essential to the maintenance of full employment.

_____ 8. We agree with the belief that money matters, but the weight of empirical evidence suggests that money is not all that matters.

_____ 9. Money is extremely important, but fiscal policy as well as net exports and "animal spirits" also contribute to fluctuations in aggregate demand.

Exercise 3: Interpreting Reduced-Form Evidence

Some economists contend that inflation is the result of cost-push pressures exerted on the economy by powerful labor unions and big businesses. To support their position, they produce empirical results which clearly indicate that rising costs tend to precede rising prices in many instances. Despite the existence of such evidence, the majority of economists in the United States are highly skeptical of cost-push theories.

A. Could there be a problem of reverse causation in the data that makes it appear as though cost increases precede price increases?

_____

_____

How might the prevalence of 3-year labor contracts help account for the perception that costs lead prices?

_____

_____

B. Many economists dismiss the cost-push theory of inflation by pointing to a third factor that is believed to drive both costs and prices. What do you suppose this third factor is?

_____

_____

C. Are changes in wages and other costs in the United States more likely to be exogenous or endogenous?

_____

_____

_____

D. Assume that the Federal Reserve is more interested in keeping unemployment relatively low than it is in keeping inflation in check. Further assume that the Fed believes that unions, which are in a militant mood, will demand significant wage increases even if workers have to suffer through prolonged strikes. Fearing that unemployment will spread throughout the economy, the Fed undertakes open-market operations expanding the money supply to accommodate the anticipated union demands.

   1. If one looks at the empirical evidence in search of the cause of the resulting inflation to determine which came first, money growth or increasing wages, what will one find?

_____

_____

_____

2. Can the true "cause" of inflation be determined in this instance? Suppose unions know the Federal Reserve's reaction function, that is, the Fed's response to various economic conditions.

_____

_____

_____

Exercise 4:   Transmission Mechanism of Monetary Policy

The traditional Keynesian view of the monetary transmission mechanism can be characterized as follows:

$$M \Uparrow \Rightarrow i \Downarrow \Rightarrow I \Uparrow \Rightarrow Y \Uparrow$$

In response to monetarist challenges in the 1960s, many Keynesian economists began searching for new channels of monetary influence on economic activity. Match the names of the transmission mechanisms on the right with their schematic depictions on the left.

_____ 1. $M \Uparrow \Rightarrow$ stock prices $\Uparrow \Rightarrow$ value of financial assets $\Uparrow \Rightarrow$ likelihood of financial distress $\Downarrow \rightarrow$ consumer durable expenditures $\Uparrow$ and residential housing $\Uparrow \Rightarrow Y \Uparrow$

_____ 2. $M \Uparrow \Rightarrow$ stock prices $\Uparrow \Rightarrow$ wealth $\Uparrow \Rightarrow$ lifetime resources $\Uparrow \Rightarrow$ consumption $\Uparrow \Rightarrow Y \Uparrow$

_____ 3. $M \Uparrow \rightarrow$ loans $\Uparrow \Rightarrow$ investment $\Uparrow$ and residential housing $\Uparrow \Rightarrow Y \Uparrow$

_____ 4. $M \Uparrow \Rightarrow i \Downarrow \Rightarrow$ consumer durable expenditures $\Uparrow \Rightarrow Y \Uparrow$

_____ 5. $M \Uparrow \Rightarrow$ stock prices $\Uparrow \Rightarrow q \Uparrow \Rightarrow$ investment $\Uparrow \Rightarrow Y \Uparrow$

_____ 6. $M \Uparrow \Rightarrow i \Downarrow \Rightarrow$ investment $\Uparrow$ and residential housing $\Uparrow \Rightarrow Y \Uparrow$

_____ 7. $M \Uparrow \Rightarrow i \Downarrow \Rightarrow$ exchange rate $\Downarrow \Rightarrow$ net exports $\Uparrow \Rightarrow Y \Uparrow$

a. Interest-rate effect on consumer durable expenditures

b. Interest-rate effect on investment

c. Exchange-rate effect

d. Liquidity effect

e. Wealth effect

f. Availability hypothesis

g. Tobin's q theory

SELF-TEST

Part A: True-False Questions

Circle whether the following statements are true (T) or false (F).

T F 1. Reduced-form evidence examines whether one variable has an effect on another by looking at a sequence of steps and describing the process at each step so that the channels of influence can be better understood.

T F 2. Keynesians prefer to emphasize structural-model evidence because they believe that reduced-form models do not add insight into how money affects the economy.

T F 3. One advantage of the structural-model approach is that it can give us a better understanding of how money influences economic activity.

T F 4. Monetarists claim that simple structural models, because they may ignore important transmission mechanisms, tend to understate the importance of money's effect on the economy.

T F 5. Correlation does not necessarily imply causation.

T F 6. Because they believed that monetary policy was ineffective, early Keynesians stressed the importance of fiscal policy.

T F 7. Though nominal interest rates fell during the Great Depression to extremely low levels, real interest rates rose.

T F 8. Economic theory suggests that real interest rates are a more important determinant than nominal interest rates in explaining the behavior of investment spending.

T F 9. Historical evidence that has focused on the effects of exogenous changes in the money supply indicates that changes in aggregate output are related to changes in money growth.

T F 10. Keynesians argue that while banks may tend to ration credit in response to "tight" monetary policy, such credit rationing has no effect on economic activity.

T F 11. The availability hypothesis appears to be consistent with the drop in housing sales in 1966 and 1969 when Regulation Q ceilings became binding.

T F 12. Though Tobin's q theory provides a good explanation for the economic recovery that started in late 1982, it is inconsistent with the events of the Great Depression.

T F 13. Assume that the stock market index falls by over 500 points in one week and remains at this level long enough that people adjust their expectations downward regarding the average level of the stock market index. One should expect this event to affect the level of consumption.

T F 14. Economic theory suggests that the stock market crash of 1929 depressed consumer expenditures due to the loss of wealth and the increase in financial distress.

T F 15. There is now fairly wide agreement among economists--both monetarist and Keynesian--that monetary growth is closely linked to business cycle fluctuations.

Part B: Multiple-Choice Questions

Circle the appropriate answer.

1. Monetarists prefer reduced-form models because they believe that

   a. reverse causation is never a problem.
   b. structural models may understate money's effect on economic activity.
   c. money supply changes are always exogenous.
   d. each of the above is true.

2. Scientists tend to be skeptical of reduced-form evidence because

   a. the finding of a high correlation between two variables does not always imply that changes in one cause changes in the other.
   b. reduced-form evidence may not account for all the channels of influence.
   c. it fails to add insight to the process that leads movements in one variable to cause movements in another.
   d. if the model is poorly specified it can lead to poor predictions about the future behavior of the variable of interest.
   e. of both (a) and (c) of the above.

3. Monetarist evidence in which declines in money growth are followed by recessions provides the strongest support for their position that money matters.

   a. statistical
   b. historical
   c. timing
   d. structural

4. Early Keynesians tended to dismiss the importance of money due to their findings that

   a. indicated the absence of a link between movements in nominal interest rates and investment spending.
   b. interest rates had fallen during the Great Depression.
   c. surveys of businessmen revealed that market interest rates had no effect on their decisions of how much to invest in new physical capital.
   d. all of the above are true.

5. Monetarists contend that reduced-form evidence provides valid proof that changes in the money supply affect economic activity when it can be shown that the change in the money supply

   a. is an endogenous event.
   b. is an exogenous event.
   c. preceded the change in economic activity.
   d. was expected.

6. What were the monetarists' main conclusions from the early reduced-form evidence?

   a. One had to be careful to distinguish between real and nominal magnitudes.
   b. The early Keynesian models were misspecified because they accounted for too few channels of monetary influence.
   c. Monetarists models showed that fiscal policies had little or no effect on economic activity.
   d. Both (a) and (b) are correct.
   e. Both (b) and (c) are correct.

7. The availability hypothesis suggests that in periods characterized by "tight" money, banks may

   a. stop making any loans.
   b. continue to make loans, but only at much higher interest rates.
   c. ration credit rather than significantly raise interest rates.
   d. make available more loans to businesses with which they have had no previous

dealings.

8. The sharp drop in housing sales in 1966 and 1969 when market interest rates rose above Regulation Q ceilings is consistent with

   a. Tobin's q theory
   b. the availability hypothesis.
   c. the accelerationist hypothesis.
   d. none of the above.

9. Assume that an increase in the money supply lowers real interest rates and increases stock prices. New Keynesian structural models suggest that the increase in money supply is channeled into higher consumer expenditure through which of the following effects?

   a. Wealth effect
   b. Liquidity effect
   c. Interest rate effect
   d. All of the above
   e. Only (a) and (c) of the above

10. The liquidity effect suggests that higher stock prices lead to increased consumer expenditures because consumers

    a. feel more secure about their financial position.
    b. will want to sell their stocks and spend the proceeds before stock prices go back down.
    c. believe that they will receive higher wages in the near future because companies are now more profitable.
    d. believe none of the above.

Chapter 28

Money and Inflation

CHAPTER SYNOPSIS/COMPLETIONS

In this chapter the aggregate demand and supply analysis introduced in Chapter 26 is used to understand the role of monetary policy in creating inflation. Economists are in general agreement that inflation is always and everywhere a (1)"_____ phenomenon." Evidence from both historical and recent inflationary episodes confirms the proposition that sustained inflation results from (2)_____ monetary expansion.

The consensus must appear at first to be highly unusual, given that much of the two previous chapters has been devoted to the disagreements between monetarists and Keynesians. The apparent paradox is solved by the precise way in which economists define (3)_____. A one-shot (or one-time) increase in the price level is simply not defined as inflation by economists. Only when the price level is (4)_____ rising do economists consider such episodes to be inflationary.

Keynesians, unlike monetarists, believe that one-shot tax cuts or government-spending boosts are likely to raise aggregate demand, and thus the price level, but they contend that any effect on inflation will be merely (5)_____. In their view, fiscal actions are incapable of generating continued and sustained price increases. Thus monetarists and Keynesians agree that rapid money growth is both a sufficient and necessary condition explaining inflation.

Regarding negative supply shocks, economists are again in general agreement that it is only through monetary (6)_____ that such shocks prove inflationary. In the absence of an increase in money growth, the price level would rise, but it would not continue to do so.

One must naturally wonder why, if it is well-understood, inflation continues to plague so many countries to this day. Examination of the U.S. experience suggests that governments pursue many goals, some of which are not (7)_____ with price stability. Specifically, federal government efforts designed to reduce unemployment in the 1960s proved incompatible with the goal of general price stability. In the 1970s, a series of (8)_____ _____ _____ compounded the problem by pressuring government policymakers toward accommodation in order to prevent high rates of unemployment.

Higher wage demands by workers can lead to inflation if policymakers fear that such demands will cause rising unemployment. Additionally, the government may set its (9)_____ target too low, causing overexpansion and inflation.

A large government (10)_____ _____ is another possible source of excessive money growth. Politicians are extremely reluctant to cut government expenditures and raise (11)_____ because such actions are often politically unpopular. Thus the political process is likely to generate a bias toward large budget deficits and inflation.

Economists often find it difficult to distinguish between (12)_____ _____ and (13)_____ _____ inflation. Both types of inflation result when money growth becomes excessive. At first glance, one distinguishes between the two by looking at the behavior of employment. Demand-pull inflation is associated with (14)_____ employment, and cost-push inflation is associated with (15)_____ employment. Once inflation is underway, however, demand-pull inflations may exhibit cost-push tendencies as workers demand higher wages in expectation of higher inflation.

The German experience from 1921 to 1923 illustrates a classical scenario of (16)_____. The unwillingness of German government officials to raise taxes and their inability to borrow an amount sufficient to finance huge budget deficits left (17)_____ creation as the only available means of financing government expenditures. This scenario has been repeated many times, most recently in Argentina and Brazil. In both instances, massive government budget deficits initiated rapid expansions in the money supply, which in turn led to rapidly accelerating rates of inflation.

While these episodes, along with others, confirm that sustained (or continual) inflation can only occur if there is a continually increasing (18)_____ _____, a variety of sources are actually responsible for the inflationary monetary policies of many countries. Budget deficits, concerns over unemployment, negative supply shocks, union wage pushes, and concerns over interest rates often lead to inflationary monetary expansions.

An examination of inflation in the United States from 1960 through 1980 dismisses the importance of budget deficits in explaining rapid money growth. It appears that the concern over unemployment led to overexpansionary policies which kept unemployment low over the period 1965 to 1973. In the latter half of the 1970s, inflation resembles the (19)_____ _____ variety as unemployment rose to a level that exceeded the natural rate level.

The debate over the appropriateness of activist stabilization policy has important implications for anti-inflationary policies. Monetarists argue against the use of activist policy to reduce unemployment. They believe the effort is fruitless because any reduction in unemployment will be merely temporary, and it may hinder anti-inflationary efforts. They believe that the economy is inherently (22)_____, as wages are sufficiently (23)_____ so that deviations from the natural rate of output are quickly reversed. Further, monetarists contend that even in those instances where adjustment tends to be relatively slow, (24)_____ policies are not likely to improve circumstances. In their view, policy responses are ineffectual, or even harmful, due to the long (25)_____ _____ which plague government decision making. For this reason, monetarists tend to support monetary rules that limit the discretion of policymakers.

Keynesians are much more optimistic about the desirability and effectiveness of activist policies. They believe that available evidence indicates that wages and prices are rigid or sticky, implying prolonged deviations from the natural rate of output and unemployment. Therefore, they contend that government fiscal or monetary actions are required to restore the economy to full employment. Unlike the monetarists, Keynesians contend that fiscal policy actions will be effective and dismiss the possibility of complete (26)_____ _____.

The phenomenon of "stagflation" in the latter half of the 1970s focused greater attention on the importance of expectations. People had come to expect that macroeconomic policies would always be (20)_____; thus, when policymakers announced intentions of fighting inflation, few people believed them. Following this experience, economists in greater numbers began to question the desirability of (21)_____ policy. Some economists argued that nonaccommodating policy would yield better inflation performance with no more unemployment. Although this conclusion is not universally accepted, the recognition of the importance expectations play in economics has led to a new field of macroeconomics which is presented in Chapters 29 and 30.

EXERCISES

Exercise 1: Forces of Inflationary Monetary Policy

Monetarists and Keynesians agree that inflation is a monetary phenomenon. In other words, inflation would not persist in the absence of excessive money growth. Of interest to many economists, therefore, is the source of inflationary monetary policy. Why at times does the Fed expand the money supply at a rapid rate? Two explanations have been offered, both of which give us an insight into the forces that affect Fed decision making. List below the two explanations presented in the text that help explain expansionary monetary policy. Provide a brief explanation for each factor listed.

1. _____

_____

2. _____

_____

Exercise 2: High Employment Targets and Inflation

The Full Employment and Balanced Growth Act of 1976 would have required the federal government to adopt policies to reduce unemployment to a level of 3% by 1980 (corresponding to an output level of $Y_{3\%}$ in Figure 28A). A modified version of this bill known as the Humphrey-Hawkins Act was signed by Jimmy Carter in 1978, but it amounted to little more than wishful thinking since the Act included no specific enforcement measures.

Assume that the economy is initially at the natural-rate level of output, where the aggregate demand curve, AD_1, and aggregate supply curve, AS_1, intersect at point 1 in Figure 28A. If the original version of the Humphrey-Hawkins bill had passed, show where the government would shift the aggregate demand curve in Figure 28A and mark it as AD_2.

FIGURE 28A

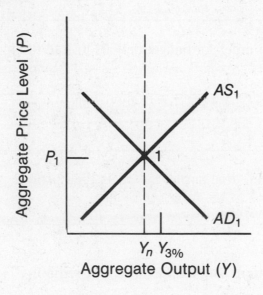

What would now happen to the aggregate supply curve? _____

Why? _____

Draw in the new aggregate supply curve as AS$_2$. Now what would the government do to aggregate demand?

_____

Draw in the new aggregate demand curve as AD$_3$. Where will the aggregate supply curve shift to now?

_____

Draw it in as AS$_3$. What is the outcome as the scenario discussed above repeats itself?

_____

Exercise 3: Budget Deficits and Money Creation

When the U.S. government is running a budget deficit, does this necessarily cause the rate of money growth to increase?

_____

What two facts must be true in order for budget deficits to lead to higher money growth?

1. _____

2. _____

Do you think that both facts were true during the 1960-1980 period? _____

Why or why not? _____

Exercise 4: Eliminating Inflation: The Importance of Credibility

The German hyperinflation provides a classic example of how mistaken policies can have dire consequences. More important, the successful cure of the hyperinflation at a relatively low cost illustrates the importance of adopting an anti-inflationary policy that the citizenry views as credible.

The German government adopted several reforms at the time it announced its intention of controlling inflation. First, the government transferred the responsibility for monetary control to a new authority. Second, new currency was issued. Third, an upper limit was placed on the issue of this new currency. Fourth, the central bank was prohibited from issuing paper money to the government. Finally, the government took immediate steps to reduce budget deficits."

In the first half of the 1980s, Argentina was beset by hyperinflation. During this period, the Argentine government and central bank adopted numerous reforms, including some of the monetary reforms enacted by the German government of the 1920s. For example, Argentina has issued new currency, several times, and since 1955 there have been more than 30 different finance ministers, each of whom vowed to stop inflation.[2] However, prior to June of 1985, Argentina made no effort to appreciably reduce its budget deficit in conjunction with its monetary reforms. Do you think that Argentina's monetary reforms were credible? Why or why not?

_____

_____

_____

Can the lack of credibility explain why the Argentine monetary reforms of the early 1980s proved unsuccessful in fighting inflation while the Germans were successful in the 1920s?

_____

_____

In June of 1985, Argentina instituted a set of policies to reduce its 1000% inflation rate. Argentina declared a one-week bank holiday, created a new currency in the interim, imposed wage and price controls, and implemented budget reforms that reduced the budget deficit from 8% to 4% of GNP. The strict anti-inflation plan proved successful in lowering the annual inflation rate to 50% by August of 1986. Disappointingly, however, the austerity plan only produced short-run benefits. By March of 1988, inflation was running at an annual rate of 207%--four times higher than predicted one year earlier by the economic team of President Raul Alfonsin. Recurrent price and wage freezes during 1987 and 1988 could not counteract the inflationary effects of budget deficits that had once again reached 8% of GNP by late 1987. Does the temporary success of the Argentine reforms suggest a key element to reducing inflation? Explain.

_____

_____

---

[1] T. M. Humphrey, Eliminating Runaway Inflation: Lessons from the German Hyperinflation, in T. M. Humphrey (Ed.), *Essays on Inflation*, Federal Reserve Bank of Richmond, 1982.

[2] E. G. Martin, In Argentina, A Peso Is a Peso Is a Peso, Which is Confusing, *The Wall Street Journal*, May 10, 1983, p. 1.

Exercise 5: Credibility and the Prevention of Inflation

In October of 1979, the Federal Reserve, under the direction of its new chairman Paul Volcker, made two dramatic announcements. First, the Fed announced that it was changing the procedure it employed for conducting monetary policy. The Fed's new monetary policy strategy would emphasize controlling monetary aggregates by targeting bank reserves. Prior to this announcement, the Federal Reserve had focused on stabilizing the federal funds interest rate within a narrow range. Second, the Fed announced an increase in the discount rate. Significantly, the second announcement coincided with the Fed's move to get inflation--then running at double-digit rates--under control. Explain why the discount rate hike may have been important. After all, the discount rates plays only a minor role in monetary policy and the Fed could have reduced money growth simply by setting its federal funds rate target higher.

SELF-TEST

Part A: True-False Questions

Circle whether the following statements are true (T) or false (F).

T F 1. If inflation is defined as a continuous rise in the price level, then it is true that inflation can be eliminated by reducing the growth rate of the money supply to a low level.

T F 2. Keynesians disagree with the monetarists'proposition that inflation is a monetary phenomenon. That is, Keynesians believe that inflation can occur even when money growth has not been excessive.

T F 3. The German hyperinflation of the 1920s supports the proposition that excessive money growth leads to higher prices, and not the other way around, since the increase in money growth appears to have been exogenous.

T F 4. In the early 1980s, both Argentina and Israel experienced hyperinflation. They differed, however, in that Israel had not overly expanded its money supply.

T F 5. A common element of the hyperinflationary episodes discussed in the text was government unwillingness to finance expenditures by raising taxes.

T F 6. The price level may rise in any one month due to factors unrelated to changes in the money supply. Thus one can conclude that continual price-level increases need not be related to changes in the money supply.

T F 7. Within the aggregate demand and supply framework, a continually increasing money supply has the effect of continually shifting the aggregate demand curve to the right.

T F 8. Keynesians argue that factors other than a continually increasing money supply may lead to sustained inflation.

T F 9. Sustained inflation occurs when unions successfully push up wages, even if the monetary authorities refuse to accommodate the higher wages by expanding the money supply.

T F 10. Inflation according to one view, is the side effect of government efforts to cure high unemployment.

T F 11. Workers will have greater incentives to push for higher wages when government policymakers place greater concern on unemployment than inflation and are thus more likely to adopt accommodative policies.

T F 12. Cost-push inflation is not a monetary phenomenon.

T F 13. At first glance, one would expect falling unemployment to be associated with demand-pull inflation.

T F 14. Huge government budget deficits have been the initiating source of inflationary monetary policies in every instance of hyperinflation.

T F 15. An examination of the period from 1960 through 1980 suggests that large government deficits are to blame for the inflationary monetary policies of this period.

Part B: Multiple-Choice Questions

Circle the appropriate answer.

1. A continual increase in the money supply, according to Keynesian analysis, will cause

    a. the price level to increase, but have no lasting effect on the inflation rate.
    b. the price level to fall.
    c. inflation.
    d. output to increase and will have no effect on either the price level or inflation.
    e. none of the above.

2. Inflation occurs whenever

    a. the price level rises.
    b. the money supply increases.
    c. the price level rises continuously over a period of time.
    d. any of the above occur.

3. In general, most economists believe that inflation can only occur if

    a. government spending increases.
    b. strong labor unions demand higher wages.
    c. negative supply shocks continuously hit the economy.
    d. the money supply is continually expanded.

4. Monetarists emphasize the importance of a constant money growth rate rule more than the balanced-budget amendment or restrictions on union power because

    a. they tend to regard excessive money growth as the cause of inflation.
    b. while they do not believe that excessive money growth is the cause of inflation, they do believe that it is related to excessive government expenditures.
    c. while they regard unions as the source of inflation, they know that they are too powerful politically to deal with.
    d. of each of the above.

5. Analysis of hyperinflationary episodes indicates that the rapid money growth leading to the inflation results when

    a. governments finance massive budget deficits by printing money.
    b. central banks attempt to peg interest rates.
    c. government taxes become too excessive.
    d. central banks lower reserve requirements too much.

6. A one-shot increase in government spending will have what effect on the inflation rate, according to the Keynesian analysis?

   a. Permanent increase
   b. Temporary increase
   c. Temporary decrease
   d. No effect

7. Assume workers know that government policymakers, because unemployment is politically unpopular, always accommodate wage increases by expanding the money supply. What type of inflation is likely to result if workers demand higher wages not fearing a rise in unemployment?

   a. Demand-pull inflation
   b. Hyperinflation
   c. Cost-push inflation
   d. Demand-shock inflation

8. If an economist were interested in testing whether federal budget deficits had been the source of excessive money growth for a particular country during the time period 1900 - 1930, he or she would be interested in the behavior of

   a. inflation
   b. the money supply-to-monetary-base ratio.
   c. interest rates.
   d. the government debt-to-GNP ratio.

9. When the government sets an unemployment target that is unrealistically low without realizing it, what is the likely result?

   a. Inflation
   b. An unemployment rate that may actually drop below the natural rate for a period of time
   c. Excessive money growth
   d. All of the above

10. Governments are likely to lose credibility in fighting inflation when

   a. government budget deficitd remain high.
   b. government policymakers continue to accommodate wage demands and negative supply shocks.
   c. the commitment to high unemployment is viewed as government's number-one goal for political reasons.
   d. all of the above are true.

Chapter 29

The Theory of Rational Expectations and Efficient Capital Markets

CHAPTER SYNOPSIS/COMPLETIONS

Chapter 29 develops the theory of rational expectations and discusses the implications of this theory as applied to financial markets, where it is known as the theory of efficient capital markets. Recently, expectations theory has received great attention as economists have searched for more adequate explanations of the observed behavior of economic variables such as unemployment, interest rates, and asset prices.

Prior to the rational expectations revolution, economists tended to model expectations as if they were formed (1)_____, meaning that people adjusted slowly over time in response to changes in economic variables. Adaptive expectations imply that people look only at the (2)_____ and (3)_____ behavior of an economic variable in forming expectations of it, never adjusting to predicted changes in economic variables.

Beginning in the 1960s a number of economists began to question the desirability of adaptive expectations models, since they imply that people never learn from their past mistakes. These economists suggested an alternative to adaptive expectations known as (4)_____ _____. As the name implies, this theory assumes that people will behave rationally when faced with new information, adjusting their expectations quickly. For example, if people believe that the Federal Reserve is about to embark on an expansionary monetary policy to reduce unemployment, people will revise their estimates of inflation upward. The possibility of this result is ignored in adaptive expectation models because people are assumed to respond only to past events; that is, people do not respond to predicted future actions.

Rational expectationists contend that individuals make (5)_____ (formulate expectations) about the future course of an economic variable based on its past behavior and on their assessment of future policies that affect the variable. These predictions--known as (6)_____ _____--will be correct on average, although they will not always be perfectly accurate. Individuals will make mistakes, but they will not be (7)_____ wrong in any one direction.

The theory of rational expectations contends that people have a strong incentive to form rational expectations since failing to do so is (8)_____. This is especially true in financial markets.

The theory of (9)_____ _____ _____ is the application of rational expectations to the pricing of securities in financial markets. Efficient markets theory suggests that security (10)_____ reflect all available information at that time. If this were not the case, an (11)_____ _____ _____ would exist giving individuals with superior information a strong incentive to capture profits by either buying (if they believe the price will rise) or selling (if they believe the price will fall) the security.

Importantly, their actions quickly eliminate the profits. If, for example, the price of IBM common stock is expected to rise because a new invention makes IBM computers more valuable to own, then those individuals with this information will attempt to buy more shares of IBM common stock before its price rises. But their actions increase the demand for IBM stock, raising its price. The price of IBM common stock will continue to rise until the optimal forecast of the rate of return falls to the (12)_____ _____. At this price, all unexploited profit opportunities are eliminated. This result does not depend on everyone being well informed.

Efficient markets theory suggests that individuals ought to be skeptical of stock brokers' (13)_____ _____ and the recommendations found in the published reports of (14)_____ _____. By the time you acquire the information, others are likely to have already used it to their benefit. Thus acting on this information will not yield abnormally high returns on average because market (15)_____ already reflect this information.

Many studies confirm the proposition that published recommendations cannot allow you to outperform the overall market. Even when economists select analysts who have done well in the past, the evidence indicates that financial analysts do not consistently outperform the overall market.

The (16)_____ _____ hypothesis contends that future changes in stock prices should for all practical purposes be unpredictable. This implication follows from efficient markets theory, since any new information that might create an unexploited profit opportunity will be quickly eliminated through the adjustment in the stock's price.

Interestingly, efficient markets theory also explains why a stock's price sometimes falls when good news about the stock is announced. This occurs when announced earnings fall short of those (17)_____ by market participants. The lower earnings mean a lower rate of return at the current price. Consequently, the stock's price must fall to bring the rate of return into conformity with the rest of the market.

So how can one get rich by investing in the stock market? The efficient markets theory suggests that relying on the published reports of financial analysts and the hot tips given to you by your broker is probably an inferior strategy when compared to the (18)" _____ and (19)_____ strategy." The buy and hold strategy will on average give the investor the same return (exclusive of transactions costs), but her net profits will be higher because she pays fewer (20)_____ _____. The only other alternative is to rely on (21)_____ _____. This, however, is a risky strategy since the government prosecutes traders using this information.

EXERCISES

Exercise 1: Definitions and Terminology

Match the following terms on the right with the definition or description on the left. Place the letter of the term in the blank provided next to the appropriate definition. Terms may be used more than once.

_____ 1. Price of a security is such that optimal forecast of its return exceeds the equilibrium return.

    a. Efficient markets theory

_____ 2. Expectations that are formed from past data on a single variable.

    b. Random walk

_____ 3. Information not available to the public, but only to those who have close contact with a company.

    c. Unexploited profit opportunity

_____ 4. Past movements of stock prices are of no use in predicting the future movement of stock prices.

_____ 5. A method for predicting future stock prices using past price data.

    d. Insider information

_____ 6. Expectations formed using optimal predictions of future movements in relevant variables.

    e. Technical analysis

_____ 7. The best guess of the future using all available information.

_____ 8. Theory that indicates that hot tips, financial analysts' published recommendations, and technical analysis cannot help the investor to outperform the market.

    f. Adaptive expectations

    g. Rational expectations

_____ 9. The application of rational expectations to the pricing of securities in financial markets.

_____ 10. A situation in which someone can earn a higher than normal return.

    h. Optimal forecast

Exercise 2: Interest Rates and Rational Expectations--Efficient Markets

Three different outcomes for long-term interest rates are possible when the Federal Reserve slows the growth of the money supply. Describe the possible conditions leading to each of these outcomes listed below.

A. No change in long-term interest rates

_____

_____

_____

B. A decline in long-term interest rates

_____

_____

_____

C. A rise in long-term interest rates

_____

_____

_____

D. What does the example here suggest about the difficulty of conducting monetary policy when expectations are rational?

_____

_____

_____

Exercise 3: Implications of Efficient Markets Theory

A. Information is assimilated rapidly in the stock market. If you read in *The Wall Street Journal* that Montana Power Company has just been granted a utility rate increase, can you profit from this knowledge by rushing out to purchase this stock?

_____

_____

_____

B. How would your answer to part A change if you had happened to get advance word on the Public Service Commission's decision from your brother-in-law?

_____

_____

_____

C. When there is a pronounced price change in a stock, the SEC will carefully study the buy and sell orders, and who has been involved in them to determine if anyone traded on the basis of insider information. Does such activity by the SEC indicate that the stock market is not informationally efficient?

_____

_____

_____

SELF-TEST

Part A: True-False Questions

Circle whether the following statements are true (T) or false (F).

T F 1. The speed with which inflation expectations respond to accelerating money growth is an important factor determining whether interest rates rise or fall when money growth increases.

T F 2. Expectations that are formed solely on the basis of past information are known as rational expectations.

T F 3. The theory of rational expectations argues that optimal forecasts need not be perfectly accurate.

T F 4. Expectations that do not take account of available relevant information may still be rational.

T F 5. An important implication of rational expectations theory is that when there is a change in the way a variable behaves, the way expectations of this variable are formed will change as well.

T F 6. If expectations are formed rationally, forecast errors of expectations will on average be positive and can thus be predicted ahead of time.

T F 7. If the optimal forecast of a return on a financial asset exceeds its equilibrium return, the situation is called an unexploited profit opportunity.

T F 8. In an efficient market, all unexploited profit opportunities will be eliminated.

T F 9. Everyone in a financial market must be well informed about a security if the market is to be considered efficient.

T F 10. The efficient markets theory suggests that published reports of financial analysts can guarantee that individuals who use this information will outperform the market.

T F 11. The overwhelming majority of statistical studies indicate that financial analysts do indeed pick financial portfolios that outperform the market average.

T F 12. According to the efficient markets hypothesis, picking stocks by throwing darts at the financial page is an inferior strategy compared to employing the advice of financial analysts.

T F 13. Mutual funds that outperform the market in one period are highly likely to consistently outperform the market in subsequent periods due to their superior investment strategies.

T F 14. Efficient markets theory indicates that one should be skeptical of hot tips.

T F 15. Stock prices always rise when favorable earnings reports are released.

Part B: Multiple-Choice Questions

Circle the appropriate answer.

1. Suppose you read a story in the financial section of the local newspaper that announces the proposed merger of Apple Computer, Inc. and Microsoft Corporation. The announcement is expected to greatly increase the profitability of Apple. If you should now decide to invest in Apple stock, you can expect to earn

   a. above average returns since you will get to share in the higher profits.
   b. above average returns since your stock will definitely appreciate as the profits are earned.
   c. a normal return since stock prices adjust to reflect changed profit expectations almost immediately.
   d. none of the above.

2. Assume that you own a ranch and lease land from the Bureau of Land Management (BLM), which allows you to graze cattle on the government land at a price that is below the market equilibrium price. If the government should raise the price for grazing cattle on BLM land, you can expect the value of the ranch to

   a. fall since ranching is no longer as profitable.
   b. be unaffected. (The value of the ranch is not dependent on the price of grazing rights.)
   c. rise since the value of the BLM land rises.
   d. rise since the value of the BLM land falls.

3. In countries experiencing rapid rates of inflation, announcements of money supply increases are often followed by immediate increases in interest rates. Such behavior is consistent with which of the following?

   a. Rational expectations
   b. Expectations of higher inflation in the near future
   c. A tight current monetary policy
   d. Both (a) and (b) of the above
   e. Both (a) and (c) of the above

4. Efficient markets theory suggests that purchasing the published reports of financial analysts

   a. is likely to increase one's returns by an average of 10%.
   b. is likely to increase one's returns by an average of about 3 to 5%.
   c. is not likely to be effective strategy for increasing financial returns.
   d. is likely to increase one's returns by an average of about 2 to 3%.

5. After the announcement of higher quarterly profits, the price of a stock falls. Such an occurrence is

   a. clearly inconsistent with efficient markets theory.
   b. possible if market participants expected lower profits.
   c. consistent with efficient markets theory.
   d. not possible.

6. Since a change in regulations permitting their existence in the mid-1970s, discount brokers have grown rapidly. Efficient markets theory would seem to suggest that people who use discount brokers

   a. will likely earn lower returns than those who use full-service brokers.
   b. will likely eam about the same as those who use full-service brokers, but will net more after brokerage commissions.
   c. are going against evidence that suggests that the financial analysis provided by full-service brokers can help one outperform the overall market.
   d. are likely to be poor.

7. Efficient markets theory suggests that stock prices tend to follow a "random walk." Thus the best strategy for investing stock is

   a. a "churning strategy" of buying and selling often to catch the market swings.
   b. turning over your stock portfolio each month, selecting stocks by throwing darts at the stock page.
   c. a "buy and hold strategy" of holding onto stocks to avoid brokerage commissions.
   d. to do none of the above.

8. Rational expectations theory suggests that forecast errors of expectations

   a. tend to be persistently high or low.
   b. are unpredictable.
   c. are more likely to be negative than positive.
   d. are more likely to be positive than negative.

9. Unexploited opportunities are quickly eliminated in financial markets through

   a. changes in asset prices.
   b. changes in dividend payments.
   c. accounting conventions.
   d. exchange-rate translations.

10. Stockbrokers have at times paid newspaper reporters for information about articles to be published in future editions. This suggests that

   a. your stockbroker's hot tips will help you outperform the overall market.
   b. financial analysts' reports contain information that will help you earn a return that exceeds the market average.
   c. insider information may help ensure returns that exceed the market average.
   d. each of the above is true.

Chapter 30

Rational Expectations: The Implications for Policy

CHAPTER SYNOPSIS/COMPLETIONS

Chapter 30 discusses the implications of rational expectations theory for macroeconomic stabilization policies. Rational expectations theory arose in the 1970s as an attempt to explain "stagflation" and the failure of government policies to prevent this unhappy state. How can the apparent ineffectiveness of government stabilization policies be explained? This chapter introduces models that address this issue.

In his famous paper, "Econometric Policy Evaluation: A Critique," Robert Lucas argues that stabilization policies formulated on the basis of conventional econometric models will fail to stabilize the economy since (1)_____ about policy will alter the intended effects. Lucas argues that while conventional econometric models may be useful for forecasting economic activity, they cannot be used to (2)_____ the potential impact of particular policies on the economy. The short-run forecasting ability of these models provides no evidence of the accuracy to be expected from simulations of hypothetical policy alternatives.

To understand Lucas's argument, one needs to recognize that conventional econometric models contain equations that describe the relationships between hundreds of variables. These relationships (parameters), estimated using past data, are assumed to remain (3)_____. Lucas contends that such models will likely provide (4)_____ results about the effects of a policy change (say, a monetary expansion); the actual effects are likely to be different than predicted because the change in policy will mean that the way expectations are formed will change, causing the real-world relationships (parameters) to change. Thus the effects of a particular policy depend heavily on the public's expectations about the policy.

Two schools of rational expectations economists have formed: the new classical rational expectations school and the nonclassical rational expectations school. (5)_____ _____ rational expectationists contend that anticipated macroeconomic policies have no effect on aggregate output and employment. This conclusion rests on the assumption that all wages and prices are completely (6)_____ with respect to expected changes in the price level. For example, if policymakers are known to act in certain systematic ways, the public will come to anticipate policy changes, causing the (7)_____ _____ curve to shift. People will respond to expected expansionary macropolicies by raising wages and factor prices. The aggregate demand curve shifts out, but the aggregate supply curve shifts in, neutralizing the impact on aggregate output. The (8)_____ _____ rises, but output remains unchanged at the natural-rate level.

Policymakers can affect the level of aggregate output and employment in the new classical rational expectations model only through policy surprises. (9)_____ policies will cause the aggregate demand curve to shift while leaving the aggregate supply curve unchanged, resulting in a change in the price level and aggregate output. Only unanticipated macropolicies can affect the level of output in the new classical model; anticipated policies cannot affect the level of output. This conclusion is referred to as the (10)_____ _____ _____. The proposition depends critically on two assumptions: rational expectations and perfect wage and price flexibility.

Many economists find the assumption of wage and price flexibility unacceptable. They note that the prevalence of long-term labor and supply contracts create (11)_____ which prevent wages and prices from fully responding to expected changes in the price level.

Nonclassical rational expectations economists argue that the existence of long-term labor contracts--both explicit and implicit--leads to wage and price stickiness. In contrast to the new classical school, the assumption of rational expectations does not imply that (12)_____ policies will be ineffectual in altering the level of aggregate output. The public may understand the consequences of a newly announced macropolicy yet be unable to fully respond in the face of contracted fixities.

(13)_____ rational expectations economists agree that unanticipated policies are more effective than anticipated policies in changing the level of aggregate output. Anticipated policies are effective in altering the level of aggregate output, but unanticipated policies have a larger impact.

The nonclassical model suggests that activist stabilization policies can be used to affect the level of output in the economy, but policymakers must be cognizant of the (14)_____ _____ _____. In other words, since expectations affect the outcome of policies, making predictions about a proposed policy's effects is more difficult than is implied by the traditional model.

New classical economists are less optimistic. They contend that (15)_____ macropolicies can only be counterproductive. Activist policies are likely to be destabilizing and inflationary.

A significant implication of rational expectations is that anti-inflationary policies can achieve their goal at a lower cost if these policies are viewed as (16)_____ by the public. The traditional model suggests that fighting inflation will be quite costly in terms of lost output and higher unemployment. Arthur Okun's rule of thumb indicates that a reduction of one point in the inflation rate requires a (17)_____ percent loss in a year's GNP, a staggering cost for such a small gain. Recall that Okun's rule of thumb holds in a world where anti-inflation policies are not viewed as credible. To the extent that such policies foster credibility, fighting inflation will be less costly.

Evidence indicates that credible policies do reduce the adverse consequences of anti-inflationary policies. Actions designed to reduce government (18)_____ _____ appear to be particularly important in this regard. It appears that anti-inflationary policies that do not address budget-deficit problems may be viewed with little credibility and prove to be relatively costly. Some economists contend that recessions in Great Britain and the United States in the early 1980s were more severe because deficit issues went unresolved. Although this conclusion is controversial, it indicates the importance expectations play in economic theory.

EXERCISES

Exercise 1: The Effect of Anticipated Policy

Suppose the economy is initially at point 1 in Figure 30A, at the intersection of the AD_1 and AS_1 curves. If Congress decides to cut military spending in an attempt to ease world tensions, draw in Figure 30A the new aggregate demand curve AD_2. If this spending cut were widely anticipated, draw in the new aggregate supply curve AS_{NC} if the new classical model is the best description of the economy.

FIGURE 30A

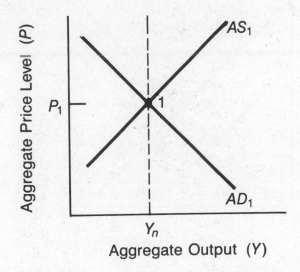

What is the effect on output and price level? _____

_____

If, instead, the nonclassical rational expectations model is the best description of the economy, draw in the new aggregate supply curve AS_N when the policy is anticipated.

What is the effect on output and price level? _____

_____

Would output rise by more or by less than your answers above if the traditional model best describes the economy?

_____

_____

Exercise 2: The Effects of Unanticipated Policy

Suppose the economy is initially at point 1 in Figure 30B, at the intersection of the AD_1 and AS_1 curves. If Congress reduces military spending in an attempt to ease world tensions, but reduces it by less than expected (where the aggregate demand curve for the expected policy is AD_e), draw in the new aggregate demand curve AD_2 and the new aggregate supply curve AS_{NC} if the new classical model is the best description of the economy.

FIGURE 30B

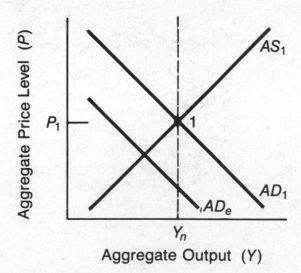

Does aggregate output fall as a result of the decline in government spending?

_____

If, instead, the nonclassical rational expectations model is the best description of the economy, draw in the new aggregate supply curve AS_N when the spending reduction is less than anticipated. Will aggregate output fall in this case?

_____

If, the traditional model best describes the economy, will aggregate output fall in response to the spending reduction?

_____

Exercise 3: The Lucas Critique and Monetary Policy

Suppose that the Fed follows a monetary rule designed to stabilize nominal interest rates. If interest rates suddenly rise, what will most likely be the Fed's response? If people come to expect this response, will the Fed's efforts be helped or hindered? Explain.

_____

_____

_____

_____

Exercise 4: A Comparison of the Schools of Thought

In the space provided next to each statement, indicate whether the statement reflects a view held by Keynesians (K), monetarists (M), new classical rational expectationists (NC), or nonclassical rational expectationists (N). Use more than one letter if appropriate.

_____ 1. Any policy move that is widely expected will have no impact at the time it is taken, since it will have already been discounted by the public.

_____ 2. No systematic economic policy can be devised that is capable of affecting anything other than the inflation rate.

_____ 3. The private economy is inherently unstable; thus monetary and fiscal policy can be important in stabilizing the economy whether or not the policy is anticipated.

_____ 4. There is no serious need to stabilize the economy, and even if there were a need, it could not be done, for stabilization policies would be more likely to increase than to decrease instability.

_____ 5. Only policy moves that people do not expect will cause changes in aggregate output and employment.

_____ 6. Traditional econometric models cannot be relied on to evaluate the potential impact of particular policies on the economy. In other words, the short-run forecasting ability of these models provides no evidence of the accuracy to be expected from simulations of hypothetical policy rules.

_____ 7. The existence of long-term labor contracts are one source of rigidity that prevents instantaneous price and wage adjustment. Thus, even with rational expectations, anticipated monetary and fiscal policies may affect output in the short run.

_____ 8. The policy ineffectiveness proposition does not hold in a world such as ours where both explicit and implicit long-term labor contracts impart a degree of wage and price rigidity in the economy.

Exercise 5: A Comparison of Rational Expectations Models with the Traditional Model

Listed below are statements that reflect the beliefs of economists regarding stabilization policy. If the statement most accurately reflects views held by the new classical economists, write NC in the space provided. If the statement most closely reflects views held by nonclassical rational expectationists, place an N in the space provided. If the statement does not reflect views held by either school of rational expectationists, place a T in the space. You may use more than one letter if the statement reflects views held by more than one of the groups.

_____ 1. An unanticipated expansion in the money supply will boost employment in the short run, but after a period of from 12 to 24 months, prices win begin to rise.

_____ 2. Stabilization policy--what some might call an activist policy--can and should be employed in an effort to eliminate the high level of unemployment.

_____ 3. An increase in government spending or a tax cut would be appropriate at this time. Unemployment is too high and inflation is almost nonexistent. In addition, the announcement of such a plan would bode well for stock prices--this is the policy the market has been expecting to hear from Washington.

_____ 4. Mr. President, since you have decided that an anti-inflation policy of slower money growth and higher taxes is appropriate at this time, I think it wise that you make the announcement at your televised press conference tonight. Remember, it is important for you to convince the public that you plan to stick with the contractionary strategy even if unemployment begins to rise.

_____ 5. Fighting inflation is extremely costly--probably more costly than it's worth--and announcing an anti-inflationary policy in advance does nothing to lower that cost.

_____ 6. An activist stabilization policy will have no predictable effect on output, and it cannot be relied on to stabilize economic activity.

Exercise 6: The Effects of Announced Policy and Credibility

Assume for a moment that you are president of the United States and currently running for reelection. The unemployment rate is 8.8% and the inflation rate is 4.0%. In a private meeting with the chairman of the Federal Reserve Board you are given assurances that the rate of monetary growth will accelerate in the next few months in an attempt to lower the unemployment rate. Does it matter if you publicly announce the chairman's assurances if the traditional model best describes the economy?

_____

_____

If the new classical model best describes the economy?

_____

_____

If the nonclassical rational expectations model best describes the economy?

_____

_____

If no one believes you when you make your announcement, how does it affect the answers above?

_____

_____

SELF-TEST

Part A: True-False Questions

Circle whether the following statements are true (T) or false (F).

T F 1. Robert Lucas in his famous critique argued that econometric model simulations provide no useful information with which to evaluate the effects of alternative economic policies.

T F 2. A monetary acceleration may have different effects in 1990 than in 1991 if the public's expectations about the policy are different in those two years.

T F 3. Even when the public expects a rise in short-term interest rates to be permanent, the impact on long-term rates will be small.

T F 4. The new classical economists argue that neither anticipated nor unanticipated policies affect the level of unemployment.

T F 5. The new classical economists argue that only unanticipated increases in the money supply can affect the general level of prices.

T F 6. If the Fed is interested in temporarily lowering unemployment, it will want to announce its intentions to expand the money supply.

T F 7. While an expansionary monetary policy can never lead to a decline in output in the traditional model, such a result is possible in the new classical model.

T F 8. Anticipated policies have no effect on aggregate output or the rate of unemployment in the nonclassical rational expectations model.

T F 9. The expansion of aggregate output will be smaller for an anticipated policy than for an unanticipated policy in the nonclassical rational expectations model.

T F 10. It is the existence of rigidities such as sticky wages and prices, not adaptive expectations, that explains why anticipated policies can affect output in the nonclassical rational expectations model.

T F 11. If expectations about policy are formed adaptively, then anticipated policies will actually have greater output effects than unanticipated policies.

T F 12. According to new classical economists, policymakers' attempts to stabilize the economy will be ineffective and may even make conditions worse.

T F 13. The assumption of rational expectations suggests that policymakers cannot be as certain about the effects of any proposed policy since history may not provide an accurate guide.

T F 14. If expectations are formed rationally, and prices and wages are completely flexible, then the best anti-inflation policy is likely to consist of a gradual reduction in the money supply over a period of several years.

T F 15. If the government reduces budget deficits, an anti- inflationary policy is less likely to be regarded as credible.

Part B: Multiple-hoice Questions

Circle the appropriate answer.

1. Robert Lucas argues that using an econometric model that has been constructed on the basis of past data

   a. may be appropriate for short-run forecasting, but is inappropriate for evaluating alternative policies.
   b. may be appropriate for alternative policies, but is not appropriate for evaluating short-run forecasting.
   c. is appropriate for both short-run forecasting and policy evaluation.
   d. is not appropriate for either short-run forecasting or policy evaluation.

2. An anticipated expansion in the money supply will have no effect on aggregate output in which model?

   a. Nonclassical rational expectations model
   b. Traditional model
   c. New classical rational expectations model
   d. All of the above

3. In which of the following models does an anticipated increase in money growth affect the price level?

    a. Traditional model
    b. New classical model
    c. Nonclassical rational expectations model
    d. All of the above models
    e. None of the above models

4. The nonclassical rational expectations model indicates that anticipated policies affect aggregate output because of rigidities resulting from

    a. long-term contracts.
    b. adaptive expectations.
    c. the reluctance of some firms to alter prices and wages frequently, creating what can be considered implicit contracts.
    d. All of the above.
    e. Only (a) and (c) of the above.

5. The traditional model is distinguished from both the new classical and the nonclassical rational expectations model by the following:

    a. The traditional model assumes that expectations are formed adaptively, that is, on past behavior of the relevant variable.
    b. The traditional model does not distinguish between anticipated and unanticipated policies.
    c. The traditional model assumes that the price level remains fixed.
    d. Both (b) and (c) of the above.
    e. Both (a) and (b) of the above.

6. Assume that the economy is characterized by sticky wages and prices, and rational expectations. If the Fed wishes to reduce unemployment by expanding the money supply, how will the preannouncement of such a policy influence the policy's effectiveness?

    a. The preannouncement eliminates the policy's effectiveness.
    b. The preannouncement diminishes the policy's effectiveness.
    c. The preannouncement has no effect on the policy's effectiveness.
    d. The preannouncement enhances the magnitude of the policy's effectiveness.

7. Kristin argues at a meeting of the Federal Open Market Committee that the committee should vote to quickly expand the money supply in an attempt to return the economy to full employment. One can infer from her argument that Kristin is

a. either a new classical economist or a traditional economist.
b. either a new classical economist or a nonclassical rational expectations economist.
c. definitely not a new classical economist.
d. definitely not a nonclassical rational expectations economist.

8. If people form rational expectations, an anti-inflation policy will be more successful if it

a. is credible.
b. comes as a surprise.
c. is unanticipated.
d. does all of the above.

9. At a meeting of the Federal Open Market Committee, Michael argues that any decision regarding a contractionary monetary policy should be postponed until Congress votes on a deficit-reduction package currently before it. Michael seems to be implying that

a. an anti-inflationary policy would make more sense if people saw evidence of lower deficits.
b. an anti-inflationary policy might be too costly in terms of lost output if such a policy was not believed to be credible.
c. both (a) and (b) of the above are possible.
d. neither (a) nor (b) of the above are a concern.

10. Assume that irrefutable evidence proves that while anticipated monetary expansions cause aggregate output to expand, unanticipated monetary expansions proved more potent than anticipated policies. What economic model would the evidence support?

a. New classical model
b. Nonclassical rational expectations model
c. Traditional model
d. Uninformed median-voter model

Answer Key

ANSWERS TO CHAPTER 1

Chapter Synopsis/Completions

1. inflation
2. highest
3. business cycles
4. decline
5. spending
6. saving
7. high
8. interest rates
9. money
10. financial institutions
11. bank
12. save
13. spend
14. financial intermediation
15. financial
16. exchange rates
17. interest
18. stock market
19. stronger
20. expensive

Exercise 1

1. e
2. a
3. f
4. b
5. g
6. c
7. h
8. d
9. j
10. i

Exercise 2

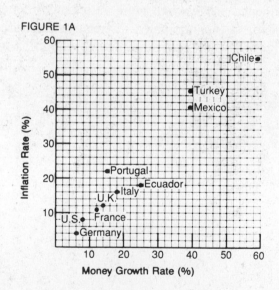

FIGURE 1A

Exercise 3

A. One would predict a fall in prices and economic output. This is in fact what happened. The worst depression of the nineteenth century lasted from 1839 to 1843.

B. He is referring to an upswing in the business cycle.

Exercise 4
1. B
2. S
3. S
4. F
5. S
6. F

Self-Test

Part A	Part B
1. T	1. d
2. T	2. c
3. F	3. c
4. F	4. a
5. T	5. d
6. F	6. c
7. T	7. b
8. T	8. a
9. F	9. b
10. T	10. b
11. T	
12. T	
13. F	
14. F	
15. T	

ANSWERS TO CHAPTER 2
Chapter Synopsis/Completions

1. money
2. currency
3. money supply
4. stock
5. flow
6. transactions
7. specialization
8. medium of exchange
9. unit of account
10. store of value
11. barter
12. time
13. liquid
14. paper currency
15. checks
16. electronic funds transfer system
17. theoretical
18. empirical
19. medium of exchange
20. business cycle
21. monetary aggregates
22. initial

Exercise 1
1. Medium of exchange
2. Unit of account
3. Store of value

Exercise 2
1. M
2. S
3. U
4. U
5. S
6. U
7. M
8. M
9. U
10. S

Exercise 3

In this example the Run DMC CD has actually served the function of money. It has served as a medium of exchange, since Barbi took an inferior position (trading for the Run DMC CD) in hopes of getting something she valued more than she gave up. This is exactly what you do when you accept money in exchange for your labor efforts. It really is not money that you want, but the things that money can be exchanged for.

Individual	Initial CD	Intermediate CD	Final CD
A	R	S	S
B	S	R	T
C	T	T	R

Exercise 4

Number of Goods	Number of Prices in a Barter Economy	Number of Prices in a Money Economy
5	10	5
25	300	25
50	1225	50
500	124,750	500
5000	12,497,500	5000

Exercise 5

1. M1, M2, M3, L
2. L
3. M2, M3, L
4. M1, M2, M3, L
5. L
6. M2, M3, L
7. M2, M3, L
8. M3, L
9. M2, M3, L

Self-Test

Part A	Part B
1. T	1. a
2. F	2. b
3. T	3. c
4. F	4. b
5. T	5. d
6. F	6. c
7. T	7. d
8. T	8. d
9. T	9. d
10. T	10. a
11. T	
12. F	
13. F	
14. F	
15. F	

ANSWERS TO CHAPTER 3

Chapter Synopsis/Completions

1. spenders
2. direct
3. indirect
4. financial intermediaries
5. consumers
6. equity
7. secondary
8. over-the-counter
9. capital
10. short
11. equity
12. primary
13. exchanges
14. money market
15. liabilities
16. Depository institutions
17. Contractual savings
18. one year
19. capital
20. information
21. soundness
22. monetary
23. home
24. reserves
25. Eurobonds
26. Euroequities

Exercise 1

1. I
2. D
3. D
4. I
5. D
6. I
7. I
8. D
9. I
10. D

Exercise 2

	Money Market Instrument	Capital Market Instrument
Traded in an Organized Exchange		Corporate bonds Common stocks
Traded in an Over-the-counter Market	U.S. Treasury bills Negotiable CDs Federal Funds Commercial paper	U.S. Treasury Bonds Corporate Bonds Common stocks

Exercise 3

Part A
1. a, b, d, f, h
2. a
3. a
4. b
5. a, e
6. e, g
7. e, f, h
8. e, g
9. c
10. b, c

Part B
1. a, c
2. a, c
3. a, c
4. a, c
5. b
6. d
7. b
8. f
9. f
10. e, g, h

Exercise 4

Part A
1. U.S. government agency securities
2. State and local government bonds
3. Bank commercial loans
4. Commercial and farm mortgages
5. Corporate bonds
6. Consumer loans
7. U.S. government securities
8. Residential mortgages
9. Corporate stocks

Part B
1. Federal funds
2. Bankers' acceptances
3. Eurodollars
4. Repurchase agreements
5. Commercial paper
6. U.S. Treasury bills
7. Negotiable bank CDs

Part C

Long-term government securities have increased relative to other capital market securities, as the federal government ran consistently large (historically) persistent budget deficits in the 1980s.

Exercise 5
1. b
2. e
3. a, b, d, e, f
4. a, b, d, e
5. a, b, d
6. a
7. c
8. g

Self-Test

Part A
1. T
2. T
3. T
4. T
5. F
6. F
7. F
8. T
9. F
10. T
11. F
12. T
13. T
14. F
15. T

Part B
1. c
2. a
3. e
4. c
5. d
6. b
7. d
8. c
9. d
10. b

ANSWERS TO CHAPTER 4

Chapter Synopsis/Completions

1. maturity date
2. fixed payment
3. face
4. coupon rate
5. discount
6. present value
11. closer
12. longer
13. understates
14. rise
15. return
16. maturity

7. yield to maturity
8. value or price
9. negatively
10. coupon

17. interest rates
18. sure or certain
19. expected rate of inflation
20. credit market

Exercise 1

1. $\$453.51 = \$500/(1 + .05)^2$
2. $\$413.22 = \$500/(1 + .10)^2$
3. $\$341.51 = \$500/(1 + .10)^4$
4. The present value falls.
5. The present value falls.

Exercise 2

Part A

1. $\$1,000 = \$600/(1 + i) + \$600/(1 + i)^2$
2. $\$1,041$
3. Above
4. $\$975$
5. Below

Part B

1. Below, because the price of the bond is above the par value.
2. $\$1,079 = \$100/(1 + i) + \$100/(1 + i)^2 + \$1,100/(1 + i)^3$
3. $\$1,052$
4. Below
5. $\$1,136$
6. Above

Exercise 3

Price of the Discount Bond	Maturity	Yield on a Discount Basis	Yield to Maturity
$900 (365 days)	1 year	9.86%	11.1%
$950 (182 days)	6 months	9.89%	10.8%
$975 (91 days)	3 months	9.89%	10.7%

The table indicates that as the maturity of the discount bond shortens, the yield on a discount basis understates the yield to maturity by a smaller amount.

Exercise 4

Coupon Rate	Maturity Date	Price	Yield to Maturity	Current Yield
7 3/8s	Jan. 1990	100 11/32	7.17%	7.35%
10 1/2s	Jan. 1990	105 22/32	7.15%	9.93%
10 1/2s	Nov. 1992	110 14/32	7.79%	9.51%
9 3/8s	Feb. 2006	107 5/32	8.58%	8.75%
10 3/8s	Nov. 2007-2012	115 3/8	8.72%	8.99%

The 7 3/8 of January 1990, the 9 3/8 of February 2006, and the 10 3/8 of November 2007-2012 are the bonds for which the current yield is a good measure of the interest rate. The reason for this is that the 7 3/8 of January 1990 is selling at a price close to par, while the 9 3/8 of February 2006 and the 10 3/8 of November 2007-2012 have a long term to maturity.

Exercise 5

1. 110 percent, which is calculated as follows: The initial price of the consol is $1000 = $100/0.10 while next year the price is $2000 = $100/0.05. The return is therefore 110 percent = 1.10 = ($2000 - $1000 + $100)/$1000.

2. 14.8 percent, which is calculated as follows: The initial price of the coupon bond is $1000, since the interest rate equals the coupon rate when the bond is at par. Next year, when the bond has 1 year to maturity, the price is $1048 = $100/(1 + 0.05) + $1000/(1 + 0.05). The return is therefore 14.8 percent = 0.148 = ($1048 - $1000 + $100)/$1000.

The consol is a better investment because when the interest rate on two bonds has the same decline, the bond with the longer maturity --the consol-- has a larger increase in its price.

Exercise 6

1. 6%   2. -10%   3. 3%   4. 0%

You would rather be a lender in situation 1 because the real interest rate is the highest, while you would rather be a borrower in situation 2 because the real interest rate is lowest.

Self-Test

Part A		Part B	
1.	T	1.	d
2.	F	2.	c
3.	F	3.	d
4.	T	4.	b
5.	F	5.	b
6.	T	6.	c
7.	F	7.	c
8.	F	8.	a
9.	T	9.	d
10.	F	10.	d
11.	T		
12.	F		

13. F
14. T
15. F

ANSWERS TO CHAPTER 5

Chapter Synopsis/Completions

1. asset
2. wealth
3. expected returns
4. risk
5. liquidity
6. positively
7. luxury
8. positively
9. expected return
10. negatively
11. positively
12. Diversification
13. perfectly
14. greater

Exercise 1

1. L   2. N   3. N   4. L   5. N

Exercise 2

1. 10%
2. 14%
3. 11%
4. 10%
5. 7%

Exercise 3

Variable	Change in Variable	Change in Asset Demand
Wealth	–	–
Liquidity of asset	–	–
Riskiness of asset	–	+
Expected return of asset	–	–
Riskiness of other assets	–	–
liquidity of other assets	–	+
Expected return of other assets	–	+

Exercise 4

	Low Energy Prices	High Energy Prices
1.	-10%	20%
2.	2.5%	17.5%
3.	5%	5%

4. You would buy Energy Intensive Products, Inc., because it reduces the uncertainty of your return the most. In other words it provides the greatest amount of risk reductions.

5. The general principle is that the less returns on two securities move together (stock in Solar Energy Ltd. and Energy Intensive Products, Inc.) the more benefits there are from diversification by holding both.

Self-Test

Part A	Part B
1. T	1. b
2. F	2. a
3. T	3. a
4. F	4. d
5. T	5. a
6. F	6. c
7. F	7. b
8. F	8. d
9. T	9. c
10. T	10. b

ANSWERS TO CHAPTER 6

Chapter Synopsis/Completions

1. loanable funds
2. demand
3. inversely
4. expected return
5. supply curve
6. lower
7. market equilibrium
8. increases
9. increases
10. decreases
11. increases
12. greater
13. rises
14. Fisher effect
15. liquidity preference
16. increase
17. rises
18. rises
19. rises
20. falls
21. decline
22. opposite
23. higher

Exercise 1

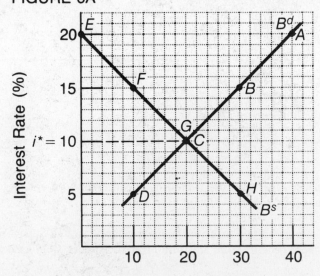

FIGURE 6A

2. The equilibrium interest rate is 10% where the quantity demanded equals the quantity supplied.

3. When the interest rate is 20%, then there is a condition of excess demand, the price of bonds will rise and the interest rate will fall.

Exercise 2

1. D -->
2. <-- D, S -->
3. D -->
4. S -->
5. S -->

6. <-- D
7. D -->, S -->
8. D -->
9. D -->
10. <-- D

Exercise 3

The new supply and demand curves are B^s_2 and B^d_2, and the market equilibrium moves from point 1 to point 2. As can be seen in Figure 6B the interest rate rises to i_2.

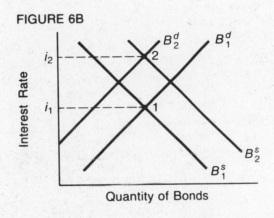

FIGURE 6B

Exercise 4

The new supply and demand curves are M^s_2 and M^d_2, and the market equilibrium moves from point 1 to point 2. As the figure is drawn, the interest rate rises, but if the shift of the demand curve is greater, then the interest rate could fall, instead of rise. What we are seeing here is a combination of the liquidity effect and the income effect of a money supply decrease. Since they have opposite effects the overall impact on the interest rate is ambiguous.

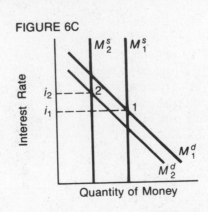

FIGURE 6C

Exercise 5

FIGURE 6D

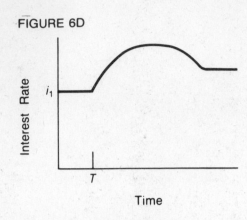

FIGURE 6E

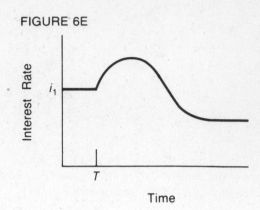

Self-Test

Part A		Part B	
1.	T	1.	b
2.	F	2.	a
3.	F	3.	b
4.	F	4.	b
5.	T	5.	b
6.	F	6.	c
7.	T	7.	a
8.	F	8.	d
9.	T	9.	d
10.	F	10.	d

ANSWERS TO CHAPTER 7

Chapter Synopsis/Completions

1. risk structure
2. default risk
3. left
4. right
5. risk premium
6. rises
7. liquidity
8. higher
9. increases
10. reduces
11. flower
12. income tax
13. term structure
14. yield curve
15. perfect substitutes
16. upward
17. segmented markets
18. expected returns
19. risk premium
20. substitutes
21. higher
22. positive
23. upward
24. rise
25. fall
26. sharply

Exercise 1

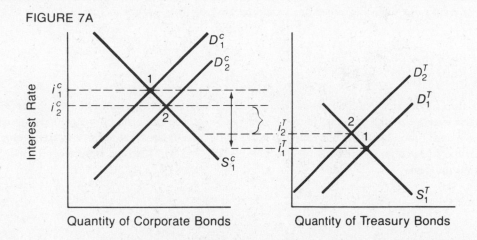

FIGURE 7A

Part A

1. The interest rate on corporate bonds would probably rise. Both the demand and supply curves shift to the right. If the supply curve shifts out more than the demand curve as in Figure 6.7, the interest rate rises.
2. The interest rate on Treasury bonds rises.
3. The risk premium depends on the size of the interest rate increase on corporate bonds relative to that on Treasury bonds. The analysis in the chapter suggests that the risk premium would probably fall.

Part B

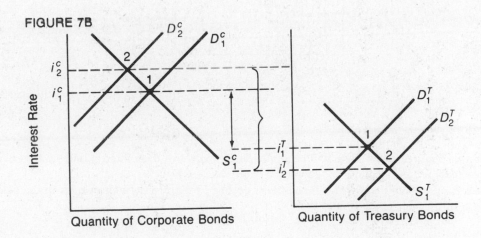

FIGURE 7B

1. The interest rate on corporate bonds rises.
2. The interest rate on Treasury bonds falls.
3. The risk premium rises.

Exercise 2
1. 8%   2. 7.5% = 10% * (1 - 0.25)

304

You would prefer to hold the tax-exempt municipal bond because it has a higher after-tax return. Since you would prefer the municipal bond with a lower interest rate, this example indicates that municipal bonds will have lower market interest rates than they otherwise would because of their tax advantages.

Exercise 3
1. $6\% = 0.06 = [0.06 + 0.06 + 0.06]/3$
2. $6\% = 0.06 = [0.07 + 0.06 + 0.05]/3$

The expected returns are identical. Our analysis of the expectations hypothesis indicates that when the 3 year interest rate equals the average of the expected future 1 year rates over the life of the 3 year bond, the expected returns on strategies 1 and 2 are equal. In our example here, the 3 year interest rate of 6% is the average of the 1 year rates over the life of the 3 year bond ($6\% = [7\% + 6\% + 5\%]/3$), so the expected return from the two strategies must be the same.

Exercise 4

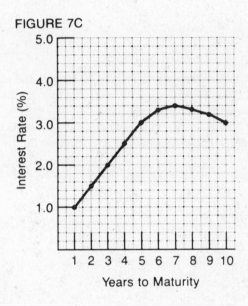

FIGURE 7C

Exercise 5

A. The market is predicting that there will be a mild decline in short- term interest rates in the near future and an even steeper decline further out in the future.
B. The market is predicting that there will be a steep decline in short- term interest rates in the near future and a sharp increase further out in the future.

Self-Test

Part A	Part B
1. F	1. c
2. T	2. c
3. F	3. d
4. F	4. a
5. F	5. a
6. T	6. e
7. F	7. d

8. T	8. b
9. F	9. d
10. T	10. b
11. T	
12. F	
13. T	
14. F	
15. F	

ANSWERS TO CHAPTER 8

Chapter Synopsis/Completions

1. financial intermediaries	12. Transactions costs
2. adverse selection	13. Adverse selection
3. moral hazard	14. moral hazard
4. negative	15. information
5. bonds	16. net worth
6. one-third	17. credit worthiness
7. financial intermediaries	18. free-rider
8. external	19. equity
9. Collateral	20. incentive compatible
10. complicated	21. restrictive covenants
11. information asymmetries	22. financial crises

Exercise 1

1. j	6. e
2. i	7. d
3. h	8. c
4. g	9. b
5. f	10. a

Exercise 2

1. B	5. B
2. B	6. B
3. B	7. B
4. B	8. M

Exercise 3

Part A.
1. Increases in interest rates
2. A sharp decline in the stock market
3. Unanticipated decline in the price elevel
4. An increase in uncertainty in financial markets
5. Bank panics

Part B.
1. Sharp increases in interest rates
2. A steep stock market decline

3. An increase in financial market uncertainty
4. A failure of major financial or non-financial firm

Self-Test

Part A	Part B
1. F	1. a
2. T	2. e
3. F	3. a
4. T	4. d
5. F	5. e
6. T	6. e
7. T	7. a
8. T	8. d
9. F	9. d
10. T	10. b
11. F	
12. T	
13. T	
14. T	
15. F	

ANSWERS TO CHAPTER 9

Chapter Synopsis/Completions

1. equity capital	15. default
2. sources	16. high
3. Reserves	17. diversifying
4. vault cash	18. lower
5. required reserves	19. fixed
6. excess	20. overnight loan
7. secondary reserves	21. negotiable CDs
8. transformation	22. asset
9. gains	23. interest-rate risk
10. deposit outflows	24. more
11. liquidity	25. gap
12. excess	26. duration
13. insurance	27. Interest rate
14. more	28. off-balance-sheet

Exercise 1

1. j	6. g
2. d	7. c
3. a	8. i
4. f	9. h
5. b	10. e

Exercise 2
Part A
1. Other assets

2. Loans
3. Securities
4. Deposits with other banks
5. Cash items in process of collection
6. Reserves

Part B
1. Bank equity capital
2. checkable deposits
3. Borrowing
4. Nontransactions deposits

Exercise 3
Part A

First National Bank

Assets		Liabilities	
Reserves	+ $2,000	Checkable Deposits	+ $2,000

Part B

First National Bank		Second National Bank	
Assets	Liabilities	Assets	Liabilities
Reserves - $1,000	Checkable Deposits - $1,000	Reserves + $1,000	Checkable Deposits + $1,000

Part C
Both banks end up with an increase of $1,000 in reserves.

Exercise 4
Part A

Assets		Liabilities	
Reserves	$19 million	Deposits	$94 million
Loans	$75 million	Bank capital	$10 million
Securities	$10 million		

No. The bank does not need to make any adjustment to its balance sheet because it initially is holding $25 million of reserves when required reserves are only $20 million (20% of $100 million). Because of its initial holding of $5 million of excess reserves, when it suffers the deposit outflow of $6 million it can still satisfy its reserve requirements: Required reserves are $18.8 million (20% of $94 million) while it has $19 million of reserves.

Part B

Assets		Liabilities	
Reserves	$15 million	Deposits	$90 million
Loans	$75 million	Bank capital	$10 million
Securities	$10 million		

Yes. The bank must make an adjustment to its balance sheet because its required reserves are $18 million (20% of $90 million), but it is only holding $15 million of reserves. It has a reserve deficiency of $3 million.

Part C

$3 million. As we see above the bank has a reserve shortfall of $3 million, which it can acquire by selling the $3 million of securities.

Part D

Assets		Liabilities	
Reserves	$18 million	Deposits	$90 million
Loans	$75 million	Bank capital	$10 million
Securities	$ 7 million		

Part E

Assets		Liabilities	
Reserves	$15 million	Deposits	$80 million
Loans	$75 million	Bank capital	$10 million
Securities	$ 0 million		

The bank could fail. The required reserves for the bank are $16 million (20% of $80 million), but it has $15 million of reserves. The proceeds from the distress sale of loans could result in loss that exceeds bank capital, causing the bank to become insolvent.

Exercise 5
1. Finding borrowers who will pay high interest rates, yet are unlikely to default on their loans.
2. Purchasing securities with high returns and low risk.
3. Attempt to minimize risk by diversifying both holdings of loans and securities.
4. Manage the liquidity of its assets so that it can satisfy its reserve requirements without bearing huge costs.

Exercise 6
1. Banks now aggressively set target goals for asset growth and then acquire funds by issuing liabilities as they are needed.
2. Checkable deposits became a less important source of bank funds, while negotiable CDs and bank borrowings have increased in importance.
3. Banks have increased the proportion of their assets in loans.

Exercise 7
A. $30 million - 50 million = -$20 million.
B. Profits will decline.
C -$20 million * 0.02 = -$400,000.
D. Profits will increase by $600,000 (= $20 million * 0.03).

Self-Test

Part A	Part B
1. F	1. d
2. T	2. c
3. F	3. d
4. T	4. d
5. F	5. e
6. T	6. a
7. F	7. c
8. T	8. b
9. F	9. c
10. T	10. a
11. T	
12. F	
13. F	
14. F	
15. T	

ANSWERS TO CHAPTER 10

Chapter Synopsis/Completions

1. bank holding companies
2. national
3. state
4. dual
5. banknotes
6. bank examinations
7. problem banks
8. FDIC or deposit
9. run
10. payoff
11. purchase and assumption
12. merger
13. payoff
14. regulation
15. capital
16. branch banking
17. bank holding
18. payoff method
19. international trade
20. International Banking Act

Exercise 1

1. f
2. e
3. a
4. h
5. b
6. d
7. c
8. g

Exercise 2

A.

National banks	a, c, d
State banks	a, d
Bank holding companies	d
Savings and loan associations	a, b, g
Mutual savings banks	a, b, d
Credit unions	d, e, f
International banking facilities	d

B. Under the Treasury prposal each bank would be regulated by only one regulatory agency and the number of bank regulatory agencies would be reduced to two: a new regulatory agency, the Federal Banking Agency, would regulate the national banks, and the Federal Reserve would regulate the state banks.

Exercise 3

One possibility would be to limit deposit insurance to, say, $10,000, on the assumption that someone with more than $10,000 in a bank account ought to inform themselves about the bank's practices. Such scrutiny would give bank managers an incentive to avoid assets deemed too risky by depositors. Of course, such a policy would force many individuals to open numerous accounts at many banks to benefit from the deposit coverage they now enjoy (assuming this would be allowed). This added cost needs to be weighed against the proposed benefits before one can determine the desirability of this proposal. Another possibility is for the FDIC to tie deposit insurance premiums to the riskiness of a bank's assets. By charging risky banks more for deposit insurance, these banks would pay a penalty for taking on greater risk. See chapter 11 in the text for a more complete discussion of these and other related issues.

Exercise 4

A. A high degree of concentration does not imply an absence of competition, as long as entry is allowed. Competition may therefore be enhanced as banks open up branch offices in new markets. The largest three banks in a state may hold 70% of all bank deposits, yet any individual may have the option of choosing between seven or eight banks. Thus concentration and competition need not be related if entry is allowed.

B. The experience of Canada and California suggest that entry is more important than branching in determining the competitiveness of banking markets.

C. The higher concentration of the savings and loan industry is explained by the more liberal branching regulations for savings and loans; almost all states permit statewide branching and since the early 1980s branching across state lines has been permitted through acquisitions of troubled thrifts.

Self-Test

Part A		Part B	
1.	F	1.	d
2.	T	2.	c
3.	T	3.	a
4.	T	4.	b
5.	F	5.	a
6.	T	6.	e
7.	T	7.	e
8.	F	8.	a
9.	T	9.	b
10.	T	10.	c
11.	T		
12.	T		
13.	T		
14.	T		
15.	T		

ANSWERS TO CHAPTER 11

Chapter Synopsis/Completions

1. Federal Deposit Insurance Corporation
2. withdraw
3. moral hazard
4. adverse selection
5. chartering
6. capital
7. examinations
8. financial disruption
9. Regulation Q
10. brokered
11. interest rates
12. lowered
13. regulatory forbearance
14. moral hazard
15. FSLIC
16. Thrift Supervision
17. Resolution Trust Corporation
18. housing
19. principal-agent
20. bureaucratic gambling

Exercise 1

1. Banks with deposit insurance are likely to take on greater risks than they otherwise would. This is the moral hazard problem.

2. Deposit insurance attracts risk-prone entrepreneurs to the banking industry. This is the adverse selection problem.

3. Deposit insurance reduces the incentives of depositors to monitor the riskiness of their banks' asset portfolios. This is the free-rider problem (see chapter 8).

Exercise 2

Part A.

1. Adverse selection problems can be reduced through a chartering process that prevents crooks or risk-prone entrepreneurs from getting control of banks.

2. Moral hazard problems can be reduced through regulatory restrictions that prevent banks from acquiring certain risky assets such as common stocks or junk bonds.

3. High bank capital requirements raise the cost of a bank failure to the owners, thereby reducing the incentives of bank owners to take on too much risk, and reducing the moral hazard to depositors.

4. Regular bank examinations reduce moral hazard problems by reducing opportunities for bank owners to skirt regulations concerning asset holdings and minimum capital requirements.

Part B.

Regular bank examinations, restrictions on asset holdings, and minimum capital requirements help to reduce the adverse selection problem because, given fewer opportunities to take on risk, risk- prone entrepreneurs will be discouraged from entering the banking industry.

Exercise 3

Part A.
1. The failure of a large bank could lead to greater uncertainty in financial markets, potentially causing a major financial crisis that could result in adverse macroeconomic consequences. The too-big-to-fail policy is intended to prevent greater financial market instability and adverse economic conditions.

Part B.
1. One implication is that individuals holding deposits in excess of the $100,000 insurance limit are fully protected. This suggests that depositors with uninsured deposits in large banks get a better deal than those in banks that are not-too-big-to-fail. It is also evident that the policy is not limited to the eleven largest banks, and may indicate that banks, which are even smaller than the Bank of New England, could be too-big-to-fail, no matter how poorly they are managed. Bank performance may suffer as a result of the increased incentives for moral hazard by big banks.

2. The alternative to the purchase and assumption method for dealing with failed banks is the payoff method.

3. These banks are liquidated, implying that uninsured depositors usually suffer some loss, as happened to depositors of Freedom National Bank (see Box 11.1 in text).

Exercise 4

Part A.
1. A burst of financial innovation in the 1970s and early 1980s that produced new financial instruments and markets widened the scope for greater risk taking.

2. Financial deregulation opened up more avenues to savings and loans and mutual savings banks to take on more risk.

3. An increase in federal deposit insurance from $40,000 to $100,000, and the use of brokered deposits made it easier for high-rolling financial institutions to attract funds.

4. In the early stages of the 1980s banking crisis, financial institutions were harmed by the sharp increases in interest rates from late 1979 until 1981 and the severe recession in 1981-82.

Part B.
Regulators adopted a policy of regulatory forbearance toward insolvent financial institutions in the 1980s.

Part C.
1. The FSLIC lacked sufficient funds to cover insured deposits in the insolvent S&Ls.

2. The regulators were reluctant to close the firms that justified their regulatory existence.

3. The Federal Home Loan Bank Board and the FSLIC were reluctant to admit that they were in over their heads with problems.

Exercise 5

1. The abolishment of the Federal Home Loan Bank Board and the FSLIC, both of which had failed in their regulatory tasks.

2. The transfer of the regulatory role of the Federal Home Loan Bank Board to the Office of Thrift Supervision, a bureau within the U.S. Treasury Department.

3. The expansion of the responsibilities of the FDIC, which is now the sole administrator of the federal deposit insurance system.

4. The establishment of the Resolution Trust Corporation to manage and resolve insolvent thrifts placed in conservatorship or receivership.

5. To replenish the reserves of the Savings Association Insurance Fund, the deposit insurance premiums for S&Ls were increased.

6. FIRREA imposes new restrictions on thrift activities. Under these restrictions, S&Ls can no longer purchase junk bonds, must limit their commercial real estate loans to four times capital, and must hold at least 70% of their assets in investments that are housing related.

Exercise 6

Regulators' desire to escape blame for poor performance, led them to adopt a perverse strategy of "regulatory gambling", whereby capital requirements were lowered and insolvent institutions were allowed to continue operating in the hope that conditions in the thrift industry would improve. Rather than mandate stricter controls, politicians encouraged lax monitoring and regulatory forbearance, even hampering regulatory efforts to close insolvent thrifts by cutting regulatory appropriations. Politicians, who were receiving generous campaign contributions from the savings and loan industry, like regulators, hoped that the industry would rebound.

Exercise 7

1. Eliminating governmentally-administered deposit insurance.

2. Lowering the amount of deposits covered by insurance.

3. Eliminating the too-big-to-fail policy.

4. Coinsurance.

5. "Narrow Bank" deposit insurance.

6. Private deposit insurance.

7. Risk-based deposit insurance premiums.

8. Eliminating branching restrictions.

9. Market-value accounting for capital requirements.

Self-Test

Part A	Part B
1. F	1. e
2. T	2. e
3. T	3. c
4. T	4. c

5. F	5. e
6. T	6. a
7. T	7. c
8. T	8. e
9. F	9. e
10. F	10. e
11. F	
12. T	
13. T	
14. T	
15. T	

ANSWERS TO CHAPTER 12

Chapter Synopsis/Completions

1. borrowers	12. credit
2. financial intermediation	13. factoring
3. Life insurance	14. money market mutual fund
4. long	15. no-load
5. Property	16. brokers
6. casualty	17. dealers
7. retirement income	18. specialists
8. underfunding	19. Investment banks.
9. Pension Benefit Guarantee	20. Underwriting
10. Sales finance	21. Glass-Steagall
11. consumer finance	22. competitive

Exercise 1

1. d	6. e
2. c	7. h
3. a	8. b
4. g	9. j
5. f	10. i

Exercise 2

1. d	5. b
2. c	6. a
3. e	7. f
4. h	8. g

Exercise 3

Financial Intermediary	Long-Term Assets	Short-Term Assets
Life insurance companies	x	
Property and casualty insurers		xx
Private pension funds	x	
Finance companies		x
Money market mutual funds		x
Tax-exempt money market mutual funds		xx

Exercise 4

Malpractice insurers finding that premiums no longer sufficiently cover their anticipated liability can be expected to write fewer policies in this field. Some insurers may discontinue offering these policies altogether in favor of other, more profitable lines of insurance. If physicians are unable to purchase malpractice insurance for certain specialties because of the high degree of risk, they will either be forced to self-insure by charging higher fees and avoiding risky cases or change to a specially that insurance companies are willing to cover.

Exercise 5

1. f	6. c
2. b	7. j
3. g, h	8. c
4. d	9. e
5. e	10. c

Exercise 6

A. The individual has less incentive to monitor the activities of the pension fund trustees. The government does, however, have an incentive to closely monitor pension fund activities since it is the government, and ultimately the taxpayer, who loses if a pension fund should fail. (Students who have have just read chapter 11 may wonder how diligently regulators monitor pension funds.)

B. The California Teachers Retirement System is underfunded due to lawmakers' reluctance to reduce the benefits of a politically powerful constituency. The approximately 400,000 retired and active teachers in the system will exert strong pressure on California assemblymen. On the other hand, the average taxpayer will have little incentive to inform himself on this issue. Politicians wanting to improve their chances for reelection may be hard pressed not to vote against a bill opposed by such a formidable group. Social Security underfunding is the result of the same type of forces. The aged are a politically powerful group because they vote in such high numbers. So powerful is this group that politicians who vote for Social Security benefit reductions often find themselves quickly voted from office.

Self-Test

Part A		Part B	
1. T		1. e	
2. F		2. b	
3. T		3. c	
4. T		4. a	
5. T		5. b	
6. T		6. b	
7. F		7. c	
8. F		8. d	
9. T		9. a	
10. T		10. d	
11. T			
12. T			
13. T			
14. T			
15. F			

ANSWERS TO CHAPTER 13

Chapter Synopsis/Completions

1. profits
2. interest
3. volatile
4. interest rate
5. variable rate
6. lower
7. mortgages
8. financial futures
9. hedge
10. options
11. cost
12. securitization
13. regulations
14. loophole mining
15. disintermediation
16. money market mutual funds
17. regulator
18. stability
19. Regulation
20. NOW
21. inflation

Exercise 1

1. c
2. a
3. f
4. g
5. d
6. h
7. e
8. i
9. b

Exercise 2

1. AR
2. RC
3. RC
4. ER
5. AR
6. AR
7. ER
8. ER
9. RC
10. AR

Exercise 3

2. -
3. +
4. +
5. +
6. -
7. +

Self-Test

Part A
1. F
2. T
3. T
4. T
5. F
6. F
7. F
8. T
9. T
10. T
11. T
12. T
13. F
14. T
15. F

Part B
1. e
2. a
3. d
4. b
5. d
6. b
7. a
8. d
9. d
10. b

ANSWERS TO CHAPTER 14

Chapter Synopsis/Completions

1. central bank
2. banks
3. depositors
4. borrowers
5. Federal Reserve System
6. monetary policy
7. currency in circulation
8. reserves
9. monetary base
10. government
11. discount loans

12. reserves
13. sells
14. open market operations
15. required reserves
16. multiple
17. securities
18. simple deposit multiplier
19. required reserve ratio
20. currency
21. excess
22. less or smaller

Exercise 1
Part A

First National Bank		The Fed	
Assets	Liabilities	Assets	Liabilities
T-bills + $100,000 Reserves - $100,000		T-bill + $100,000	Reserves - $100,000

Reserves in the banking system have fallen by $100,000.

Part B

First National Bank		The Fed	
Assets	Liabilities	Assets	Liabilities
Reserves - $100,000	Discount Loans - $100,000	Discount Loans - $100,000	Reserves - $100,000

Reserves in the banking system have again fallen by $100,000.

Exercise 2

A. $100
B. $100, the amount of its excess reserves.

C.

Pittsburg State Bank

Assets	Liabilities
Reserves - $100	
Loans + $100	

Exercise 3

Part A

A. The deposit liabilities of Bank A increase by $1000, implying that required reserves increase by $200 (20 percent of $1,000). Bank A can safely lend $800. In the process of lending $800, checkable deposits increase by $800. Thus checkable deposits at Bank A are $1,800 higher than before the Fed open market purchase.

Part B

Bank	Change in Deposits	Change in Loans	Change in Reserves
A	+ $1000.00	+ $800.00	+ $200.00
B	+ 800.00	+ 640.00	+ 160.00
C	+ 640.00	+ 512.00	+ 128.00
D	+ 512.00	+ 409.60	+ 102.40
.	.	.	.
.	.	.	.
.	.	.	.
Total All Banks	+ $5000.00	+ $4000.00	+ $1000.00

Exercise 4

1. The simple deposit multiplier formula is $D = (1/r_D)R$.

2. The $10 billion dollar sale of government bonds causes bank reserves to fall by $10 billion. This is partially offset by the $5 billion in discount loans that increase bank reserves by $5 billion. Thus on net, bank reserves fall by $5 billion.

3. The change in checkable deposits is calculated by multiplying the $5 billion decline by 5 (= 1/0.20). Checkable deposits fall by $25 billion in the simple model.

Self-Test

Part A		Part B	
1.	T	1.	d
2.	F	2.	c
3.	F	3.	c
4.	T	4.	b
5.	F	5.	c
6.	T	6.	d
7.	F	7.	a
8.	F	8.	c
9.	F	9.	d
10.	F	10.	a

11. T
12. F
13. T
14. T
15. T

ANSWERS TO CHAPTER 15

Chapter Synopsis/Completions

1. high-powered money
2. reserves
3. open market operation
4. monetary base
5. identical
6. currency
7. certain
8. deposits
9. borrowing
10. nonborrowed

11. borrowed
12. nonborrowed
13. borrowed
14. overstates
15. currency in circulation
16. time deposit-checkable deposits
17. money multiplier
18. reduce
19. fall
20. increase

Exercise 1

1. d
2. f
3. g
4. h

5. a, c
6. b
7. e

Exercise 2
Part A

Banking System

Assets		Liabilities
Securities	+ $100	
Reserves	- $100	

The Fed

Assets		Liabilities	
Government Securities	- $100	Reserves	- $100

Change in the monetary base = -$100
Change in Reserves = -$100.

Nonbank Public

Assets		Liabilities
Securities	+ $100	
Checkable deposits	- $100	

Banking System

Assets		Liabilities	
Reserves	- $100	Checkable deposits	- $100

The Fed

Assets		Liabilities	
Government Securities	- $100	Reserves	- $100

Change in the monetary base = -$100
Change in Reserves = -$100.

Part C

Nonbank Public

Assets		Liabilities
Securities	+ $100	
Currency	- $100	

The Fed

Assets		Liabilities	
Government Securities	- $100	Currency in circulation	- $100

Change in the monetary base = -$100
Change in Reserves = 0.

In all cases, the open market sale leads to a $100 decline in the monetary base. In part C, reserves do not change, while they decline by $100 in parts A and B.

Exercise 3
A. $m = [1 + \{C/D\}]/[r_D + r_T\{T/D\} + \{ER/D\} + \{C/D\}]$

B. $\{C/D\} = \$280b/\$800b = 0.35$
$\{T/D\} = \$2400b/\$8000b = 3$

{ER/D} = \$40b/\$800b = 0.05
m = 1.35/0.6 = 2.25

C. B = M/m = \$1080/2.25 = \$480 billion
R = B - C = \$480 - \$280 = \$200
RR = r_D(D) + r_T(T) = 0.11(800) + 0.03(2400) = \$160
ER = R - RR = \$200 - \$160 = \$40

D. m = 1.35/0.57 = 2.368
M = \$480 * 2.368 = \$1137

E. M = C + D
M = [{C/D}]D + D
M = 1.35 * D
D = \$1137/1.35 = \$842
C = \$842 * .35 = \$295

F. RR = 0.08(842) + 0.03(2526) = \$143
ER = \$480 - \$295 - \$143 = \$42
ER = 0.05 * D = 0.05 * \$842 = \$42

Exercise 4
A. m = 1.3/0.5 = 2.6
M = m * B = 2.6 * \$300 = \$780

B. C + D = 0.3D + D - 1.3D = \$780
C = \$180
D = \$600
RR = 0.1(600) + 0.02(3000) = \$120
R = B_n - C = 300 - 180 = \$120

C. m = 1.3/0.6 = 2.167
M = 2.167 * \$300 = \$650
D = \$650/1.3 = \$500
C = 0.3 * \$500 = \$150
RR = 0.1(500) + 0.02(2500) = \$100
ER = B - C - RR = \$300 - \$150 - \$100 = \$50
ER = {ER/D} * D = 0.1 * \$500 = \$50

Exercise 5

Change in Variable		Money Supply Response
B	−	+
r_D	−	−
{C/D}	−	−
r_T	−	+
DL	−	+
{ER/D}	−	−
{T/D}	−	−

Self-Test

Part A	Part B
1. T	1. e
2. F	2. c
3. F	3. a
4. T	4. b
5. F	5. d
6. T	6. d
7. F	7. a
8. T	8. c
9. F	9. b
10. T	10. a
11. T	
12. F	
13. F	
14. F	
15. T	

ANSWERS TO CHAPTER 16

Chapter Synopsis/Completions

1. Currency-checkable deposit
2. wealth
3. expected returns
4. risk
5. liquidity
6. fall
7. interest rates
8. bank panics
9. fall
10. FDIC
11. increased
12. cash or currency
13. interest
14. money market deposit account
15. deposit outflows
16. excess reserves
17. money multiplier
18. nonborrowed monetary base
19. bank
20. withdraw
21. rise
22. excess reserves
23. money multiplier

Exercise 1

1. negatively
2. negatively
3. positively
4. positively
5. positively
6. positively
7. negatively
8. negatively
9. positively
10. positively, negatively

Exercise 2

A. The currency-checkable deposit ratio will fall.

B. The money multiplier will rise as the currency-checkable deposit ratio falls.

C. A rise in crime increases the cost of carrying cash and is likely to speed the transition from heavy reliance on cash to greater reliance on checks.

Exercise 3

Variable	Change in in Variable	Effect on Money Supply
1. Time deposit-checkable deposits ratio	-	-
2. Discount rate	-	-
3. Required reserve ratio on time deposits	-	-
4. Nonborrowed base	-	+
5. Required reserve ratio on checkable deposits	-	-
6. Expected deposit outflows	-	-
7. Currency-checkable deposits ratio	-	-
8. Market interest rates	-	+

Exercise 4

A. $m = 2.64 = [1 + 0.40]/[0.10 + 0.02(1.5) + 0.40]$
   $M = \$581$ billion $= 2.64 * 220$

B. $m = 2.38 = [1 + 0.50]/[0.10 + 0.02(1.5) + 0.50]$
   $M = \$524$ billion $= 2.38 * 220$
   $B = \$244$ billion $= 581/2.38$

Exercise 5

A. $m = 2.46 = [1 + 0.45]/[0.10 + 0.02(2.0) + 0.45]$
   $M = \$615$ billion $= 2.46 * 250$
   $B = \$252.5$ billion

Since all other factors remain constant, a one percent increase in the money supply is generated by a one percent increase in the monetary base, which equals $2.5 billion (0.01 * $250 billion).

B. 6.3%. $M = 654 = 252.5 * \{(1 + 0.4)/[0.10 + 0.02(2.0) = 0.4]\}$. The growth rate $= (654 - 615)/615 = 0.063 = 6.3\%$. This example shows that the Fed may not have precise control over the money supply during short time periods.

Self-Test

Part A		Part B	
1.	T	1.	b
2.	T	2.	c
3.	T	3.	e
4.	F	4.	c
5.	F	5.	a
6.	T	6.	b
7.	T	7.	a
8.	T	8.	e
9.	F	9.	c
10.	T	10.	a
11.	T		

12. T
13. T
14. T
15. T

ANSWERS TO CHAPTER 17

Chapter Synopsis/Completions

1. banking panic
2. lender of last resort
3. Board of Governors
4. Chairman
5. four
6. Federal Open Market Committee
7. New York
8. Chairman
9. appropriations
10. Treasury securities
11. fourteen
12. Paul Volcker
13. interest
14. Bureaucratic
15. banks
16. inflationary
17. undemocratic

Exercise 1

1. c
2. c
3. a
4. a
5. a
6. b
7. b
8. a, c
9. a
10. a

Exercise 2

Two explanations seem possible. First, the Fed may have feared that Congress would overreact and set Regulation Q ceilings much too low for too long, causing severe economic harm to affected groups. Thus the Fed may have felt that its action was a least worst strategy. Second, the Fed may have feared losing permanent control over Regulation Q. The Theory of Bureaucratic Behavior suggest that bureaucracies want to maximize their power and prestige. The potential loss of power over Regulation Q would diminish the overall power of the Fed and might encourage Congress to usurp other duties from the Fed. Additionally, since lower Regulation Q ceilings allow the Treasury to borrow more cheaply, the Fed may have been attempting to avoid a potential conflict with the executive branch as well.

Exercise 3

Making the Fed a branch of the U.S. Treasury would eliminate the Fed's current source of revenue. The Treasury Department would allocate part of its annual budget to Fed activities, but presumably this allocation would not vary from changes in money growth. If inflationary expansions in the money supply result from the Fed's desire to increase the revenue available for expenditures on its activities, then making the Fed a branch of the Treasury eliminates the incentive to overly expand the money supply.

Exercise 4

A. Such statements put the Fed on notice that if policies become too unpopular with the electorate, the Fed risks losing its coveted independence.

B. Germany Switzerland, and the United States have central banks that are relatively more independent than their counterparts in France, Italy, and Great Britain. This finding is consistent with the view that political pressure imparts an inflationary bias to monetary policy.

Exercise 5
Part A
1. Greater focus on long-run objectives.
2. Less pressure to finance deficits and less pressure to pursue inflationary policies.
3. More likely to pursue policies in the public interest even if politically unpopular.

Part B
1. Greater accountability. If the Fed makes mistakes there is no way of voting them out, thus system is undemocratic.
2. Coordination of fiscal and monetary policy would be easier.
3. President is ultimately held responsible for economic policy, yet he does not have control over monetary policy, an important element determining economic health.
4. Lack of evidence indicating that an independent Fed performs well.

Self-Test

Part A
1. T
2. T
3. F
4. F
5. T
6. T
7. F
8. T
9. T
10. T
11. T
12. T
13. F
14. T
15. T

Part B
1. a
2. c
3. d
4. c
5. c
6. c
7. b
8. c
9. d
10. d

ANSWERS TO CHAPTER 18

Chapter Synopsis/Completions
1. reserves
2. monetary
3. open market
4. purchase
5. currency
6. transportation (or clearing)
7. cash items in the process of collection
8. deferred availability cash items
9. increase
10. tax and loan
11. fall
12. reduce
13. decline
14. open market operations
15. government budget constraint
16. monetary base
17. interest rates
18. purchase
19. printing money
20. monetizing the debt

Exercise 1
Part A
1. securities
2. discount loans

3. gold and SDR certificate accounts
4. coin
5. cash items in the process of collection
6. other Federal Reserve assets

Part B
1. Federal Reserve notes outstanding
2. bank deposits
3. U.S. Treasury deposits
4. foreign and other deposits
5. deferred availability cash items
6. Other Federal Reserve liabilities and capital account

Exercise 2

	Change in Factor	Response of Monetary Base
Treasury Currency	−	−
Gold and SDR accounts	−	−
Other Fed assets	−	−
Other Fed liabilities	−	+
Securities	−	−
Float	−	−
Treasury deposits	−	+
Discount loans	−	−
Foreign deposits	−	+

Exercise 3

A. Federal Reserve float is the rise in reserves created whenever a check drawn on one bank does not clear within two days after being deposited in another bank. Reserves in the banking system rise whenever the bank in which the check is deposited is credited with reserves before the bank on which the check is drawn has its reserves debited.

B. Large unpredictable fluctuations in float reduce the Federal Reserve's short-run control over the monetary base.

C. The movement toward an electronics payments system promises to significantly reduce float. A complete electronics payment system would eliminate float altogether.

Exercise 4

A. As the Treasury pays its bills, checks are deposited in banks or cashed, causing reserves in the banking system or currency in circulation to increase. All else constant, this increase in the monetary base will lead to an increase in the money supply.

B. If the Fed wants to offset this temporary increase (everyone knows that Congress always raises the debt ceiling) in the monetary base it will sell government securities draining the additional reserves from the system. (This is referred to as a defensive open market operation and is discussed in Chapter 19).

Exercise 5

To calculate the change in the monetary base, one adds the changes in the first six items (Federal Reserve assets), and subtracts from this sum the changes in the last three items (Fed liabilities). This difference gives the change in the monetary base for the given week.

Subtotal 1 = + 5768

Subtotal 2 = + 9296

Change in monetary base = 5768 - 9296 = -3528. Thus the monetary base dropped $3.528 billion during the week.

Exercise 6

A.

1. The government can increase taxes.
2. The government can borrow from the public.
3. The government can borrow from the Fed.

B. When the government borrows from the Fed, the monetary base increases.

C. Monetizing the debt or it is sometimes called printing money.

D. No, because the Fed does not have to monetize it--that is, buy the Treasury debt. On the other hand, if the Fed wants to prevent a rise in interest rates, then it will purchase bonds to keep interest rates low and the result will be expansion of the monetary base.

Self-Test

Part A		Part B	
1.	T	1.	e
2.	T	2.	b
3.	F	3.	c
4.	F	4.	a
5.	F	5.	c
6.	F	6.	b
7.	F	7.	c
8.	T	8.	d
9.	T	9.	d
10.	T	10.	b
11.	F		
12.	T		
13.	T		
14.	T		
15.	F		

ANSWERS TO CHAPTER 19

Chapter Synopsis/Completions

1. open market operations
2. discount rate
3. reserve requirements
11. quantity
12. liquidity
13. seasonal credit

4. open-market operations
5. dynamic
6. defensive
7. purchase
8. reserve repos
9. flexible
10. interest rate

14. extended credit
15. lender of last resort
16. discount borrowing
17. market rate
18. money multiplier
19. 100%
20. money supply

Exercise 1

1. g
2. a
3. d
4. h
5. c

6. b
7. e
8. i
9. j
10. f

Exercise 2

Part A
Open market operations are the most important monetary policy tool because they are the most important determinant of changes in the monetary base, the primary source of fluctuations in the money supply.

Part B
1. Dynamic open market operations
2. Defensive open market operations

Part C
1. Open market operations occur at the initiative of the Fed.
2. Open market operations can be used to any degree.
3. Open market operations are easily reversed.
4. Open market operations can be implemented quickly.

Exercise 3

Part A
1. Adjustment credit
2. Seasonal credit
3. Extended credit

Part B
Many deposits exceed the $100,000 limit that the FDIC promises to pay. Thus the lender of last resort prevents bank failures due to large depositor withdrawals. In addition, the FDIC contingency fund is limited and a wave of bank failures could seriously jeopardize the solvency of the system leading to a severe financial panic that only a lender of last resort might prevent.

Exercise 4
A. Disadvantage
B. Disadvantage
C. Advantage

Exercise 5

Part A

1. Small changes in reserve requirements are too costly to administer, so it is too blunt a tool to be used effectively.

2. Raising reserve requirements can cause immediate liquidity problems for banks with small amounts of excess reserves.

Part B

1. The main advantage is that the narrowly defined money would be controlled exactly because the money multiplier would exactly equal one.

2. The main disadvantage is that there would surely be financial innovation that would create money substitutes. Thus the narrowly defined money supply would probably cease to be the economically relevant measure of the money supply.

Self-Test

Part A		Part B	
1.	F	1.	d
2.	F	2.	a
3.	T	3.	a
4.	T	4.	c
5.	T	5.	c
6.	T	6.	d
7.	F	7.	a
8.	F	8.	b
9.	F	9.	b
10.	T	10.	b
11.	T		
12.	T		
13.	T		
14.	F		
15.	T		

ANSWERS TO CHAPTER 20

Chapter Synopsis/Completions

1. high employment
2. economic growth
3. price stability
4. interest rate stability
5. financial market stability
6. foreign exchange market stability
7. natural rate of unemployment
8. higher
9. intermediate targeting
10. operating target
11. policy tools
12. increase
13. money supply
14. measurable
15. controllable
16. predictable effect
17. crisis
18. money supply

Exercise 1

Part A

1. high employment
2. economic growth

3. price stability
4. interest rate stability
5. stability in financial markets
6. stability in foreign exchange markets

Part B

Economists do not believe that it would be desirable to lower the unemployment rate to zero. By "full" unemployment, economists mean the natural rate of unemployment--the level of unemployment consistent with labor market equilibrium.

Exercise 2

Part A
1. monetary aggregates such as M1, M2, or M3
2. short- or long-term interest rates

Part B
1. reserve aggregates such as reserves, nonborrowed reserves, or the monetary base
2. interest rates such as the federal funds rate or the T-bill rate

Exercise 3
1. Measurability
2. Controllability
3. The ability to predictably affect goals

Exercise 4
1. The Fed could tie the discount rate to a market interest rate to decrease fluctuations in discount borrowing.
2. The Fed could focus less on stabilizing interest rates, thereby gaining improved control over the money supply.

Self-Test

Part A		Part B	
1.	T	1.	a
2.	F	2.	c
3.	F	3.	e
4.	F	4.	b
5.	T	5.	c
6.	T	6.	e
7.	F	7.	e
8.	T	8.	b
9.	T	9.	a
10.	F	10.	b
11.	F		
12.	T		
13.	T		
14.	T		
15.	F		

ANSWERS TO CHAPTER 21

Chapter Synopsis/Completions

1. currency
2. deposits
3. forward
4. appreciated
5. more
6. less
7. same
8. purchasing power parity
9. depreciate
10. identical
11. traded
12. tariffs and quotas
13. productivity
14. exchange rate
15. expected return
16. interest parity
17. capital mobility
18. interest rate
19. fall
20. higher
21. appreciates
22. depreciation
23. expectations
24. dirty
25. increase
26. depreciation

Exercise 1

1. e
2. i
3. g
4. b
5. m
6. n
7. a
8. l
9. f
10. j
11. c
12. k

Exercise 2

1. 2 francs per dollar
2. $500
3. 200 francs
4. Depreciation of the franc; appreciation of the dollar
5. $250;less
6. 400 francs; more
7. When a country's currency appreciates, its goods abroad become more expensive and foreign goods in that country become cheaper (holding domestic prices constant in the two countries).

Exercise 3

Part A
1. $10
2. 1800 pesos
3. None, because Argentine wheat is more expensive in both countries and the goods are identical.
4. $5
5. 3600 pesos
6. None, because American wheat is more expensive in both countries and the goods are identical.
7. 500 pesos per dollar, because only at this exchange rate will[both American and Argentinian wheat be purchased.
8. 300 pesos per dollar; a depreciation of the dollar

Part B
1. Tne value of the dollar will fall to 250 pesos per dollar.
2. The dollar will appreciate by 2%.

Exercise 4

Change in Factor		Response of the Exchange Rate
Domestic interest rate	−	−
Foreign interest rate	−	+
Expected domestic price level	−	+
Expected tariffs and quotas	−	−
Expected import demand	−	+
Expected export demand	−	−
Expected productivity	−	−

Self-Test

Part A	Part B
1. T	1. c
2. T	2. a
3. F	3. b
4. F	4. a
5. T	5. c
6. F	6. c
7. T	7. a
8. F	8. e
9. F	9. a
10. T	10. a
11. F	
12. F	
13. T	
14. F	
15. T	

ANSWERS TO CHAPTER 22

Chapter Synopsis/Completions

1. balance of payments
2. credits
3. current account
4. trade balance
5. official reserves transaction
6. monetary base
7. reserve currency
8. fixed
9. balance of payments
10. long-term loans
11. speculative attack
12. managed float
13. exchange rate
14. gain
15. rise
16. sterilization
17. contractionary
18. increase
19. depreciation
20. reserve currency
21. inflationary
22. gold standard
23. monetary discipline
24. stable

Exercise 1

1. b
2. e
3. d
4. g
5. a

6. j
7. i
8. f
9. c
10. h

Exercise 2

U.S. Balance of Payments in 1994 (billions of dollars)

	Receipts(+)	Payments(-)	Balance
Current account:			
1. Merchandise exports	+500		
2. Merchandise imports		-600	
3. Trade balance			-100
4. Net investment income		-40	
5. Net services	+20		
6. Net unilateral transfers		-15	
7. Current Account Balance			-135
Capital account:			
8. Capital outflows		-50	
9. Capital inflows	+100		
10. Statistical discrepancy	+60		
11. Official reserves transactions balance			+110
Method of financing:			
12. Increase in U.S. Official reserve assets		-5	
13. Increase in foreign official assets	+25		
14. Total financing of surplus			+25

Exercise 3

FIGURE 22A

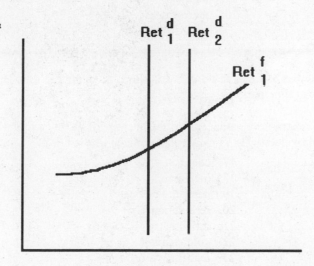

Exchange Rate, E_t

Ret^d_1 Ret^d_2 Ret^f_1

Expected Return

Self-Test

Part A

1. F
2. T
3. F
4. T
5. F
6. F
7. T
8. F
9. T
10. F
11. T
12. F
13. T
14. T
15. T

Part B

1. c
2. b
3. a
4. d
5. d
6. c
7. e
8. c
9. c
10. b

ANSWERS TO CHAPTER 23

Chapter Synopsis/Completions

1. income
2. velocity
3. fixed
4. equation of exchange
5. quantity theory of money
6. flexible
7. price level
8. interest rates
9. liquidity preference theory
10. transactions
11. precautionary
12. speculative
13. interest rates
14. fall
15. nominal
16. positive
17. transactions
18. procyclical
19. money
20. interest rates

Exercise 1

A. Velocity is the average number of times that a dollar is spent in buying the total amount of final goods and services produced during a given time period.

B. The equation of exchange relates nominal income to the quantity of money and velocity. It states that the quantity of money multiplied by velocity (MV) must equal nominal income (PY).

C. quantity theory of money

Exercise 2

1. 600
2. 1000
3. 2
4. 4
5. 800

Exercise 3

Part A
1. transactions motive
2. precautionary motive
3. speculative

Part B
  Speculative motive

Part C
  Risk

Exercise 4

1. Q	7. K
2. C	8. K
3. C	9. Q
4. K	10. Q
5. F	11. K
6. F	12. F

ANSWERS TO CHAPTER 24

Chapter Synopsis/Completions

1. aggregate demand	11. expenditure multiplier
2. consumer expenditure	12. consumer expenditure
3. investment spending	13. mpc
4. government spending	14. smaller
5. disposable income	15. full employment
6. marginal propensity to consume	16. IS
7. autonomous	17. investment spending
8. inventory investment	18. higher
9. planned	19. income
10. cut(reduce)	20. interest rates

Exercise 1

1. g	9. k
2. h	10. m
3. i	11. d
4. b	12. f
5. a	13. c
6. l	14. e
7. j	15. n
8. o	

Exercise 2

Part A

Point	Disposable Income (DI)	Change in DI	Change in C	Autonomous Consumption	Total Consumption
A	0			50	50
B	100	100	75	50	125
C	200	100	75	50	200
D	300	100	75	50	275
E	400	100	75	50	350
F	500	100	75	50	425

Part B

FIGURE 24A

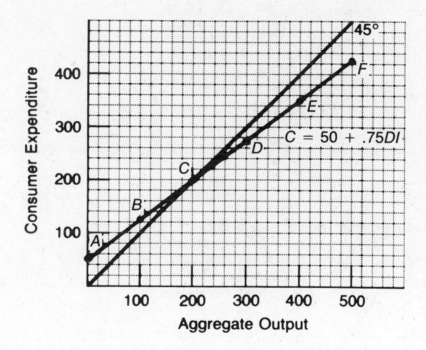

Exercise 3
Part A

FIGURE 24B

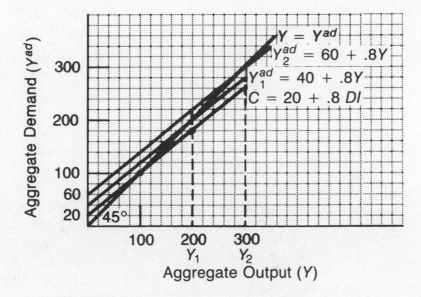

B. $Y_1 = 200$

C. $Y_2 = 300$

D. 5

Exercise 4
A. $Y^{ad} = 100 + 0.9Y + 100 + 200 = 400 + 0.9Y$
B. Inventory investment $= -100 = (Y - Y^{ad}) = 3000 - 400 - 0.9(3000)$
C. Output will increase since business will expand production in the second time period.
D. 4000: Because $Y - Y^{ad} = 0 = Y - 400 - 0.9Y$; $0.1Y = 400$; $Y = 4000$
E. 4000: The same level where unplanned inventory investment is zero.

Exercise 5

	Consumer Expenditure		Planned Investment Spending	Gov't Spending	Equilibrium Aggregate Income
	Autonomous	Induced			
Decrease in rate of interest	0	+	+	0	+
Decrease in MPC	0	−	0	0	−
Decrease in tax rate	0	+	0	0	+
Increase in planned investment spending	0	+	+	0	+
Increase in autonomous consumer expenditure	+	+	0	0	+
Decrease in MPS	0	+	0	0	+
Decrease in government spending	0	−	0	−	−

338

Exercise 6
A. 5 = 1/(1 - 0.8)
B. -4 = -0.8(5)
C. Change in G = 40
    Change in T = 50

Exercise 7

FIGURE 24C

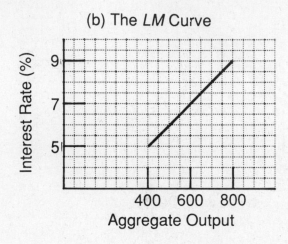

(b) The *LM* Curve

Exercise 8

FIGURE 24D

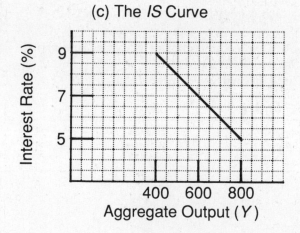

(c) The *IS* Curve

Self-Test

Part A		Part B	
1.	F	1.	d
2.	T	2.	b
3.	T	3.	a
4.	F	4.	c
5.	T	5.	b
6.	F	6.	d
7.	F	7.	a
8.	T	8.	a
9.	T	9.	b
10.	F	10.	e
11.	T		
12.	T		
13.	T		
14.	F		
15.	T		

ANSWERS TO CHAPTER 25

Chapter Synopsis/Completions

1. monetary policy
2. fiscal policy
3. IS
4. investment
5. right
6. LM
7. demand
8. excess
9. interest rate
10. aggregate output
11. fall
12. right
13. leftward
14. money
15. rise
16. LM
17. IS
18. ineffective
19. crowded out
20. real
21. rise
22. downward
23. right

Exercise 1

Part A
1. increase in autonomous consumer expenditures
2. increase in autonomous investment
3. increase in government spending
4. decline in taxes

Part B
1. increase in autonomous consumer expenditures
2. increase in autonomous investment
3. increase in government spending
4. decline in taxes

Part C
1. increase in the money supply
2. decline in money demand

Part D
1. decline in the money supply
2. increase in the money demand

Exercise 2
1. M
2. F
3. F
4. M

5. M
6. F
7. B

Exercise 3

FIGURE 25A

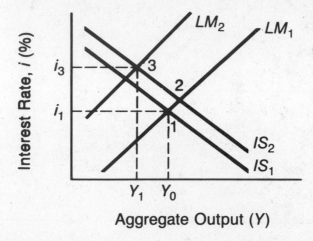

The LM curve must have shifted to the left (to LM₂), moving the economy to point 3. The leftward shift in the LM curve is best explained by the combination of two factors. First, the Fed, in an attempt to slow inflation which had reached double-digit levels in 1979 and 1980, slowed money growth. Second, people's concerns about recession and rising unemployment led to an increase in money demand. Both these factors cause the LM curve to shift to the left and thus reinforce each other. Some economists have argued that the Fed was slow to realize the increase in money demand. Had the Fed known earlier it is possible that the Fed would not have slowed money growth so sharply.

Note that the contractionary monetary policy explains the decline in real GNP, while the combination of an expansionary fiscal policy and contractionary monetary policy pushed interest rates up. In 1982, these interest rates adjusted for inflation (real interest rates) proved to be very high, leading to concerns that the fiscal-monetary policy mix of the Reagan administration would prove harmful to investment.

Exercise 4

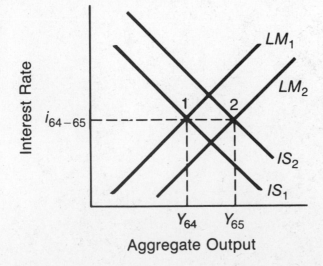

Exercise 5

FIGURE 25C

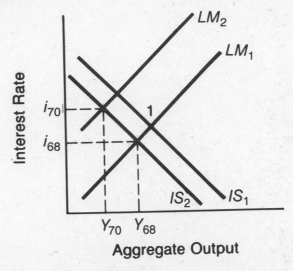

The prime rate of interest rose from 6.3% in 1968 to 7.91% in 1969 and 1970, while the unemployment rate rose from 3.6% in 1968 to 4.9% in 1970.

Exercise 6
1. F
2. M
3. M
4. F
5. M

Exercise 7
A. =>
B. <= .
C. <=
D. <=
E. =>
F. <=

Self-Test

Part A
1. F
2. T
3. T
4. F
5. T
6. T
7. F
8. T

Part B
1. a
2. d
3. d
4. b
5. c
6. c
7. b
8. b

9. F	9. a
10. F	10. a
11. F	
12. T	
13. F	
14. F	
15. T	

ANSWERS TO CHAPTER 26

Chapter Synopsis/Completions

1. price
2. monetarists
3. money supply
4. interest rates
5. increase
6. money
7. right
8. autonomous
9. right
10. fixed
11. expand
12. rise
13. aggregate output

14. price level
15. aggregate supply
16. natural rate
17. temporary
18. price level
19. shocks
20. stagflation
21. temporary
22. stable
23. flexible
24. activist
25. time lags
26. crowding out

Exercise 1
Parts A and C

FIGURE 26A

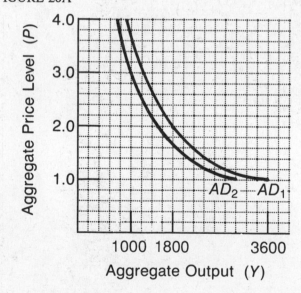

Part B

Aggregate spending will fall from 3600 to 3000

Exercise 2
Part A
1. increase in the money supply
2. increase in government spending
3. increase in net exports
4. reduction in taxes
5. improved consumer optimism
6. improved business optimism

Part B
1. decline in the money supply
2. decline in government spending
3. decline in net exports
4. increase in taxes
5. increase in consumer pessimism
6. increase in business pessimism

Exercise 3
1. $< =$
2. $< =$
3. $= >$
4. $< =$
5. $< =$
6. $= >$

Exercise 4

FIGURE 26B

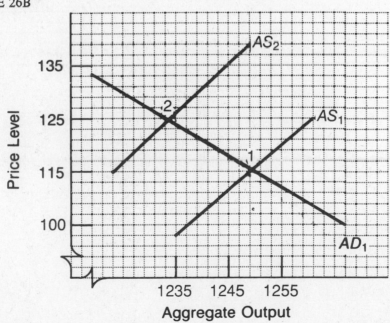

Since the actual unemployment rate exceeds the natural unemployment rate in 1974, the labor market was slightly "easy" at this time, suggesting that the aggregate supply curve would have shifted out, all else constant. Most of the blame for the shifting of the aggregate supply curve must go to OPEC which had significantly raised the price of oil in 1974, crop failures, and the lifting of wage and price controls.

Exercise 5

The large decline in aggregate demand from 1929 to 1933 is clearly evident in the data as both real GNP and consumer prices fall significantly. It appears that between 1933 and 1936 that the aggregate demand curve had shifted out due to more expansionary monetary and fiscal policy. The aggregate supply curve appears to have shifted out. This is also consistent with the theory presented in Chapter 23, which indicates that when unemployment is above the natural rate there will be downward pressure on wages. Thus the behavior of aggregate demand and supply during the Great Depression is consistent with our more modern theory.

FIGURE 26C

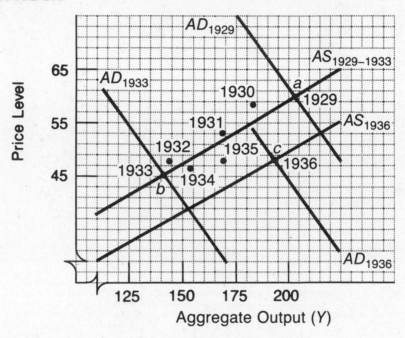

Exercise 6

1. B		6. K
2. N		7. K
3. K		8. M
4. M		9. B
5. M		10. B

Exercise 7

Part A
1. data lag
2. recognition lag
3. legislation lag
4. implementation lag
5. effectiveness lag

Part B
He is referring to the political business cycle.

Self-Test

Part A		Part B	
1.	T	1.	c
2.	T	2.	c
3.	F	3.	b
4.	T	4.	c
5.	T	5.	e
6.	F	6.	d
7.	T	7.	d
8.	T	8.	a
9.	F	9.	c
10.	F	10.	b
11.	T		
12.	T		
13.	F		
14.	F		
15.	T		

ANSWERS TO CHAPTER 27

Chapter Synopsis/Completions

1.	monetarists	14.	money
2.	Keynesians	15.	timing
3.	consensus	16.	statistical
4.	evidence	17.	historical
5.	reduced form	18.	historical
6.	channels	19.	ration
7.	mechanism	20.	residential construction
8.	structural	21.	stock
9.	forecasts	22.	interest rate
10.	specified	23.	wealth
11.	reverse causation	24.	liquidity
12.	third factor		
13.	real		

Exercise 1

1.	R	6.	S
2.	S	7.	S
3.	R	8.	S
4.	K	9.	R
5.	R		

Exercise 2

1.	K	6.	M
2.	M	7.	K
3.	M	8.	K
4.	S	9.	K
5.	M		

Exercise 3

A. If workers and other resource suppliers anticipate future price increases, they may attempt to hedge against inflation by increasing their prices now, especially if longer term contracts are prevalent. When parties enter into longer term agreements they will have expectations of what the future will be like. If high rates of inflation are anticipated, wages will tend to reflect these anticipations. Thus, it is possible that wages rise in anticipation of higher prices rather than cause higher prices.

B. Many economists would argue that changes in monetary growth drive both input costs, such as wages, and prices.

C. Cost-push theories of inflation are not well accepted in the United States since most economists regard input prices as endogenously determined. But in Great Britain and Italy where unions are viewed as more powerful than in the United States, cost-push theories are more generally accepted. While the evidence is mixed and highly controversial, inflation in Great Britain and Italy appears to exhibit some cost-push elements.

D.
1. Higher rates of money growth will precede higher wage rate growth.
2. It is very difficult to say that one is the cause and the other is not. If unions know in advance that their wage demands will be accommodated by the Federal Reserve, they will have little incentive not to make those demands. Therefore, both contribute to the inflation. Absent increased money growth, inflation would not occur. Absent higher wage demands, money growth would not increase.

Exercise 4
1. d
2. e
3. f
4. a
5. g
6. b
7. c

Self-Test

Part A
1. F
2. T
3. T
4. T
5. T
6. T
7. T
8. T
9. T
10. F
11. T
12. F
13. T
14. T
15. T

Part B
1. b
2. e
3. b
4. d
5. b
6. d
7. c
8. b
9. d
10. a

ANSWERS TO CHAPTER 28

Chapter Synopsis/Completions

1. monetary
2. excessive
3. inflation
4. continually
5. temporary
6. accommodation
7. compatible
8. negative supply shocks
9. unemployment
10. budget deficit
11. taxes
12. cost-push
13. demand-pull
14. high
15. low
16. hyperinflation
17. money
18. money supply
19. cost-push
20. accommodating
21. activist

Exercise 1

1. Concern over unemployment. Expansionary macropolicies reduce unemployment in the short run, but raise the price level in the long run. Such policies may prove inflationary if the unemployment target is set too low. Alternatively, monetary authorities may expand the money supply in response to cost-push pressures that threaten to raise unemployment.

2. Budget deficits. If deficits push interest rates upward, the Fed may automatically accommodate them if it pursues an interest-rate targeting strategy. Even if the Fed does not attempt to peg interest rates, the Fed may feel pressure to expand the money supply to keep interest rates from rising.

FIGURE 28A

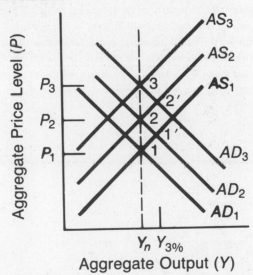

The target level of unemploymnent is below the natural rate level so $Y_{3\%}$ is above Y_n, as is drawn in the figure. Hence in trying to reach an output level of $Y_{3\%}$, the government will shift the aggregate demand curve to AD_2. Because the resulting level of output at point 1' is above the natural-rate level, the aggregate supply curve shifts in to AS_2 and output falls to the natural-rate level. To raise aggregate output to $Y_{3\%}$, the government again pursues expansionary policy to shift the aggregate demand curve to AD_3. The aggregate supply curve again shifts up to AS_3 because $Y > Y_n$. The outcome of this process is that the price level continually rises from P_1 to P_2 to P_3 and so on. The result is a demand-pull inflation.

Exercise 3

U.S. government budget deficit does not necessarily lead to monetary expansion because the Fed is not obligated to monetize the debt.

1. The budget deficit must lead to upward pressure on interest rates.
2. The Fed will try to prevent any rise in interest rates.

Although the Fed may have tried to prevent interest rate rises in the 1960-1980 period, the budget deficits could not have led to upward pressure on interest rates since the debt-to-GNP ratio did not rise in this period. Thus the budget deficits in this period could not have been the source of higher money growth.

Exercise 4

A comparison of the Argentine experience with that of post-World War I Germany suggests that changing the person in charge and issuing new currency may be insufficient by itself to rid a country of inflation. The German government constrained itself by limiting currency issue and moving toward a balanced budget. The deflation proved costly as the German economy went into recession. However, one can reasonably assume that the recession would have been longer and deeper had their policies not been viewed as credible by the citizenry. Especially important to achieving credibility is the reduction of budget deficits, since many people associate large deficits with inflation. Unfortunately, the failure of past reforms probably means that even serious reforms may, at first, be regarded with skepticism. Thus one might anticipate that deflationary policies will prove relatively more costly in Argentina than they did in 1920s Germany. The initial success of the Argentine anti-inflation program differed from previous attempts by addressing the problem of government budget deficits. Reducing the budget deficit likely changed inflationary expectations, contributing to the dramatic drop in the Argentine inflation rate in 1986. The government's failure to constrain budget deficits explains, in part, the return of triple-digit inflation rates.

Exercise 5

The rate hike appears to have been important in changing expectations. The Fed wanted to get inflation under control but feared that a deflationary monetary policy would cause high unemployment. Therefore, the Fed wanted its new strategy to be regarded as credible. It believed that the discount rate increase would signal to financial market participants its concern over inflation. The switch to reserve targeting was probably aimed at economists. Few others would understand the distinction between reserve targeting and interest-rate targeting. News reports following the announcement confirms this impression. The financial pages of most newspapers emphasized the discount-rate increase, while discussions among economists focused on the change in the targeting procedure.

Self-Test

Part A	Part B
1. T	1. c
2. F	2. c
3. T	3. d
4. F	4. a
5. T	5. a
6. F	6. b
7. T	7. c
8. F	8. d
9. F	9. d
10. T	10. d
11. T	
12. F	
13. T	
14. T	
15. F	

ANSWERS TO CHAPTER 29

Chapter Synopsis/Completions

1. adaptively
2. current
3. past
4. rational expectations
5. predictions (or forecasts)
6. optimal forecasts
7. persistently
8. costly
9. efficient capital markets
10. prices
11. unexploited profit opportunity
12. equilibrium return
13. hot tips
14. financial analysts
15. prices
16. random walk
17. expected
18. buy
19. hold
20. brokerage commissions
21. insider information

Exercise 1

1. c
2. f
3. d
4. b
5. c
6. g
7. h
8. a
9. a
10. c

Exercise 2

A. If the Federal Reserve action was widely anticipated, long- term interest rates are likely to be unaffected. Since asset prices, and hence financial market yields, reflect currently available information, efficient markets theory suggests that the anticipated Federal Reserve action will not change long-term interest rates.

B. If the policy, once it is implemented, changes expectations so that people become convinced that the slower growth of money will be permanent, long-term interest rates might fall as people revise their expectations of inflation downward.

C. Finally if the policy should come as a surprise but expected inflation is not reduced, then long-term interest rates are likely to rise as the excess demand for money leads to failing bond prices (see Chapter 6).

D. Thus, when the Fed slows the growth of the money supply, predicting the interest-rate outcome requires some knowledge of people's expectations. While there is dispute as to whether or not unexpected money growth influences long-term interest rates, this example illustrates that expectations can play an important role in determining the effectiveness of monetary policy.

Exercise 3

A. No, by the time you purchase Montana Power Company stock its price will already reflect the increase in expected profits, and, therefore, you should not expect to earn an above normal profit from this purchase.

B. The information you receive from your brother-in-law is known as insider or advance information. Insider information can allow you to earn a higher-than-normal rate of return, though you risk going to jail if you and your brother-in-law get caught.

C. No, the stock market is still informationally efficient if people can profit from insider information as long as an investor in that market cannot make an above-normal return by gathering information available to the public. Apart from inside information, financial economists generally believe that the stock market comes close to the ideal of an informationally efficient market, although the stock market crash of October 1987 may lead to a reassessment of this conclusion.

Self-Test

Part A		Part B	
1.	T	1.	c
2.	F	2.	a
3.	T	3.	d
4.	F	4.	c
5.	T	5.	c
6.	F	6.	b
7.	T	7.	c
8.	T	8.	b
9.	F	9.	a
10.	F	10.	c
11.	F		
12.	F		
13.	F		
14.	T		
15.	F		

ANSWERS TO CHAPTER 30

Chapter Synopsis/Completions

1. expectations
2. evaluate
3. constant
4. misleading
5. New classical
6. flexible
7. aggregate supply
8. price level
9. Unanticipated
10. policy ineffectiveness proposition
11. rigidities
12. anticipated
13. nonclassical
14. Lucas policy critique
15. activist
16. credible
17. 9
18. budget deficits

Exercise 1

The Fed will buy securities, but if expectations are rational, then the Fed's efforts in stabilizing nominal interest rates will be hampered. People realizing that higher rates of money growth will eventually prove inflationary, will bid up nominal interest rates further. (Recall that the nominal interest rate is the sum of the real interest rate and the expected rate of inflation, so that if inflation expectations rise by more than the real interest rate falls, the nominal rate rises.)

Exercise 2

In the new classical model, the aggregate supply curve shifts out to AS_{NC} and the economy goes to point NC. Aggregate output does not fall, while the price level falls to P_{NC}.

In the nonclassical model, the aggregate supply shifts out but only to AS_N and the economy goes to point N. Aggregate output falls below Y_N and the price level falls to P_N, which is higher than that found in the new classical model.

In the traditional model, the aggregate supply curve does not shift out at all and the economy goes to point T. Aggregate output falls to Y_T, which is lower than in the other models, and the price level falls to P_T, which is higher than in the other models.

FIGURE 30A

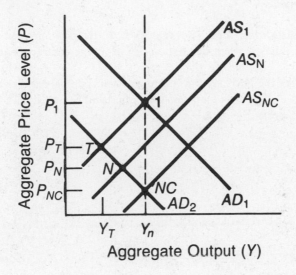

Exercise 3

FIGURE 30B

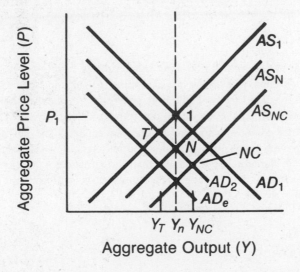

In the new classical model, the aggregate supply curve shifts out to AS_{NC} (where output would equal Y_n if the realized aggregate demand curve were AD_e). The economy goes to point NC, at which point aggregate output has risen to Y_{NC}. Aggregate output does not fall but rather rises.

In the nonclassical rational expectations model, the aggregate supply curve shifts out by less than in the new classical model. As drawn, the aggregate supply curve shifts to AS_N and the economy is at point N with the level of output unchanged. Thus aggregate output need not fall. However, the nonclassical aggregate supply curve can lie above or below the AS_N drawn in the figure, and output could fall as well as rise in the nonclassical rational expectations model.

In the traditional model, the aggregate supply curve does not shift, so the economy ends up at point T. Only the traditional model gives the unequivocal result that output falls from the contractionary policy (to Y_T).

This example illustrates that in either the new classical or nonclassical, rational expectations model a contractionary policy does not necessarily lead to a decline in output and can even lead to a rise in output if the policy is less contractionary than expected.

Exercise 4
1. NC
2. NC
3. K
4. M, NC
5. NC
6. NC
7. N
8. K,M,N

Exercise 5
1. NC, N, T
2. T
3. T
4. N, NC
5. T
6. NC

Exercise 6

In the traditional model, your announcement will not effect the aggregate supply curve; expectations about the Fed's policy will not effect the outcome. In the new classical model, your announcement will shift up the aggregate supply curve if it is believed and so the Fed's policy will not be as expansionary as the chairman of the Fed hopes. The chairman would prefer that you keep quiet about his intentions. The nonclassical rational expectations model leads to a similar conclusion as the new classical model. The Fed's policy will not be as expansionary as the chairman hopes; again, he would prefer you to keep quiet. However, the announced policy is likely to be more expansionary in the nonclassical model than in the new classical model. If no one believes you when you make your announcement, then the aggregate supply curve will not shift even in the new classical or nonclassical rational expectations model.

Self-Test

Part A

1. T
2. T
3. F
4. F
5. F
6. F
7. T
8. F
9. T
10. T
11. F
12. T
13. T
14. F
15. F

Part B

1. a
2. c
3. d
4. e
5. e
6. b
7. c
8. a
9. c
10. b